D0772378

The Way of the Heavenly Sword

THE WAY OF THE HEAVENLY SWORD,

*The Japanese Army
in the 1920's*

Leonard A. Humphreys

STANFORD UNIVERSITY PRESS, STANFORD, CALIFORNIA

Stanford University Press
Stanford, California
© 1995 by the Board of Trustees of the
Leland Stanford Junior University
Printed in the United States of America

CIP data appear at the end of the book

Stanford University Press publications are distributed exclusively by Stanford University Press within
the United States, Canada, Mexico, and Central
America; they are distributed exclusively by
Cambridge University Press throughout the rest of
the world.

Original printing 1995
Last figure below indicates year of this printing:
04   03   02   01   00   99   98   97   96

36^{75} MW 7/8/97 (BRL)

To Sally, our children, and our grandchildren

Preface

Japan's military system underwent three transformations in the century following the Meiji Restoration of 1868. The first ended the reign of the samurai as the dominant, feudal military power and provided Japan with modern military forces organized along the lines of European armies (and navies). The warrior class in the Tokugawa era (1600–1868) had as its goal the maintenance of the status quo and the perpetuation of its own power. Its replacement, the Meiji military system, prepared the unified nation to repel the advance of Western imperialism and, later, to share in the division of imperialist spoils in East Asia.

The third metamorphosis was the conversion from the Imperial Japanese Army (and Navy) to the Japan Ground, Maritime, and Air Self-Defense Forces after the devastating defeat of the Pacific War. These Self-Defense Forces, with whom I worked closely for six years, are the mixed product of the Cold War and Japan's 1947 "peace" Constitution. Much maligned for many years by large numbers of Japanese, they may well be among the finest nonnuclear military forces in the world today.

But this book is about the second, less well defined transformation of the Japanese military, from *Nihongun* or *kokugun* (Japan's army or the nation's army) to *kōgun* (the imperial or emperor's army). Its beginnings can be traced to the period immediately following the Russo-Japanese War of 1904–5, but the real impetus to radical change came only after World War I. I believe that although the transformation was complete by the time of the Manchurian Incident in 1931, the mechanism for the new structure had probably been in place since mid-1929. The book, then, is about the disintegration of the Meiji military system, whose architect and guiding hand, until his death in 1922, was Yamagata Aritomo, Japan's preeminent political-military figure.

The emergent *kōgun* had several characteristics that distinguish it from its predecessor. (The book concentrates almost exclusively on the army, which was the more politically involved and powerful of the two military services.)[1] First, it had no single strong leader like Yamagata to keep the factionalized officer corps under control. Second, it cleaved to the irrationalist view that an army with superior morale, inculcated by intense spiritual training, could triumph over an enemy with marked material superiority. Third, this army considered that it had the prerogative to interfere in the political and foreign affairs of the nation, in spite of an imperial prohibition on such activity, and it used political persuasion and modern propaganda techniques to bring the people into line with its own view of the world. Fourth, this army's worldview was apocalyptic, and it led the nation quickly down the path to external confrontation and war. Unlike the change to the Meiji military system or to the Japan Self-Defense Forces, both of which were sponsored by responsible governments, the transformation of the 1920's was accomplished internally by the military elite itself.

The imperial army and its leaders have been the subject of extensive historical study by both Japanese and foreign historians for the period from the Manchurian Incident to the end of the Pacific War. These *Nihon o horoboshita mono* (fellows who ruined Japan), as one author entitled his book, have for a long time been the recipients of obloquy, but there has been surprisingly little interest until recently in the people or the process that wrought the army of "double patriots" that dominated the Japanese political system after 1931. This book is no revisionist tract; it seeks only to understand what happened. It attempts to assign responsibility, but not censure or blame. I think that in the final decade of this turbulent century, most of us can agree that what the Japanese army did in the period of its ascendancy, terrible as it was, lies innately within the capability of all human beings.

World War I was a turning point for Japan and its army. Soon afterward, perceptive younger officers realized that their army had fallen far behind those of Europe in its ability to wage a modern war and that staid army leadership, apparently more intent on parochial infighting than modernization, would not or could not effect the necessary changes to keep abreast of world military trends. To make matters worse, in their view, the ideas of the people and the army were drifting apart, a perhaps fatal condition in a world where all peoples must fight to survive.

I am convinced that Japanese military thought from even before the Russo-Japanese War was informed by a crude social Darwinism — not of the individualistic or eugenic form but of the collective variety. It saw Japan as an organismic whole fighting for survival in a hostile world of similarly competing entities (a common view, of course, in Europe and America at the time). In Japan this conception revived confidence in a Confucian ideal that embodied all the nation in a great family working as one to ensure the preservation of the state, its emperor, its people, and its collective values. The army sought to position itself at the forefront of this absolutely vital cause and to exhort and cajole all the people in its support. The military judgment that Japan was in a very poor position to survive in this struggle gave it added impetus to seek concerted action to enhance the defensive capabilities of the state. Lacking the resources of the other great powers, the Japanese military reached two somewhat contradictory and ultimately fatal conclusions: (1) they must seize the necessary resources to survive from already failed neighbors, and (2) they must win in a war against materially superior enemies by preparing their soldiers with the psychological armor of an indomitable spirit. I hope that this book sheds some light on the process that led to these conclusions and on the people who involved themselves in it.

The idea for this volume took shape in 1968 and reached its first milestone as a doctoral dissertation in 1974. Since then, short periods of intense activity to update it, make obvious and necessary changes, and generally ready the manuscript for publication have interspersed longer periods of life and teaching. The present work is the final result. I make no apologies for the long wait, for I feel that it is a much stronger presentation of the Japanese army officers' world in the 1920's than it could have been had it appeared even four or five years earlier. There is still a great deal left to know and do, but one must stop somewhere.

I do apologize to my readers for the large number of direct quotations that interrupt the pages of my narrative, but I want as much as possible to allow Japanese military men, commentators, and historians to present their ideas in their own words, at least insofar as possible within the constraints of translation.

Japanese names follow the customary Japanese order, but common geographic names — for example, Tokyo, Osaka, and Kyushu — omit the macrons over the vowels. Chinese names appear in pinyin. In some well-known names the Wade-Giles spelling follows in parentheses — for example, Zhang Zuolin (Chang Tso-lin). A few very familiar names, such as Chiang Kai-shek (Jiang Jieshi in pinyin) have been left in Wade-Giles to prevent misunderstanding.

Over the years many schools and libraries have given me generous institutional support and encouragement in preparing my manuscript. Among them I must single out Stanford University; the Hoover Institution on War, Revolution, and Peace; the National Diet Library of Japan; the War History Office of the Defense Research Institute, in the Japan Defense Agency; and the University of the Pacific, where I have been privileged to teach for the past 23 years.

Some of the many individuals who have helped me in this enterprise are no longer living, but this does not lessen in any way my debt to them or my appreciation for the contribution of their time and knowledge. Among those whose names I must include here are Tsunoda Jun, Hata Ikuhiko, and Takahashi Masae, whose own work and personal aid have given this narrative critical direction. I must also thank the officers, enlisted men, and civilians of the Japan Defense Agency and Self-Defense Forces, without whose cooperation and support my work would not have been possible, among them General Yamada Masao, former chief of staff of the Ground Self-Defense Force, and former imperial Japanese army officers Nishiura Susumu and Inaba Masao of the War History Office. My list of friends and teachers, whose help has been indispensable, would be incomplete without mentioning former IJA major general Utsunomiya Naokata, General Sugita Ichiji, who served in both the IJA and the Self-Defense Forces, and former colonel Katō Takeo of the IJA. I must also express my thanks to my professors Nobutaka Ike, Thomas C. Smith, and Peter Duus for their encouragement and assistance. Finally, I want to thank Cathy Tanner and Pamela Altree, of the University of the Pacific, who magically transferred my sloppy scrawls to floppy disks.

Contents

(Photographs follow page 100)

The Way of the Heavenly Sword

_____

The Background to Army Politics

The secret of victory or defeat lies in the spirit
of the men and not in their weapons.
                    Rai San'yō, 1780–1832

The great imperial Japanese army review in Tokyo on the last day of April
1906 was a spectacle long remembered by the people of the capital. Eight
months after the government signed the Treaty of Portsmouth, which
ended the bloody conflict with Russia, the triumphant army gathered in
final conclave to renew its pledge of service to the emperor and the nation,
and to receive an expression of appreciation from the sovereign and the
adulation of the people. The spontaneous and violent popular reaction
against the treaty that had erupted in Tokyo and echoed in protests across
the nation in September 1905 had spent itself on the civil government.
There was no hint of resentment against the heroic generals and admirals
or the brave soldiers and sailors whom they commanded. These were the
days when people informally referred to Japan's army with pride as the
kokumin no guntai or *kokugun*, the people's or nation's army. The transition to *kōgun*, or emperor's army, was not yet in motion.

On that fine spring day even the frightful losses of the war were forgotten for the moment as 30,000 soldiers formed ranks to receive imperial
recognition for their sacrifice and gratitude for their victories. The Meiji
emperor, in the 39th year of his eventful reign, personally inspected the
host, and with battle-torn regimental flags flying gallantly, the troops
passed their sovereign in review.

Japan had entered the war in 1904 with thirteen standing infantry
divisions. Sizable contingents represented each of them that day in Tokyo.
The four new regular infantry divisions, created in the midst of the fighting and still in service on the continent, were represented by their commanding generals and staffs. Separate cavalry, artillery, engineer, trans-

port, and local reserve infantry units swelled the ranks to fill the expanse of the broad Aoyama parade ground.

A galaxy of successful generals, men whose names were by now familiar to every Japanese, stood before the officers and men in ranks. Marshal Ōyama Iwao, Japan's senior field general, who led the armies to victory in the war with China in 1895 as well as in the war with Russia, commanded the review. His brilliant wartime chief of staff Gen. Kodama Gentarō and the five stalwart commanding generals of the Manchurian and Yalu River field armies accompanied him to a position before the imperial reviewing stand.

When the marshal stepped forward to present the troops, the emperor spoke briefly to him in the formal language of the court: "We warmly celebrate here today our army's triumphal return, and we perceive that military discipline remains vigorous and the ranks in good order. We deeply rejoice at this, and we will continue to rely on ye for ever more strenuous efforts to develop and advance the army of this imperial land."[1]

At the end of the formal portion of the day's festivities, the troops paraded the thronged streets of the city to the cheers of the people. In effect, the Japanese army had performed its final duty of the Russo-Japanese War and could now turn its full attention to the immediate postwar tasks of appraisal, planning, and renewal.

National Army, Localized Leadership

To the Japanese nation the army was an army of the people, and indeed, the ranks were filled with young men from all over Japan with a satisfactory distribution on the basis of class and clan backgrounds. The conscription law of 1872 and subsequent adjustments had transformed the feudal clan forces of the Meiji Restoration wars, largely *shizoku* (samurai), into a national army by 1895. Yet a glance at the army's leadership left no doubt that as late as 1906, 38 years after the restoration, the positions of authority were not distributed on any national basis.

The feudal clan, or *han*,[2] origins of the men who held the key positions in the army's central headquarters are illustrative. Marshal Yamagata Aritomo of the Chōshū clan, twice prime minister of Japan and by far the most politically powerful man in the army, held sway as chief of the general staff throughout the war and only days before the review had relinquished that position to Gen. Kodama Gentarō, his protégé and fellow clansman. The army minister was Terauchi Masakata (often Masa-

take), another Chōshū protégé of Yamagata's. Of Terauchi's most powerful assistants, the vice minister and the chief of the bureau of military
affairs, the former was one of the army minister's close personal followers,
the latter a Chōshū clansman.

The army field commanders, who fought the war in Manchuria and
stood before the emperor on that spring day in 1906, included Ōyama,
Kuroki Tamemoto, Nozu Michikane, and Kawamura Sōroku of Satsuma,
and Nogi Marusuke of Chōshū. Of the field army commanders only the
talented Oku Yasukata stood outside the Satsuma-Chōshū (*Satchō*) circle.
Chōshū and Satsuma dominated the army, but within this coalition the
positions of real power clearly belonged to Yamagata and his Chōshū
faction.

Four important fiefs of western Japan, Satsuma, Chōshū, Tosa, and
Hizen, had joined to overthrow the feudal Tokugawa regime in 1868. The
aim of the *Satchōdohi* alliance was to unify Japan and restore the nation to
imperial rule in the face of the threat of Western imperialism. Satsuma and
Chōshū, the stronger pair, provided a preponderance of the military man-
power and leadership during the battles for imperial restoration.

Saigō Takamori, the Great Saigō, was the preeminent military leader
of that day. As counselor to the Lord of Satsuma, he was responsible for
the decision that brought the traditionally rival Satsuma and Chōshū *han*
together for a joint struggle to displace the Tokugawa. Saigō led the victorious "loyalist" coalition forces east to Edo (Tokyo). When he spared
the Tokugawa capital the agony of siege by persuading the shogun's army
to surrender without giving battle, the feat elevated him to hero status.

When the fighting ended, Saigō, piqued at his clan's small share of the
political spoils, retired to Satsuma taking his troops with him, but in 1870
the new government prevailed upon him to join it in order to lend an air of
unity and credibility to the shaky *han* coalition in Tokyo that presumed to
represent the emperor's national authority.

Between 1870 and 1873, as an active and powerful figure in the emperor's government, Saigō divided his time between military and civil
duties. A busy man, he left the specifics of military organization and planning in the hands of an innovative young Chōshū general who had been
eloquent in persuading Saigō to join the government for the good of the
nation. Maj. Gen. Yamagata Aritomo had recently returned from Europe,
where he studied Western military systems. Earlier, he had played a brave
but relatively inconspicuous part in the battles of the restoration, in which
he worked closely with the leading Chōshū military leader Ōmura Masujirō. Ōmura held a post equivalent to vice minister of military affairs

immediately after the restoration, but assassins cut short his bureaucratic career in 1869. After a period of confusion, Yamagata, once assured of Saigō's support and Satsuma's participation in the urgent business of army development, accepted an appointment as the assistant vice minister of military affairs.[3] From this post he turned to the task of building a national military force.

With Saigō's cooperation Yamagata organized an imperial bodyguard, the Goshinpei, furnished with troops from the Satsuma, Chōshū, and Tosa clans, each group preserving its separate identity within the whole. This was Japan's first step toward the national army it so desperately needed to face the encroaching Westerners or the even more likely possibility of internal disturbance.

Saigō's participation was essential in the next step to centralize government power, the dissolution of the *han*, or fiefs, into which Japan had been divided for centuries. In August 1871 the emperor abolished the *han* and redivided the country into administrative prefectures controlled from Tokyo. This structural reform opened the door to the formation of Japan's first truly national military force, and Yamagata moved quickly to take advantage of the opportunity. In February 1872 the government authorized the establishment of a separate army and navy. Two months later the Goshinpei converted to the first imperial guard (*konoe*) unit, which Yamagata and then Saigō commanded. If one considers the perceived threat from foreign imperialists and the more present danger from all manner of native malcontents during the chaotic period immediately after the restoration, when the newly created imperial government faced the world and the nation without money, without military power, and indeed, without true nationwide authority, it is not surprising that a loyal military force was the most urgent priority.

In the meantime, with the great singleness of purpose for which he was noted, Yamagata fought and won the battle for a universal military conscription system. Conscription was an extremely delicate issue for a society struggling free of feudalism. Many restoration leaders of the *shizoku* class, including Saigō, resisted the idea of relinquishing the monopoly on military service that had provided the basis for their hereditary power. Most of the nation's former samurai, already stripped of any political power they had enjoyed, feared the consequences of such a change to their own social and economic positions, and generally speaking, the usually inarticulate peasants also opposed conscription, for they could see no advantage in national military service for their sons. Saigō, a champion of *shizoku* privilege, must have agonized over the dilemma, but he tacitly accepted Yamagata's proposal as the only way to form a truly national army, and a compromise version of Yamagata's conscription plan went into effect in January 1873 under the slogan "All the people soldiers."[4]

The cooperative spirit between the Satsuma and Chōshū military leaders for the greater good of the nation ended abruptly, however, when in October 1873 the impetuous Saigō, disagreeing once again with his colleagues on many policy issues, quit the government after an acrimonious dispute over Japan's relations with Korea. Saigō's resignation demonstrated the great ingrained strength of feudal loyalties, because many Satsuma men in the imperial guard deserted to follow Saigō back to their native fief (now redesignated Kagoshima Prefecture).

While Yamagata carefully constructed the new army step-by-step, adding schools and training facilities on French and then German models, Saigō opened an academy in remote southern Kyushu that soon became a focal point of *shizoku* opposition to the central authority. Having gradually legislated away *shizoku* privileges and reduced the class to equality with the common people as part of the modernizing process, the imperial government faced the outrage of many disgruntled samurai and had already used military force to suppress some minor uprisings. In February 1877 *shizoku* resentment exploded in the Satsuma Rebellion, which found Saigō, the hero of the restoration, the leader of a large-scale revolt against the very government he had fought to establish. The Satsuma Rebellion caught the remaining Satsuma men in the army in the same sort of dilemma as the one faced by officers from the southern United States at the outbreak of the American Civil War. A number of them left to cast their lot with Satsuma and Saigō. In the end, Yamagata's drafted soldiers, mostly of peasant stock but largely led by officers of *shizoku* lineage, proved more than a match for Saigō's warriors. In a seven-month campaign the new army defeated them, ending the samurai cause and Saigō's life.

It is little wonder that, in a country divided for centuries into fiefs that limited geographic as well as social mobility, provincialism remained strong. Formal emancipation from the feudal system and exhortations to develop a sense of national identity did not change traditions and loyalties that had persisted for centuries. The Satsuma Rebellion is one outstanding example of provincial as well as *shizoku* class assertions from a *han* with proud and ancient traditions and a proportionally large and loyal samurai population.

Han loyalties powered Tokyo politics in the early post-restoration era, and political relationships in the military service were no different. Life in early Meiji military units must have been turbulent. *Han* chauvinism entered into every aspect of military life; no one ever forgot his own clan background, and neither Satsuma nor Chōshū braves were distinguished for their humility. Saigō once wrote that commanding the imperial guard was like bedding down with a bomb.

Ōmura Masujirō, the outstanding leader of Chōshū forces in the restoration, was an outspoken Chōshū chauvinist and particularly suspicious of Satsuma. Once in office, he showed open favoritism toward his own clansmen. When Yamagata succeeded Ōmura, his deep commitment to the imperial cause and his recognition of the need to centralize the government and modernize the nation forced him to give precedence to national concerns, but he never forgot his Chōshū ties, placing his greatest trust in the many able Chōshū clansmen who rallied round him. Saigō's withdrawal from the government and his subsequent rebellion cast a shadow of suspicion over the many Satsuma men in the army who placed loyalty to the nation (or self-interest, perhaps) above the cause of Satsuma or the *shizoku* class. The upshot of Satsuma's temporary and partial defection was to tip the balance of army internal political power in some immeasurable degree to Chōshū.[5] Under Yamagata's leadership Chōshū never yielded this political advantage. The strength of the Satsuma faction in the army officer corps should not be underestimated, however. After 1877 loyal Satsuma officers quickly regained their equilibrium and claimed a firm second place in the army behind Chōshū. They continued to compete with Chōshū men, who admitted their claim to recognition by awarding them a generous share of the rank, prestige, honors, and positions in the army structure while retaining ultimate control in their own hands. Chōshū was not so generous, however, in its treatment of officers outside this informal *Satchō* coalition.

In the Meiji era between 1873 and 1912, the emperor approved the promotion of 33 men to the rank of *taishō* ("full" general). Of them, 5 were members of the imperial family and can be effectively eliminated from any calculus assessing *han* power and influence. Eleven of the remaining 28 were from Chōshū, 9 from Satsuma, and 8 from all the rest of Japan (71 percent *Satchō*). Seven of these *taishō* were eventually elevated to the status of *gensui*, or field marshal. (The *gensui* remained on active duty and served on the emperor's supreme military affairs council, *gensuifu*, for life. Three of these *gensui* were from Satsuma, and 3 were from Chōshū (86 percent *Satchō*); first among them was Yamagata Aritomo. In the same period the army promoted 153 officers to the rank of *chūjō* (lieutenant general). Thirty-six came from Chōshū, 25 from Satsuma, and

8 from Tosa (40 percent *Satchō*). Among *shōshō* (major generals) the disparity in numbers between *Satchō* and the rest of Japan is less pronounced. Thus, the discrimination against the promotion of non-*Satchō* officers rose with rank. In fairness, these figures are somewhat misleading because they do not reflect the progressive increase in the ratio of non-*Satchō* to *Satchō* officers as the opportunity to join the military forces opened to men from all over Japan. Among the older officers the proportion of *Satchō* men was higher, but this fact may have been lost on younger officers who saw only the continuing domination of the *Satchō* cliques as an obstacle to their own aspirations.

Yamagata's Army and Civil Politics

After his success in the campaign against Saigō's Satsuma rebels, Yamagata emerged as the real arbiter of army affairs. As he advanced in rank and in the emperor's confidence, he became a mighty figure on the national political scene, serving in such civil capacities as home minister, minister of justice, prime minister, and privy councillor. The emperor appointed Yamagata a personal adviser, and when the powerful extra-constitutional body known as the *genrō*, or elder statesmen, formed, Yamagata was a leading figure in it, and in time its most powerful member. In spite of his importance as a national leader, Yamagata never loosened the tight grip on his army power base, and his interest in army affairs did not slacken until the waning days of his long life.

The fundamental principle of his leadership was to deny the military any participation in politics and, conversely, to prevent the civil political world from interfering in the performance of the military function. This was a lesson he drew from his experiences in the decade of turbulence between the restoration and the Satsuma Rebellion. He remained steadfast to the principle of the separation of civil and military power until he died. To this end, he founded the military police (*kenpei*) in 1881 to ensure the apolitical posture of military personnel, and in 1882 he prevailed upon the emperor to issue the "Imperial Rescript to Soldiers and Sailors," which explicitly told the military to stay out of politics (an injunction later circumvented or ignored and never applied to Yamagata himself).

On the other hand, he prompted the army to adopt a version of the German general staff system, which led in 1878 to a separation of the army's administrative and operational functions, vesting them in the co-equal positions of army minister and chief of the general staff.[6] Under this structure, the army achieved final unity of command only in the person of the emperor in his role as commander-in-chief of the armed forces. In exercising the operations function, the new system provided the chief of staff with direct access to the emperor (*iaku no jōsō*), which the army minister did not enjoy at the time, since he reported to the emperor through the civil authority of the prime minister. At Yamagata's insistence, the Meiji Constitution (1889) removed this disability by making each minister of state directly responsible to the emperor, granting to each, including the service ministers, access to the throne. With this constitutional proviso Yamagata successfully divorced both the administrative and operational functions of the army (and navy) from civil cabinet controls.[7]

Since at the time it had become routine to select the army and navy ministers from among military officers on active duty, the Meiji Constitution did not specify that they be officers in uniform. Later on, when speculation arose among the political parties that civilian service ministers might be a possibility, following the practice of some western European states, Prime Minister Yamagata plugged this loophole with the Imperial Ordinances (nos. 193 and 194) of May 1900. They specified that the posts of army and navy minister were to be held only by generals and lieutenant generals or admirals and vice admirals on active duty. After the ordinances were given Diet approval with little or no discussion, Yamagata completed his dual military-civil system of government, fully establishing the doctrine of *tōsuiken no dokuritsu*, or independence of military command.[8]

Yamagata's system had dangerous flaws, however. There could be no unity of the administrative and operational functions of the military in the commander-in-chief because the emperor could not participate in the decision-making process without jeopardizing his sacrosanct position as the repository of sovereignty and national morality. As principal military adviser to the emperor, Yamagata fulfilled this role for him, but after Yamagata died, the system of dual command within the army led at times to competition and serious political rivalry between the army minister and the chief of the general staff.

As Yamagata's system evolved, it became clear that it would work effectively to prevent civil interference with the military, but the converse was not true. By refusing or removing an army (or navy) minister, the military services could destroy civilian cabinets and upset the orderly process of constitutional government, a familiar pattern in Japan's political history from 1912 on. Later, when the army became a hotbed of internal political activity, it could, and did, use the lever of ministerial appointment to overbear the civil government's authority by forcing the army's will on the entire political system. Unable to curb army power, political parties came in time to seek alliances with the army to strengthen themselves against political rivals, and civilian politicians danced to the army's tune.

The fateful consequences of these rulings on domestic politics in the decades between the end of the Meiji era and the Pacific War are well known. The chapters that follow examine them only in relation to the internal politics of the army.

Yamagata's Chōshū Clique and Its Rivals

As the army grew to maturity under his steady hand, Yamagata saw to it that talented young officers of Chōshū lineage on whom he could depend moved steadily into more and more responsible positions in the army and the government.

Gen. Katsura Tarō, a highly talented staff officer with German training, who as a junior officer instituted the German general staff system in the fledgling army, became the army minister in 1898, and in 1901 he formed his first of three governments. The first Katsura cabinet carried Japan through the Russo-Japanese War. Katsura attained the court rank of prince and the status of *genrō* before his death in 1913.

Lt. Gen. Count Kodama Gentarō, ambitious and energetic, rose quickly to high positions in the army as vice minister, minister, vice chief, chief of the general staff, and wartime chief of staff of the Manchurian Army in the war with Russia. While he lived, he was a real power among Chōshū men, but he died exhausted at the age of 54 in 1906.

After Kodama's death Terauchi Masakata acceded to undisputed leadership of the Chōbatsu, or Chōshū clique. He became army minister in 1902 and held that important post for Chōshū for almost ten years, longer by far than any other man. He rose to the rank of marshal in 1916 and became prime minister shortly thereafter. Nicknamed "the truncheon general" (*biriken shōgun*), Marshal Count Terauchi is well known for having browbeaten the last Korean monarch into signing away the dying kingdom's remaining shred of freedom as Japan annexed the peninsula in August 1910. As the "king of Korea," he governed there from October 1910 until October 1916, when he returned to Japan to be prime minister. Terauchi, a less talented man than Kodama with no outstanding war record, epitomized the Chōshū clique's tenacious hold on army power. The years of his army ministry were the zenith of Chōshū power in the army as well as without.[9]

The last of the Chōshū giants was Gen. Baron Tanaka Giichi. An outstanding staff officer and imaginative military planner, Tanaka was 30 years junior to Yamagata and 16 years junior to Kodama and Terauchi. A great deal more is said of Tanaka's career on subsequent pages.

Like Chōshū, Satsuma was prolific in its production of able military leaders. After Saigō Takamori, his young cousin Ōyama Iwao is rightfully the best known among them. There is no question that the cherubic Ōyama ranks among Japan's more able officers, but he was a field commander, not a political general. Heaped with honors for his brave and loyal service, Ōyama was included among the *genrō*. Until his death in 1916 Marshal Ōyama was the doyen of the army's Satsuma faction, but unlike Yamagata, to whom he was four years junior, he had neither the inclination nor the political power to further the careers of his fellow clansmen.

Any recitation of outstanding Satsuma generals should include Marshal Nozu Michikane and Gen. Kuroki Tamemoto, of Russo-Japanese War fame, neither of whom was a strong political figure. On the other hand, Gen. Kawakami Sōroku and Nozu's son-in-law Marshal Uehara Yūsaku were politically active. Kawakami's reputation for brilliant staff work made him virtually unchallengeable as a military plans officer in the general staff headquarters. Thus entrenched, he stood up to Yamagata and remained an obstacle to complete Chōshū domination of the army until his untimely death in 1899. Uehara, younger than the other Satsuma stalwarts, blossomed as an army political figure in the Taishō era (1912–26). Like his younger Chōshū counterpart, Tanaka Giichi, Uehara is a principal character in the chapters that follow.

The rock on which Chōshū control anchored was Yamagata's close relationship to the Meiji emperor and, later, his towering prestige as a *genrō*, during the first years of the reign of the Taishō emperor. In the latter period especially, few Japanese statesmen had the temerity to attempt major decisions without consulting the *ōgosho*, or grand old man. To do so was to court disaster.

Circumstances made *Satchō* shared control of the army a natural outgrowth of the restoration. The same may be said for Chōshū's gradual rise to primacy after the Satsuma Rebellion. It is not surprising that under these conditions Satsuma and Chōshū together provided a preponderance of the army's leaders through the Sino-Japanese and even to the Russo-Japanese War. The successful young leaders of the restoration became the experienced generals of Japan's turn-of-the-century continental wars. At some point, however, the normal advancement of *Satchō* generals became, or appeared to become, a conscious effort to perpetuate a monopoly on military leadership. *Satchō* rivalry and compromise tended to fill the top positions with officers of the two clans to the exclusion of the non-*Satchō* majority.

Although he could also move against Chōshū colleagues who crossed him, it is not difficult to find examples of Yamagata's favoritism in advancing members of his own clan. The careers of Katsura, Kodama, Terauchi, and Tanaka are eloquent proof. Yamagata once even requested (in vain) that the emperor approve an accelerated promotion for Kodama. Katsura also accrued a personal following, but it was in the decade of Terauchi's ministry that the seeds of serious internal discontent were sown. By the time of Terauchi's tenure, the proportion of non-*Satchō* officers had risen appreciably. In addition, the regional *yōnen gakkō* (army youth school) system, founded in 1887, had begun to feed its graduates into the lower ranks of the officer corps and the geographic distribution of the corps broadened even more rapidly after that. At the same time, Terauchi's personnel policies were notoriously partisan. He not only showed marked favoritism toward Chōshū officers, but he openly suppressed the careers of Satsuma men as well. While in office he forced the retirement of 7 high-ranking generals, 3 of whom were Satsuma officers; none were Chōshū. Five of the 7, including all 3 of the Satsuma generals, were senior to Terauchi. He also retired 44 lieutenant generals, of whom only 10 were from Chōshū. Of these 10, 4 were promoted to general on retirement. His hand-picked vice minister was his devoted disciple. Two successive Chōshū generals and an officer beholden personally to Terauchi held the key office of chief of the military affairs bureau in the Terauchi decade.[10] When Terauchi finally resigned in 1911, Tanaka Giichi, Chōshū's rising star, came to head the military affairs bureau, a position that gave him direct (and frequent) access to Yamagata.

After the Russo-Japanese War, just as after the war with China, the nation showered its military leaders with decorations and noble rank. In 1907, 64 army officers received appointments to or advanced in the nobility, among them Terauchi, previously a commoner, who soared miraculously up to viscount, skipping the rank of baron entirely. The army minister's feat was all the more curious when one realizes that he did all his fighting from an office in Tokyo. The emperor granted 21 Chōshū and 10 Satsuma officers noble rank, just short of a majority of the total so honored.[11] In addition, he selected 35 naval officers for elevation to noble status. This imperial recognition for military service materially heightened the political profile of both the army and the navy on the national scene, as well as that of Chōshū within the army.

The Effects of the Russo-Japanese War

In spite of human losses and a stupendous burden of debt, Japan emerged from the Russo-Japanese War a great power. The war with China had gained a colony in Taiwan, a stranglehold on Korea, and a commercial position in China analogous to that of the Western powers, and it had led to freedom from the "unequal treaties" imposed by the Westerners before the restoration. The war with Russia enlarged Japan's continental position by transferring to Japan the Russian leasehold on China's Guandong (Kwantung) Peninsula, together with the South Manchurian Railway (SMR), which ran north from Guandong into the heart of Manchuria, and it removed Russian pressure from Korea. The war strengthened Japan's industrial power and further developed the structural base for a modern economy. Victory over a major Western power imparted a confidence that allowed the Japanese to reflect on themselves and place increasing value in their own traditions. A critical examination began of earlier, often indiscriminate, borrowing from the West. The army, as a principal actor in this dramatic change in the nation's fortunes, basked in the favor of the people. Its prestige was never higher.

Nor did Japan's feats on the battlegrounds of Manchuria go unnoticed in the West. War correspondents from Europe and America covered the fighting in precise detail. The heroic charges of the Japanese infantry under the withering fire of Russian rifles and machine guns at Port Arthur (for this was the first major war in which that terrible weapon found extensive use) became famous throughout the Western world, where dying gloriously for one's country was never more fashionable. Japan's British allies led the way in extolling the indomitable spirit of the Japanese foot soldier, and that spirit was quickly recognized and applauded as the difference between defeat and shining victory. The Japanese had achieved something thoroughly admirable by the nationalist and imperialist standards of the day, and the world paid homage to their fighting spirit.

Within the army pride and confidence surged. It was manifest that the time had come to reexamine military doctrine on the basis of Japanese victories, not on the learned experience of the Western powers. The army had come of age; it had mastered the art of modern warfare and would thereafter stand on its own. The overriding lesson of the war appeared to be the decisive role of morale or spirit in combat. Japan's centuries-old samurai tradition had strongly emphasized the importance of the intangible qualities of the human spirit (*seishin*) in warfare, and this war served to reestablish their primacy. Since esprit was the universally acclaimed key to Japan's victory, the leadership tended to emphasize the irrational quality *seishin* and rest content with attained levels in the rational elements of war — technology and its practical utilization through organization and training. After fifty years of borrowing from the West the army, like the people, was now relieved and proud to find new relevance in the nation's traditional values.

Since the restoration national defense had held the highest priority for the Meiji government. To reward the army for its success in war and praise its leaders for advancing the nation's fortunes was to reconfirm the singular importance of a strong military as an instrument of successful national policy. The army quite naturally translated this affirmation into the necessity for its support, and it made demands on the nation for men and material to maintain the defense of Japan's new continental frontier. The temptation to enter the political arena to fight for the support of army priorities was overwhelming, and in time it rationalized away such flimsy obstacles to political action as the "Imperial Rescript to Soldiers and Sailors."

The engine that powered army external politics was the fear of Russia. Of all the nations to contact Japan in the waning days of the Tokugawa era, none posed a closer or more persistent threat than the tsar's empire. The proximity of the Russians to Japan, the competition between the two countries in the islands bordering the Sea of Okhotsk and, later, on the Asian continent, and the seemingly insatiable appetite of tsarist imperialism made Russia a nightmare for the Japanese. Only Yamagata's Anglo-Japanese alliance of 1902 gave Japan the necessary international backing to stand against Russia in 1904. The army knew the truth about the war — how narrow the victory, how uncertain the peace. Diplomatic rapprochement with Russia in the agreements of 1907 and 1910 (designed to thwart America's efforts toward an "open door" in a closed Manchuria) notwithstanding, the army's primary enemy remained Russia and only Russia. This is the salient fact of the Japanese army's external political history.[12] Only once — in the Pacific War — did the army turn its attention elsewhere, and it paid dearly for that lapse.

The certainty of a new war with Russia and the perception that Japan's spiritual ascendancy was the key to victory led the army to fret a great deal about the moral quality of the soldiers and of the people from whom they came. Since army leaders traced *Yamato damashii*, the superior Yamato or Japanese spirit, to the traditional values of old Japan, they worried about the impact of rapid change and modernization on the moral fiber of the society. As a result, the army tended to be somewhat suspicious of Japan's modern sector, especially the new urban society. The army saw the corruption of Japan's military virtues in imported industrialization yet depended on it for modern arms.

To preserve the valuable traditions of loyalty, valor, and frugality, which in its view typified the Japanese of old, the army began to show a great deal of interest in agricultural Japan—the countryside where feudal traditions and the hard honest life of old Japan survived best. (In Japan's military lore the weakest infantry divisions were from Kyoto and Osaka, the big cities; the strongest were from rural Japan. The more remote the region, the stronger the unit.) It also broadened its interest in education because the officers perceived changes in the attitudes of the drafted soldiers. The army was no longer receiving stolid, malleable yeomen of rural Japan with only one or two years of formal education. Postwar draftees had six or more years of school, and increasing numbers of young men came from the morally suspect urban areas. For an army that relied on the *seishin* of its soldiers for victory, it was essential that the content of the soldier's education foster and support the army's spiritual ideal.[13]

The Changes to the Army Standing Orders

The preservation of moral values in the society were long-range concerns, however. The immediate problem was to apply the lessons of the war to the military system in preparation for wars to come. The emperor's prepared statement before the great parade at Aoyama on good order and discipline was a broad clue to the army's solicitude. On 1 December 1908, the army ministry issued the first of the changes to standing orders in a completely revised *guntai naimusho*, or handbook of interior administration, which regulated life in army camps and barracks in detail. In addition to a heavy emphasis on spiritual training and the inculcation of the military virtues, the new handbook veered sharply from the old rational European standards of interior management to a family system based on transposed Confucian relationships. From this time, the army looked upon itself as a great "family of soldiers who suffer and rejoice together and live or die as one."[14] Implicit in the handbook was the idea that the army had a mission to shape national character through the education and training of its soldiers—later expressed in the phrase "The army is the school of the people."[15] In the implementation of this concept, the army actually isolated itself from the people by restricting soldiers' time off base and strictly censoring their reading material.

The revised *naimusho* separated the soldiers from the people, but two years later, in November 1910, the army introduced a new mode of communication more favorable to its interests. If the army was to be a school for the people, it was imperative that a means of official contact be maintained. The army designed the Imperial Military Reservists Association, or Teikoku Zaigo Gunjinkai, to perform this function. The Reservists Association, another army response to the perceived threat of a new war with Russia, formed local branches across the nation down to the village level, and after 1914 it included former navy men as well. General, later Marshal, Terauchi, under whose ministry the association took shape, served as its chairman for the rest of his life, but informal control centered for many years in its real founder, Col. Tanaka Giichi.

The late Meiji creation of the centralized reservist association marks an important dividing line in the Chōshū officers' efforts to build national unity and spread military values. Not only was it the army's last attempt to expand its influence through primarily military organizations. . . . It was also the army's first effort to educate civilians, for one-half of the members enrolled even though they had never served on active duty.[16]

The next step in the "derationalization" of the standing orders was to change the field manuals, a major undertaking that took several years to complete, since it required a new manual for every branch of the army. The first one, the infantry field manual, was by far the most important because of its general applicability to all army units in battle. Published in 1909, the *hohei sōten* set the tone for the army's approach to combat. Building on the experience of the Russo-Japanese War, the infantry manual, while giving lip service to a doctrine of combined arms tactics, actually placed the total burden on the infantry to attain victory. Infantry attack with small-arms fire followed by a bayonet charge was the doctrine in which army tactics centered. The activities of other branches were strictly peripheral to this main action. By its very nature, this doctrine emphasized *seishin* and almost automatically relegated technology to a secondary role. The manual also intimated that proper attention to military discipline would develop an irresistible attack spirit that would inevitably result in victory.

The confidence born of victory over Russia, inflated by self-congratulation and foreign flattery, encouraged the army to revive irrational elements from Japan's military past at the expense of rational technological and organizational features borrowed from the West. With the foreknowledge that any renewed warfare with Russia would strain Japan's material and spiritual resources to their limit, the army prepared its soldiers by clothing them in heavy psychological armor. It was said later, "No matter how powerful the enemy, we must resolve to prevail with our spiritual superiority as a matter of course."[17]

The idea that Japan would always face a primary enemy whose army was superior both in number and in material strength penetrated deeply into the minds of officers and men alike. From this time, the sole key to victory lay in *Yamato damashii,* and by a paradoxical twist in the army's mentality, efforts to achieve technological superiority or even parity assumed a secondary role. The navy, more dependent on rational technical attainments in ships and guns, never fell so completely into this terrible trap. It is significant that one of the staff officers most responsible for the preparation of the infantry manual was Col. Tanaka Giichi.

To complete the revision of standing orders, the army published new training regulations in 1913 and new field service regulations in 1914. Like their forerunners these, too, incorporated native conceptions or moral values and moved away from earlier versions based on European rational standards.

The Problem of an Integrated War Plan

While the army ministry coped with revisions to the standing orders, the general staff headquarters directed its attention to preparations for the next war. Many documents connected with these plans remain unavailable and may be lost, but we do know that the army's plan for the defense of the empire was based on Russia as the prime hypothetical enemy with China mentioned as a relatively unimportant secondary foe. The army also considered France and Germany in its analysis, usually in the context of an alliance with Russia or with Russia and China. The army was able, however, to discount any great danger from France or Germany on the basis of Japan's renewed alliance with Great Britain, while China's debilitating internal weakness ruled that country out as a serious enemy, so army planning remained narrowly focused on Russia. Nowhere in the plan did the general staff view the United States as a potential enemy. The army portion of the 1907 national defense plan called for a total of 50 infantry divisions, 25 active and 25 reserve. (It had 19 active divisions at the time.)[18]

Both the army and the navy recognized the need for a joint long-range defense plan after the war, but, given the gaping divergence in their analysis of the world situation, an integrated plan proved almost impossible to achieve. The navy had utterly destroyed Russian sea power in 1905 at the great naval battle of Tsushima, and it could no longer assign any priority to the Russians as a hypothetical enemy. For the navy the United States was a far more likely opponent, for relations with the United States had deteriorated rapidly after the war. There was a strong movement to end Japanese immigration to the U.S. west coast; the island territories the two nations acquired at the turn of the century set their national interests at cross purposes in the Pacific; and America, like Japan, had recently built a large modern navy. In headlong pursuit of an open door policy in China, America attempted to alter the exclusive nature of Russian and Japanese imperialism in Manchuria. The Japanese, who had bought their rights in China's northeast with the blood of their sons and brothers, openly resented American interference. The Japanese government's agreements with Russia to block the presumptuous Americans were perceived as rapprochement with the former enemy by most Japanese outside the army, and the navy's view that America, not Russia, was Japan's most likely potential foe prevailed. Knowing from Russia's unhappy experience that a second-best fleet is worse than no fleet at all, the navy in its portion of the defense plan called for huge expenditures on a thoroughly modern force centered on eight new battleships and eight new cruisers — the "eight-eight" fleet.

As might be expected, controversy surrounded the 1907 imperial defense plan from its inception, and after its adoption the eight-eight fleet and plans for 50 infantry divisions competed in the imperial Diet for money in an era of financial stringency caused by postwar economic dislocations and the immense burden of the war debt. The rift that developed between the services in the period between the Russo-Japanese War and World War I over defense priorities and the allocation of financial resources never closed, and the "advance north, march south" dichotomy in Japan's military thought ended only with the Pacific War. Over the next few years the army's uphill battle with the government and the Diet for funds enticed it into the political arena. Afterward, blatant army (and navy) interference in the normal process of civil government under the Meiji Constitution gradually became an endemic feature of Japan's national political scene. In reaction, the political world leveled charges of militarism against the army, and movements began in the political parties to protect constitutional government from the military's political threat. By the end of the Meiji era the army and the political world had come to view each other as competitors, and the army's popularity fell as criticism of its political interference mounted.

A Glimmer of Hope for the Army's Outsiders

Until the end of the Meiji era (1912), Chōshū remained firmly in the army's seats of power. Army Minister Terauchi ruled, backed by the awesome power of Yamagata. Terauchi was as arrogant in his dealings with the officer corps as he was in his later treatment of the hapless Koreans. He saw to it that Chōshū men or his own personal followers occupied prime positions in the army ministry and the general staff and that choice commands went to Chōshū generals. Flagrant in his favored treatment of Chōshū clansmen, Terauchi never neglected his own advancement. As we have seen, he rose from commoner to viscount in one bound, and he later achieved the court rank of count. He is accused of manipulating the qualifications for elevation to marshal in order to assure his own eligibility. He became a marshal in May 1916, shortly before the *genrō* chose him prime minister of Japan.

So firmly was Terauchi entrenched that he held the post of army minister and governor-general of Korea simultaneously from October 1910 until September 1911, when he finally resigned the ministry to devote his energy to the pacification of Korea. When his longtime vice minister and devoted follower Lt. Gen. Ishimoto Shinroku replaced him, Terauchi and Chōshū, in effect, continued to rule the army, but the ailing Ishimoto died in April 1912, offering renewed possibilities for non-Chōshū officers. Chōshū had held the ministry for more than fourteen years in an era noted for Chōshū domination in national politics as well.

Terauchi's resignation and Ishimoto's untimely death brought high hopes to the outside generals, who could now entertain the possibility of a break in Chōshū power.[19] When Ishimoto died, the army foresaw a difficult battle with Prince Saionji Kinmochi's Seiyūkai Party over the proposed increase in army strength. With this in mind, the army narrowed the choice of the man to lead the charge to two candidates, neither of them Chōshū generals. Lt. Gen. Kigoshi Yasutsuna of Ishikawa Prefecture, a protégé of Katsura Tarō, was one politically suitable choice, more for his close connections with Chōshū men than his personal strength; Lt. Gen. Uehara Yūsaku of Satsuma was the other. The army settled on Uehara as the more forceful of the pair. Although with Uehara's selection Chōshū relinquished the army ministry, this did not appear at the time to be a serious threat to its overall position because Chōshū continued to occupy the offices of the chief of the general staff and the chief of the general affairs bureau in the army ministry. As a marshal, Terauchi was still on the active list, the governor-generalship of Korea was a posting for an officer on active duty, and, of course, the ultimate power of Yamagata loomed in the background.

The story of the Saionji cabinet's staunch resistance to the army's insistent demand for an immediate increase in strength of two infantry divisions, which resulted in Uehara's resignation and the downfall of the cabinet, is well known. Uehara's term of office as the army minister lasted only from April to December 1912, but when he resigned, the army looked upon him as a political hero—a steadfast advocate of its position. His reputation rose, and his following within the ranks of the officer corps grew. It is a measure of the change in the public attitude toward the army and the split between the army and the people that the soldiers idolized Uehara while the civilian political world reviled him. The army, however, never happy with the idea of competing political ideas or even with the institution of political parties, accepted its defeat as further proof of parties' willingness to weaken the nation for their own selfish political ends.

Internal political maneuvering outside the closed circle of the Chōbatsu reopened with the resignation of Terauchi and the death of his successor. Letters written to Uehara by his friends and partisans during this time reveal the intense interest and hopeful speculation inspired by these events. Uehara had been a dark-horse candidate for army minister or vice minister in August 1911, when Terauchi left office, but to his friends' disappointment, Chōshū favoritism prevailed over excellence and the posts went to the failing Ishimoto and Oka Ichinosuke, another Chōshū minion. There was a new blow to Satsuma and the aspiring non-Chōbatsu generals in January 1912, when Hasegawa Yoshimichi, a tough-minded Chōshū general, succeeded the aging Marshal Oku Yasukata as chief of the general staff and Ōshima Ken'ichi, another Chōshū handmaiden, became Hasegawa's deputy. Ishimoto's death put a new face on the situation, however, and differences within the Chōshū clique, compounded by some recognition that the army could not be led forever by Chōshū hacks, reopened the way for Uehara, who finally received the army minister's portfolio on 5 April 1912, to the delight of the Satsuma and non-Chōshū generals. One must remember, however, that the Chōbatsu chose Uehara and that his appointment did not signify any composite inclination on Chōshū's part to renounce its comfortable position of superiority. A notable exception to this attitude was that of the young Maj. Gen. Tanaka Giichi, who supported the appointment of Uehara in both 1911 and 1912. Chōshū's leading scion, the ambitious and personable Tanaka, always had more to say about subjects of broad army interest than his rank would normally allow, and non-Chōshū officers regularly approached him in private to find out what was going on in Chōshū circles closed to them. Secure in the success of his own career, he maintained a liberal view of personnel administration and did not insist on perpetuating Chōshū control as did his compatriots of lesser talent.

In a letter to Uehara congratulating him on his appointment, Machida Keiu, a partisan and outspoken young Satsuma general, praised Tanaka in the following words;

Tanaka has extraordinary vision [for a Chōshū man]. He consistently adheres to your doctrine of attempting to rebuild the army on a sound basis through the recognition of ability [not clan affiliation]. Moreover, as child prodigy of the Chōshū line, he has great power. . . . If later on the opportunity arises and you choose Tanaka as your vice minister, in response to your friendship he will be obliged to work with you.[20]

A few years would elapse before a Uehara-Tanaka conjunction emerged at the top levels of the army hierarchy, and it would be in the general staff headquarters, not the army ministry.

Uehara plunged into the fight for the two-division increase, meeting head-on the determined resistance of Saionji's economy-minded ministers. Yamagata worked hard on the army's behalf and backed Uehara with all his resources, but to no avail. On 2 December 1912, the exasperated Uehara exercised his right of *iaku no jōsō* with Yamagata's approval and tendered his resignation directly to the emperor without even the courtesy of informing Saionji beforehand. Closing ranks, the army generals in support of Uehara denied Saionji a replacement. Yamagata refused Saionji's pleas to intervene, and on 5 December his cabinet fell.

The popular reaction to these events was devastatingly critical of the army, leading shortly to Diet action to revise the ordinances limiting the qualifications of army and navy ministers. Be that as it may, the army never wavered in the belief that the two divisions were essential to the defense of Japan against Russia or in its view that defense considerations overbore domestic, political, and financial considerations. The split between the army and the civilian world was plain.

Within the army a new champion had emerged, however. Uehara's following increased, and from this time until his death in 1933 he remained the most consistently admired figure in the army and a model for many younger officers. Because Uehara's following transcended clan lines, the clique that formed about him was probably the first to break the *hanbatsu*, or clan clique, mold, and it later became one of the primary internal political instruments for attacking the entrenched Chōbatsu.

Because the army's cynical destruction of Saionji's cabinet sparked a violent political reaction, the *genrō* could find no one willing to replace the fallen prime minister. For two weeks the nation's elders wrestled with the problem, finally prevailing upon retired General Katsura Tarō to step down from his sequestered position as the emperor's grand chamberlain to form his third cabinet. His effort was doomed from the outset. Katsura came under immediate, vehement attack from the Seiyūkai for his "greed" in leaving the emperor's service to grab the political spotlight, and the navy for its own reasons added to the chaos by refusing to provide Katsura a navy minister. In desperation Katsura turned to the emperor for an order, which forced the navy to produce an admiral to fill the position. This assured Katsura a cabinet, but for openly involving the emperor in a political issue, the Seiyūkai redoubled its attacks on Katsura.

Under these trying circumstances Lt. Gen. Baron Kigoshi Yasutsuna, Katsura's protégé, finally received his turn as army minister. Katsura had not favored the army's demand for an immediate increase in strength, and Kigoshi did not even raise the tender issue with the embattled prime minister. When the Katsura cabinet resigned in February 1913 after a hectic two months in office, Yamamoto Gonbei, a Satsuma admiral, agreed to take the reins of the government, and Kigoshi continued in office under him.

Yamamoto determined on a course of compromise with the rampaging Seiyūkai political forces in order to restore stability to the government, and he focused his attention on the troublesome Imperial Ordinances 193 and 194, which confined the positions of the service ministers to active duty officers, since these ordinances had led directly to the current impasse and the Diet was clamoring for their repeal. Yamamoto's compromise struck the words "on active duty" from the ordinances, admitting the possibility for retired flag officers of the first and second reserve to fill the ministerial posts. The compromise was a minimal concession to the politicians, but it was enough to terminate the crisis. From the army's viewpoint, however, even this compromise was totally unacceptable, for potentially it took control of the army ministry out of the hands of the active army, a step the army perceived as a breach of its right to independent command. Hasegawa Yoshimichi, the hard-nosed Chōshū chief of staff, approached the emperor, as was his right, in order to block the compromise — another attempt to involve the emperor in political action — but the emperor wisely declined to interfere.

Having lost its battle, the army turned its wrath on Army Minister

Kigoshi, who had not, in the army's opinion, made the necessary effort to stave off the disaster. The Yamamoto cabinet continued in office until spring 1914, when it fell owing to the "Siemens affair," involving peculation in the management of naval appropriations, but the army removed Kigoshi in June 1913. The army retired Kigoshi shortly thereafter, and as a final indignity his colleagues refused to recommend him for promotion to *taishō* (general) on his retirement. Kigoshi's close association with Katsura and his long, honorable service to his country availed him nothing when he faced the ire of an uncompromising army. Ironically, the shabby treatment of Kigoshi can be attributed largely to the dominant Chōshū clique.[21]

The events surrounding the fall of the Saionji cabinet and the overwhelming political attack on Katsura that followed shook to the core the *Satchō* oligarchs who ruled Japan. The aftershocks reverberated in a similar fashion among the Chōshū leaders of the army. For the Chōbatsu, determined to cling to power, the problem was to give a semblance of broader leadership to the army while preserving control in its own hands. The choice of army ministers following Uehara's resignation in December 1912 bears this out. No Chōshū general held the post again until 1918, but manageable generals beholden to Chōshū succeeded to the post one after the other. The Chōbatsu's weakened footing naturally invited criticism and verbal attack from the repressed majority of general officers who chafed under Chōshū rule, and they saw in these circumstances an opportunity to rid the army of one-clique domination—a feat accomplished earlier in the navy under Adm. Yamamoto Gonbei. The primary rallying point was the popular Uehara, whose loyalty to the army's cause and personal rectitude could not be denied. Unfortunately, Uehara fell sick a short time after leaving office, and he battled illness for several months thereafter. As was usual in such circumstances, the army placed him on a "waiting list," which often spelled retirement for general officers, but after a long recuperation he regained his health, and not even the Chōbatsu dared to suggest that he be released from active duty. In March 1914 Uehara stepped from the shadow of retirement to become the inspector general of military training (*kyōiku sōkan*), a position that, together with the army minister and chief of the general staff, composed the army's "big three" (*san chōkan*). The next year the army promoted Uehara to general, and in December 1915 he succeeded Hasegawa in the more important post of chief of the general staff.[22] There he joined Tanaka Giichi, who had ascended to the post of vice chief of staff in October.

Army Activity in China During the First World War

As so often happened in Japan's modern era, the political impasse of early Taishō found its solution in war. In September 1914, cleaving to its alliance with Great Britain, Japan declared war on the Central Powers. With a cause to support, the nation closed ranks once again, and in 1915 the army received sanction for its two new divisions. The first of these completed organization in 1916, the second in 1919, bringing the total number of active infantry divisions to 21. The new divisions, numbered 19 and 20, formed the Chōsen Army and went on permanent station in Korea.

The war with Germany did not involve the Japanese army in extensive operations. A short, leisurely campaign against the small German garrison in their Jiaozhou (Kiaochow) Bay Leased Territory delivered Qingdao (Tsingtao) and German holdings in China's Shandong Province into Japanese hands. That campaign terminated on 7 November 1914, but it was only the prelude to a series of incidents in China in which the army played an increasingly significant role.

When Uehara and Tanaka assumed their offices on the general staff in the waning days of 1915, Japan and China had already passed through their first wartime crisis over the so-called Twenty-One Demands. The army had apparently not played a major role in their formulation or in the bitter negotiations between the Ōkuma and Yuan Shikai governments, but when China was forced to agree to transfer the German rights in Shandong to Japan and expand Japan's rights in Manchuria, the army acquired new continental responsibilities.

The army demonstrated its own ability to act in China and set the precedent for further intelligence operations on the continent when, in 1916, it took charge of a government-sponsored operation to prevent China's president, Yuan Shikai, from establishing a new dynasty in China with himself as emperor. From this time, the army played a major role in Japan's affairs in China,[23] soon overshadowing all other government agencies with its power and later, at times, acting contrary to the expressed policy of the government and the foreign ministry.

In a sense, army intrusion into the normal course of diplomatic relations with China was natural during the warlord period, which followed the death of Yuan in June 1916. As China dissolved into warlordism, local leadership passed into the hands of military men. Under these circumstances, meaningful contact with China's leaders fell more and more to the army. China's warlords were soldiers; they sought the advice of soldiers. They tended to think of solving China's problems and advancing their own fortunes by military means. The army could understand the necessity for using force and could discuss the intricate military problems of troop training, tactics, strategy, arms, and equipment as no diplomatic representative could. There is little doubt that most Chinese warlords welcomed Japanese military advisers and the visits of military attachés in the hope that these men could provide the military advice and aid they desperately needed for their own survival, if not for more ambitious projects.

The new importance of the army in Japan's relations with China was clearly demonstrated when Vice Chief of Staff Tanaka Giichi made an unprecedented grand inspection tour of that country in spring 1917. Tanaka talked with most of the important warlords and political leaders of the day including Sun Yat-sen and China's new president, Li Yuanhong. The central theses of Tanaka's long conversations were the restoration of domestic unity, the advance of China's national strength, and a joint Sino-Japanese effort to end European imperialism in Asia. The foundations of Tanaka's China policy when he became prime minister a decade later rose from this visit.[24] But even more important, the army became accustomed to the idea of a role in diplomacy to accompany its forward strategy and its supplementary intelligence operations.

By 1918 the army had acquired two decades of experience in continental affairs. In that year it maintained four garrisons in China and Manchuria, including the China Garrison Army in Tianjin and Beijing, an outgrowth of the Boxer Rebellion, and the Manchuria Garrison Force, later to become the powerful Guandong (Kwantung) Army (1919). The army policed the South Manchurian Railway, which connected to the Russian-controlled Chinese Eastern Railway and was the principal line of land communication from the Guandong Peninsula to northern Manchuria, Siberia, and Russia. In addition to the four garrisons in China, the two-division Chōsen Army approached full authorized strength in Korea. Nor were troops the extent of the army's continental influence, for in 1918 it already maintained attachés in Beijing, resident military officers in major cities, and military advisers to principal warlords.[25] The combined system of military advisers, attachés, residents, and command headquarters, each with its own intelligence-collection capability, provided the army with an information network second to none in China. With extensive coverage, adequate funds, highly motivated agents, and the support of a curious group of Japanese civilian ultranationalist adventurers known as the "China *rōnin*," no one could deny that the Japanese, and especially the army, were the best informed of foreigners on the kaleido-scopic situation of China's warlord era.[26]

As its interests and power in China grew, the army trained more and more young officers as China specialists. These men, accustomed to an active role in China's rough-and-tumble warlord politics and convinced of the importance of the army's continental position in the national defense, later rose to prominence as proponents of political views within the army itself. I discuss them in greater detail later.

The Disastrous Siberian Venture

By far the most significant army action stemming from the Great War was the Allied intervention in Siberia from August 1918. This initiative embroiled Japan in the Russian civil war and ended only after a night-marish four-year occupation in that unhappy land. The intervention tore Japan's wartime political unity to shreds, involved the army and the gov-ernment in bitter controversy, and renewed factional strife within the army itself.

The collapse of the Allies' eastern front in the Russian revolutions of April and November 1917 panicked the Western Allies, who justifiably feared a new onslaught from the reunited German armies along the front in France. The Japanese initially rejected France's urgent requests to inter-vene in Russia, but later the army general staff came to view the tsarist collapse as a unique opportunity to free Japan from any future threat from Russia by detaching eastern Siberia to form an independent state. For months Yamagata and the government refused to countenance such an adventure, until the United States proposed a joint Allied expedition into Siberia to rescue an army of Czech nationalists stranded in the storm of the Russian socialist revolution.

The Czechs, originally unenthusiastic members of the Austrian army, who had been captured by the Russians, had joined the tsarist forces in the hope of freeing their Slavic homeland from Austro-Hungarian domi-nation. The Bolshevik Revolution in November 1917 and the peace ar-ranged between the revolutionary government of Russia and Germany in March 1918 left the Czechs without a war to fight, but the new Commu-nist regime finally gave them permission to leave Russia at Vladivostok via the Trans-Siberian Railroad. When the Czechs encountered obstructions on their long journey to the east, President Woodrow Wilson took it upon himself to "rescue" the little army, prompting a turnabout in the U.S. policy on intervention in Russia. The Americans, in turn, persuaded the

Japanese government to join them and the European powers in a relief expedition. Yamagata and the Terauchi government, enticed by the Americans and egged on by the army, relented.

The army's most vociferous proponent of intervention was Vice Chief of Staff Tanaka Giichi, and he had the complete support of his chief, Gen. Uehara Yūsaku. The most candid expression of Tanaka's position is preserved in a position paper written by the general himself, probably for presentation to the army minister in spring 1918.[27] In this "Tanaka shuki" the vice chief of staff openly advocated a policy of support for Asiatic Russians willing "to defend their fatherland against the eastward advance of German-Austrian influence" (i.e., Bolshevism) and asked that all continental diplomatic and military representatives be instructed to make this policy clear to the Russian people and to work for their cooperation. Support for the Russians, once firmly organized, could include military equipment, money, and the military "advisers" to lead them. The ultimate goal of the Japanese effort would be to establish a great self-governing buffer state in Siberian Russia east of Lake Baikal.

Extensive planning for an expedition proceeded under Tanaka's personal supervision, even to the point of badgering the Chinese into a military agreement that granted the Japanese army permission to move troops at will in northern Manchuria. The joint Allied intervention began in early August 1918. Once committed, the Japanese army quickly violated every expectation of their American allies by dispatching ten times the number of troops the United States originally considered necessary to accomplish the rescue mission and by occupying an immense expanse of Russian territory. Entering at Vladivostok and points along the Manchurian border, they seized every major inhabited place east along the Trans-Siberian railway from the city of Chita. The army then lent its support to willing White Russian elements, primarily unruly Cossack atamans, in order to accomplish its own grandiose scheme.

On 5 September the Japanese linked up with the Czech vanguard, which, it turned out, was quite capable of taking care of itself. A few days later the British and French contingents joined the Czechs in a harebrained scheme to reestablish the eastern front beyond the Urals. Subsequently, the European allies trekked west into the vast Russian heartland. The Japanese army, with its own separate objective in mind, refused to proceed west of Lake Baikal, and the Americans, shaken by the surprising turn of events, stayed behind to keep an eye on the Japanese, whose actions were indeed suspicious.

When the war in Europe ended with Germany's defeat in November

1918, the Allies, changing policy without serious reflection, decided on the disastrous course of intervention in the Russian civil war in support of White counterrevolutionary forces. The Allies in western Siberia teamed up with Adm. A. V. Kolchak's shaky regime at Omsk. The Japanese gave perfunctory sanction to this action, but they stood by their original decision to remain east of Lake Baikal as their army continued to pump support into Kolchak's Cossack rivals such as the notorious G. M. Semenov and the murderous Ivan Kalmykov.

Meanwhile, significant political changes had taken place in Tokyo. No sooner had the Terauchi government given the go-ahead to the army for the Siberian Expedition than internal disturbances within Japan, the "rice riots" of August 1918, toppled it. With great reluctance and after much bargaining, Yamagata agreed to the designation of Hara Kei, leader of the Seiyūkai, to form a government. Hara, who spearheaded the political parties' fight against a Siberian expedition, had given in, as had Yamagata, only after the American president had thrown his weight behind the idea. The cornerstone of Hara's position on foreign affairs was, and remained, cooperation with the United States. Hara's cabinet, Japan's first true party government, thus inherited a venture its leader had sought desperately to prevent and for which he had no enthusiasm.

In order to form his government, Hara had to make certain concessions to Yamagata, whose opposition to party cabinets was still strong, and to the army, which shared Yamagata's view. One compromise was the acceptance of the Chōshū lieutenant general Tanaka Giichi as the army minister. In position, if not in rank, Tanaka was now Uehara's equal.

Tanaka may have been presumptuous and impulsive, but he was no fool, and from his new vantage point in the cabinet, it was not long before he began to have reservations about the expedition he had so ardently advocated. Justifying his action by financial considerations, but with an eye to American and Japanese criticism of army actions in Siberia, Tanaka exercised his administrative prerogative to trim troop strength in Siberia by one-half in December 1918 over the objections of Uehara and the general staff.[28] From this time, Tanaka wavered between his loyalty to the army cause and the commonsense dictates of the situation in Siberia; finally, after months of indecision, he concluded that the expeditionary force could never realize the army's dream and must be withdrawn.

By the summer of 1919 Admiral Kolchak's White regime in central Siberia had collapsed, and his European allies began to troop back to Vladivostok. The British departed Siberia in September 1919; after many vicissitudes, the larger Czech force cleared Vladivostok one year later.

Gradually, as he came to realize that there was no chance for success in Siberia, Tanaka drew closer to the private views of most of his fellow cabinet members. Uehara, however, steadfastly maintained in the face of all evidence to the contrary that it was still possible to detach eastern Siberia and form an independent, anti-Bolshevik regime. Furthermore, Uehara argued, troop deployment in Siberia was an operational matter, not an administrative one, and as chief of the general staff he had the right to determine troop strengths and deployment as an inherent function of his office. Tanaka countered that the Siberian Expedition was not a war but an effort to aid Japan's Russian friends and allies, and therefore it came within the full administrative control of the army minister.[29] Yamagata, close to the end of his long life and unable to make clear decisions, wavered between the two opinions, coming around to Tanaka's position shortly before his death. As the argument between the two generals ran on month after month, it began to take on Chōshū-versus-Satsuma overtones that stirred up old interclan animosities that had lain dormant during the war. As Hara put it, "The general staff headquarters includes the friction of Satsuma and Chōshū, and there are many times when they are not in accord with Tanaka's opinions."[30]

The Americans removed their troops in spring 1920 in a manner that left no doubt of their disgust with Japan's activities in Siberia. Ironically, the unilateral American withdrawal undercut Hara, Tanaka, and those working to get the army out. To make matters worse, Russian partisans, who most wanted to rid Russia of Japan's presence, probably prolonged the occupation by several years when a group of them massacred Japanese garrison troops and civilians at Nikolaevsk in May 1920, presenting the army general staff with just the excuse it needed to continue the occupation. The massacre also gave Japan a credible justification for occupying the northern half of Sakhalin Island. The occupation in northern Sakhalin dragged on until 1925, but the prolonged negotiations and piecemeal withdrawal of the troops from Siberia after June 1920 need not detain us further. The withdrawals were, of course, at the initiative of the government, and the resistance to them came from Uehara and the army general staff.

In February 1921 General Tanaka sustained a serious heart attack. Torn between his duties and the warnings of his doctors, he carefully prepared for his resignation while acting on his current convictions with respect to Siberia and fulfilling the obligation he felt to Hara. Between February and May, when he resigned, the army minister laid the groundwork for the army's final withdrawal from Siberia and the Shandong

Peninsula in accord with the Hara government's foreign policy but over the continued objections of the chief of staff. With Yamagata's approval he selected his own successor, his friend and confidant Lt. Gen. Yamanashi Hanzō, so that his resignation would not cause the fall of the cabinet whose continuation Yamagata now supported. Finally, he negotiated a private agreement with Uehara, which elevated the chief of staff to *gensui* status in April 1921 with the understanding that the new marshal would leave office after a reasonable lapse of time.[31]

In July, when Marshal Uehara, faithful to his agreement, discussed his resignation with Yamagata, the quixotic old man reversed himself, insisting that Uehara remain in office because of the ill health of the Taishō emperor — a circumstance that had no conceivable bearing on Uehara's continuation. Thus, Tanaka lost his battle to bring the general staff under some kind of unified control. A few months later, when Yamagata died, Uehara emerged as the army's single most important figure. His position as *gensui* assured him an active duty role in army affairs for many more years.

2

The Army Faces Change

Wars of the future will not be won or lost on the strength of
armies alone. The ordinary people must be strong as well.

Tanaka Giichi

The Japanese nation had in the five decades before the Great War undergone and absorbed changes at an unprecedented pace, so much so that
Japan's modernization stood as a marvel in the West and an example to
the rest of Asia. The country, without succumbing to Western imperialism,
had successfully left its isolation and entered the world, and it had modernized and expanded in the manner of the dominant West by dint of
ceaseless struggle. In the enterprise the army had led the vanguard as the
nation's shield and sword. After the Great War, for the first time in the
mainstream of international politics, Japan, its people, and its army were
beset without respite by the same storm of technological, ideological, and
psychological changes that was raging in the other "modern" nations.

The builders of the Meiji system, steeped in a Japanese interpretation
of Confucian canon, which stressed harmony and balance, had sought
change primarily to cope with intolerable internal and external instability.
Their goal was not change for its own sake, but for a new harmony, a new
stability. The system they devised was not meant to absorb the shocks of
the changing world of the postwar decades. The army, a powerful and
established feature of the Japanese bureaucracy, tended to react negatively
or, at best, unenthusiastically to new ideas and new technology that might
disturb the set pattern of national success and military stability.

By the end of the Great War the leaders of the Meiji army had grown
old in the service. Although still powerful and active in 1920, the ōgosho,
Marshal Prince Yamagata Aritomo, the last of the army's founding fathers, was an octogenarian. Chief of Staff Uehara Yūsaku, born before the
restoration, had entered the army school system as a youth in the 8th year
of the Meiji era (1875). He was 64 years old in 1920; his rival, Army

Minister Tanaka, was 60. Ugaki Kazunari, a Tanaka protégé who would in a few years bear the burden of massive changes in the army, was born in the 1st year of Meiji. He graduated with the first class of the military academy.[1] Ugaki (52 in 1920) ultimately served his country as a member of the Diet under a new constitution, until his death in 1956. The Taishō army was not so young as the early Meiji army had been. Its officer corps spanned generations. It had formed traditions, an integrated system of line and staff functions, and a developed perception of its place in Japanese society. The army was a proud, independent, and powerful member of the imperial bureaucracy.

After Yamagata's death on 1 February 1922, Uehara, Tanaka, Ugaki, and the other army leaders were left to lead a far-from-exemplary military system. Like its counterpart in the civilian government, this system worked best so long as its founders, the first-generation "revolutionaries," the makers of modern Japan, remained in charge. Yamagata's death symbolized the end of the *genrō*, the peculiar extraconstitutional institution of elder statesmen that had given balance and stability to the Meiji system by its awesome presence in the background of Japanese politics for so many years.[2] When Yamagata died, Japan's military leaders (like their civilian colleagues) had already entered a new phase of doubt and insecurity, brought on not only by sharp contradictions within the army itself but also by the unstable atmosphere of a world in flux.

The Army's Anachronistic Leadership

The army's faults were quite apparent. It had acquired next to none of the new equipment — the artillery, the tanks, the airplanes, the communications — developed in Europe during the Great War. Its organization, training, and tactics dated back to the Russo-Japanese War. Everything was outmoded. The army needed a thoroughgoing renovation, but what rankled rising, younger officers was the continuing domination of the Chōbatsu, which limited their personal aspirations. Naturally, the army's shortcomings in every sphere were laid to the monopolistic personnel practices of the Chōshū clique and its repression of talented outsiders. By 1920 the younger generation of officers could see no reason for continuing Chōshū hegemony, and in keeping with the spirit of democratic action and radical activism abroad in the world, some of them were willing to risk doing something to end what had become a glaring abuse in Japan's military organization. The original Chōshū and Satsuma leadership had arisen as the result of a natural process, but its perpetuation into the Taishō period was calculated and, to those outside the charmed circle, grossly unfair. By contrast, the navy had ended Satsuma clique domination by 1914.[3]

As we have seen, the clan basis for the military cliques was built into the armed services at their inception. The basis changed later, but the formation of special interest groups remained an integral and very often dysfunctional feature of the army until its demobilization and abolition in 1945. All the Meiji era *gunbatsu*,[4] rooted as they were in the feudal clans, or *han*, were properly *hanbatsu*, or clan cliques, but this relationship was about to change.

Meiji era *hanbatsu* were small in actual participating membership. Perhaps all army officers from Yamaguchi Prefecture (as Chōshū was renamed) felt pride in their Chōshū birthright, but those who benefited most from the accident of their geographic origin were the elite among them — those who rose to the attention of Yamagata himself or of the Chōshū men who formed the core of their *hanbatsu*. In practice this came to mean the young men who graduated from the military academy high in their class and, more important, those who competed successfully for entry and did the best work at the army staff college (*rikugun daigakkō* or *rikudai*).[5] In Chapter 1 we saw how the veterans of the restoration wars constituted the bulk of the officer corps of the new imperial army by remaining in the service of the Meiji emperor. The percentage of *Satchō* officers was naturally very high under those circumstances, and, since the young Meiji emperor's "loyalist" army was composed primarily of lower-class samurai, it followed that the new army's officer corps came generally from that class. Only after the institution of the conscription system and the gradual development of the officer school system did the army attain a more balanced personnel structure that included officers from all geographic areas and most class backgrounds. However, the real shift from former samurai (*shizoku*) to officers of more general rural and urban backgrounds did not take place until the Taishō era.[6] By right of seniority, then, Chōshū (and Satsuma) clansmen formed the first elite leadership, and they perpetuated their position through the *hanbatsu* system, dominated by Chōshū men who did not, during Yamagata's lifetime, relinquish control of army personnel management. This ensured Chōshū a preponderance of promotions to high rank and assignments to preferred posts.[7]

Yamagata Aritomo's Chōshū Clique

Nationwide conscription and a military school system for advancing officer candidates opened a military career to all Japanese, but incumbent

Chōshū and Satsuma officers continued not only to lead the army but also to attract many of the best young men of Yamaguchi and Kagoshima (Satsuma) Prefectures into the army system through the example and prospect of success. Bright young Chōshū soldiers, cadets, and junior officers coming to the attention of military instructors and senior officers were moved, as they advanced in rank, into positions of responsibility, perpetuating a system not yet considered evil or unnecessarily discriminatory. Under the watchful eye of Yamagata the Meiji army grew to maturity. Yamagata's Chōshū protégés, and their protégés in turn, moved easily into high positions of responsibility in the army and the government. The last and youngest of Yamagata's Chōshū scions, the precocious Tanaka Giichi, was indulged like a spoiled youngest child, dabbling in such properly civilian matters as the Japan Youth Corps[8] without protest from his seniors and taking an unprecedented trip to Europe and America when assigned to a unit as brigade commander.[9] And like so many spoiled children Tanaka, close personally to Yamagata, openly used his favored position in the Chōshū *gunbatsu* to attain his own goals but took a cavalier attitude toward the maintenance of the clique that had fostered his success.

Shortly after Yamagata's death it is said that representatives of the Chōbatsu asked Tanaka about regular meetings to plan the preservation of the clique, and Tanaka reportedly demurred, saying, "That's all very nice, but since all Chōshū men are capable of walking by themselves [that won't be necessary]."[10] Tanaka's career had taken the model course for a successful Chōshū general, and he had received more than his share of army and public recognition for his work. It was natural that after Yamagata died, Tanaka was immediately identified as the head of a still powerful Chōbatsu in spite of his apparent unwillingness to perpetuate the *hanbatsu* system. Although Tanaka himself may have realized that the old clan cliques were an anachronism, neither possible to continue nor worthy of preservation, younger officers did not share his perception, and the general became the focus of an extraordinary "smash Chōshū" movement in the army late in the Taishō period.

Young Staff Officers Move for Personnel Reform

The army, influenced greatly by the Russian revolution and its experience in Siberia, became very sensitive to what Japanese political leaders termed dangerous thoughts in the postwar years and took active measures to prevent their spread in the army.[11] Ironically, the penetration of "dangerous" ideas, which justified subsequent radical political action and political subversion among younger officers in the army, stemmed from the failure of the army to correct abuses in its own personnel management system, and the officers' tactics of political subversion were much more effective than those of the civilian radicals, socialists, communists, or anarchists of that day.

The first stirring of active discontent among the officers occurred in October 1921, not in Japan as one might expect, but in Baden-Baden and Frankfurt, Germany. There on 27 and 28 October three good friends, all majors, all classmates in the military academy's 16th class (1904), and all recent graduates of the staff college, met and discussed ways to bring about reforms in the army.[12] The group, known to contemporaries as "the three crows," was led by Nagata Tetsuzan (Nagano Prefecture), soon to become a central figure in the army reform movement and later (12 August 1935) to die at the hand of a fellow officer, assassinated at his desk in the army ministry. In the year of his death Nagata was a major general in charge of the important military affairs bureau of the army ministry and a powerful figure in the imperial army's central headquarters.[13] At the time of the Baden-Baden meeting, Nagata was the military attaché in the Japanese legation in Bern, Switzerland.

The second member of the group was Obata Toshishirō (Kōchi Prefecture, formerly Tosa), then assigned as a military attaché to Russia but living in Berlin because the Soviets refused to admit him. Later, as a lieutenant general placed on reserve in 1936 after the February 26th Incident, Obata left the army. He subsequently served as ambassador to the Soviet Union and briefly as a state minister in the Higashikuni caretaker cabinet at the end of the Pacific War. Like Nagata, as an honor graduate, he had received a sword from the emperor on graduation from the staff college.

The third man of the trio, Okamura Yasuji (Tokyo), was returning through Europe after an assignment in China. Okamura became a general in 1941 and served in China during the war, where he ruthlessly retaliated against the Chinese communists after their "hundred regiments offensive" of 1940.[14] In 1944 he became supreme commander of the China Expeditionary Army.

Okamura's diary for 27 October 1921 cryptically tells us that the three friends made

a secret agreement concerning the dissolution of cliques, personnel reform, military organization reform, and arrangements for general mobilization. Ludendorff's total war became the topic of conversation. Obata, a specialist in Russian, hadn't read this book of Ludendorff's. England's Northcliffe was said to be a traitor. He was hated, but before a half year passed he became the propaganda minister. This was very impressive. We consider the matter of wartime propaganda.[15]

This is not much to go on, but years later, after the Pacific War, Okamura was able to talk more freely, although he was seeing things then through the long lens of time. Author Nakamura Kikuo asked him about the formation of the Issekikai, an important outgrowth of the Baden-Baden meeting. Okamura answered that Itō Masanori had written in *Gunbatsu kōbōshi* as if

in 1921 at Baden-Baden in southern Germany Nagata Tetsuzan, Obata Toshishirō, and I raised the standard of rebellion. That's an exaggeration. At the time we didn't think the least bit in terms of other countries like the Manchurian problem. What the three of us considered was the reform of the army. We took things seriously at that time. Frankly, what we meant by reform was, first, that personnel matters were all [settled by] clique, weren't they? The Chōshū clique made arbitrary personnel [decisions], and again, through [the Chōshū clique's exercise of] the army's right to command [*tōsuiken*], it had become separated from the people. We resolved to change this to a direction that was at one with the people's. That's the truth of the matter, and it was because we'd gone to Europe and seen the military situation there, wasn't it? At the time all three of us were majors. It was the beginning.[16]

These three young officers, leaders in their class, met not only to renew their friendship in a convivial atmosphere but also to conduct serious business in which they were willing to risk their reputations and careers. Okamura's diary indicates their concerns, including the great technological and organizational gap between the armies of Europe and Japan since the war. "Dissolution of cliques" and "personnel reform" showed their personal anxiety over continued Chōshū domination by its hold on the personnel system. "Military organization" and "arrangements for general mobilization" indicated their feeling that Japan was unprepared for modern warfare, unable to mass efficiently the total defense resources of the nation as outlined in Ludendorff's thesis.

The army's success in the Russo-Japanese War had given its leaders tremendous confidence in themselves, as exemplified by the plans made in conjunction with the navy for the defense of the nation. After the war with Russia military planners envisioned much larger military forces, and they drew up plans and pushed them forward without reference to political considerations, ignoring cabinets and political parties. The young officers in Baden-Baden were aware of the position of the military in society and its aims from the aura of the Russo-Japanese War that had permeated their

training at the staff college and from the stories of the war told them by
their seniors. However, their class had not participated in the war. They
had graduated from the *shikan gakkō* in October 1904, and they were
assigned almost to a man to rear area duties. Later, a clear division arose
between the *senjūha*, the "in-the-war group," and the *sengoha*, the "after-
the-war group." According to military historian Takahashi Masae, the
envy of the *sengoha*, who had missed the chance for recognition and glory
in battle, the raison d'être of the soldier, was quite apparent. "Nagata and
his friends resolved to become leaders of a new army . . . because they
understood the larger situation. But, I believe, they were conscious of this
division."[17]

Okamura's memory gives us the emphasis of the Baden-Baden meeting. To the conspirators the key to the situation was to break the Chōshū
hold on power, to remove the army from the hands of special interests,
and with the horrifying example of the Russian revolution before their
eyes, to return the army to harmony with the people. Their method would
be clandestine and subversive, as their actions after the meeting proved.
They immediately began to contact reliable like-minded military academy
classmates and men they knew in the classes just ahead and behind their
own. The first was Maj. Tōjō Hideki (Iwate Prefecture, 17th class), then
studying in Leipzig. Okamura got in touch with him immediately after the
initial meetings, probably because he was sure of Tōjō's support. Tōjō's
father, Hidenori, made a lieutenant general only on his retirement into the
reserves, bore a grudge against the Chōbatsu for his alleged unfair treatment at the clique's hands. Young Tōjō reflected his father's resentment.[18]

Okamura was the first of the three to return to Japan. Assigned to
general staff headquarters, second (intelligence) division, China section,
he began the work of recruiting.[19] As time went on younger men who
joined the movement discussed other things, but the original objectives
were to institute personnel reform, bring the army and the people back
together, and prepare the nation to withstand the rigors of total war.

As Okamura said, this was the beginning. This tiny group of discontented officers, the first to start a subversive movement within the ranks of
the army, eventually grew in number, broadened its membership to lower
ranks, changed its perspectives, and widened its concerns and activities in
a manner that changed the character of the army and, eventually, the
nation. A few years later new associations among much younger officers,
entirely unrelated to the original group founded at Baden-Baden, multi-
plied, opposed one another, resorted to extremist tactics and violence, and
joined hands in action with civilian and navy groups. In the years 1928–

31 the sudden, complicated proliferation of organizations with roots in the army officer corps found sympathy among more senior officers, while overbearing their authority, and goaded the nation toward foreign adventure and war. The Manchurian Incident and the February 26th Incident, two peaks of the crisis, were the direct result of the officers' aberrant behavior and their activism. In the last analysis they contributed heavily to the ultranationalist mood of the 1930's, which led the country into the disastrous China Incident (1937–41) and the Pacific War. The Baden-Baden meeting was not father to the ultranationalist, activist "young officers movement" in the army, but it was the first example of officers, not in authority, taking matters into their own hands to repudiate established army leadership and policy in defiance of their oath of obedience and disciplined conduct. As a whole, these movements were entirely contrary to the concept of army organization and most prejudicial to good order and discipline, but they flourished in the atmosphere of desperation that gradually enveloped Japan in the 1920's.

The Baden-Baden meeting and the movement that arose from it came about because of changes wrought by the Great War, which were political and psychological as well as military. The movement grew to embrace external aggression, particularly in China, but it remained a relatively rational approach to the solution of Japan's problems, given the social-Darwinist context of Japanese (and world) military thought at that time. In its original form this "staff officers movement" was oriented toward specific goals; in its later manifestations it tended toward hardened ideological positions, progressing from reformism to the brink of revolutionism, but there it drew back. The "young officers movement" of the late 1920's and early 1930's resulted from the increasingly desperate economic circumstances of the day and was much more intensely emotional than its predecessor. It based its thought on the highly irrational premises of Japanese nationalism and the emperor-centered Shinto faith. Its members advocated social revolution to rid the nation of unbearable injustice and intolerable economic disparities and did not shrink at terror, violence, or even open rebellion.

The Natural Evolution of the Army Clique Structure

At the time of the Baden-Baden meeting, the top posts in the army were still heavily weighted with Chōshū and Satsuma men. Yamanashi, Tanaka's surrogate, was the army minister. His vice minister was Ono Minobu (Fukuoka, a client of Satsuma), and the chief of the military affairs bureau was Sugano Hisaichi (Chōshū). The chief of staff was Uehara, and his vice chief was Kikuchi Shinnosuke (Ibaragi). The inspector general of military training was Akiyama Yoshifuru (Ehime), and his headquarters chief was Kojima Sōjirō (Okayama, a client of Chōshū). Five of the seven top posts were directly or indirectly in the hands of the *Satchō* cliques.

The striking new dimension, however, was that every one of these men, plus the three Baden-Baden conspirators and all the young field grade officers they eventually contacted, with the single exception of Uehara, was a graduate of the army staff college.[20] Ten percent or less of the graduates of the military academy attended the staff college; yet by 1921 staff college graduates had an almost complete monopoly of power and authority in the army. The men who were about to challenge them were also staff college graduates. Matsushita Yoshio, a lifelong observer and commentator on army politics, describes the shift taking place in the army *gunbatsu* as follows:

In the army from about the middle of the Taishō era, we can see the power of the "*han*-type" military clique [*hanbatsu*] — that is, the Chōshū clique — gradually deteriorating, but while the head of the Chōshū clique, Yamagata Aritomo, lived on, the clique carried immense weight in army circles. However, rise and fall is a rigid law of man's world, and the fact that at the height of its prosperity the Chōbatsu was, in the final analysis, permeated with decadence gave rise to "school-type" military cliques [*gakubatsu*], epitomized by the army staff college clique. We can say, then, that the Taishō era is a period of military cliques based on a combination of *han* and school types. After Yamagata died in February 1922, the influence of Chōshū declined markedly, and in its place the influence of the school clique at last came into its own within the army.

As the world passed from the Taishō to the Shōwa era [in 1926], the *han* coloring of army cliques faded and they were redyed with the tint of the school clique, and the [power of] the school clique loomed large in the army. It is probably correct to call Shōwa the era of the *gakubatsu*. In later years two factions, the Imperial Way Faction [Kōdōha] and the Control Faction [Tōseiha] arose within the school clique, but as military cliques they had the same characteristics and cannot be considered separate from [the school clique of] the previous period.[21]

In several ways the change from *han* to school clique was natural for the army. As the Meiji period wore on clan ties became less important for the rising generations. After the Meiji Restoration province names were quickly dropped in favor of the modern prefectural designations. With the unification of the country youngsters were educated to think in national rather than local geographic terms. The process of modernization brought with it urbanization and a relatively great amount of social and geographic mobility. All these things tended to dim the importance of old-fashioned clan affiliations. The abolition of the samurai as a class dealt the old loyalties a body blow. At the same time the modern elements of Japanese society tended to emphasize ability over ascription as a basis for advancement.

The Japanese army, in accord with Japan's traditional Confucian respect for learning, emphasized schools and schooling as a ladder to success. It followed that the army would accept academically successful individuals into positions of leadership. Before long graduation from, and class standing in, the army's prestigious staff college became the sine qua non for success, and almost all positions of prestige and power within the army came to be filled by staff college graduates. Chōshū or Satsuma credentials no longer sufficed. Since, however, Chōshū and Satsuma were already entrenched at the top of the army's bureaucratic elite, *Satchō* staff college graduates high in class standing were the men chosen for top ranks and offices. Satsuma and Chōshū provided their finest sons in the beginning, and later *Satchō* instructors and commanders gave students from the home prefecture a little unconscious (or conscious) boost out of fraternal interest.[22] In time, however, bright young officers from other parts of the country, provided through the nationwide system of military youth schools (*yōnen gakkō*), entered in increasing numbers to compete for rank and recognition. Their graduates from the staff college joined the army elite but quite naturally became conscious of their second-class status within it.

The struggle between the *hanbatsu* and *gakubatsu* of the late Taishō period was restricted to a small number of elite officers representing less than 10 percent of the officer corps.[23] It was a struggle for equality among elite elements and had nothing to do with the vast majority of *taizuki shōkō*, the unit officers, who seldom if ever breathed the heady air of the army's central sections (*chūōbu*), where the graduates of the staff college applied their special skills and where military decisions of national and international importance were made. In the Taishō period unit officers, who had never gone to the staff college and had little hope of rising to flag rank or of serving in peacetime in any but routine housekeeping and recruit training duties in the units, remained inactive. They were not heard from until the Shōwa era. In the meantime, the officers who had the most fought among themselves to see who would get more.

The Anti-Chōshū Conspiracy

The officers of the Baden-Baden group and their proselytes soon began to take aggressive and effective action against Chōshū hegemony. As they perceived the problem, the way to destroy Chōshū was to interrupt the flow of Yamaguchi Prefecture officers into the army elite. Since elite status could be achieved only through graduation from the staff college, the simple and direct method of dealing with Chōshū was to prevent its young officers from entering. In time, they reasoned, Chōshū would become unable to replenish its supply of leaders for the clique.

The staff college system presented them with the means to attempt this. Candidates for admittance to the college took two examinations: the first, a written one in their units (division headquarters); and the second, an oral in Tokyo. The oral examination held each year in December came under the supervision of young staff college military instructors, usually about the rank of major.[24] The anti-Chōshū officer instructors at the staff college oral examinations made it their business to determine which candidates were born in Yamaguchi Prefecture and see to it that none of them passed. They began this subversion of the selection process in 1922, and for four or five years few Chōshū officers gained entrance to the college.[25]

Circumstantial evidence points to the young major Tōjō Hideki as the instigator and manager of this scheme. Tōjō returned from Europe in November 1922 for his new assignment as instructor at the staff college; he left the college in March 1926. These dates correspond almost exactly to the years of the anti-Chōshū vendetta, and Maj. Gen. Horike Kazumaro identifies Tōjō as the most ardent of the Chōshū hunters.[26]

As the anti-Chōshū movement in the staff college gained momentum, Gen. Ōba Jirō, the inspector general of military training and a Chōshū man, apparently found something strange in the fact that no Yamaguchi officers were entering the staff college and attempted an investigation. But the *rikudai* was the one school not under his jurisdiction, and the chief of staff, whose school it was, would not allow it. Ōba withdrew, and the elimination of Chōshū candidates continued.[27]

These young officers did not understand that Chōshū could not continue to control the army and that the Chōshū star had waned since the Terauchi army ministry. They were attacking a hollow shell. After Yamagata's death no one with power in the Chōshū clique had either the ability or the tenacity to sustain it. In the long run the young officers' attack hastened the development of a new, more politically active type of military clique instead of destroying the old.

The Saga Clique

When the young field grade officers of the late Taishō era took direct action to destroy Chōshū's grip on the army, older elite officers had already begun to protect their positions and further their own careers by forming regional interest groups. For example, Gen. Utsunomiya Tarō, a well-liked and capable officer from Saga Prefecture (Hizen), rose to the rank of general in November 1919, but the Chōshū clique used his lack of combat experience in the Russo-Japanese War (he had served in London as military attaché) as an excuse to bar him from the most prestigious positions of responsibility. As a major he had formed, with lower-ranking Saga Prefecture compatriots in the army, the Sagabatsu, or as they themselves called it, the *Saga sakentō*.[28] Its purposes were to promote the interests of officers from Saga and to curb the influence of the Chōbatsu. Utsunomiya died in 1922, but the group continued meeting under the leadership of Lt. Gen. Mutō Nobuyoshi (later marshal). Later, Mutō's *sakentō* joined forces with Marshal Uehara Yūsaku to oppose the mainstream *gunbatsu* of Ugaki Kazunari. Members of the Saga clique included Araki Sadao, the stormy petrel of army politics between 1927 and 1934 and kingpin of the Imperial Way Faction; Araki's military academy classmate Mazaki Jinzaburō, another leader of the Imperial Way Faction and vice chief of the general staff when Araki became army minister; and Yanagawa Heisuke, an outspoken right-wing radical and vice minister of the army under Araki.

In time, the Sagabatsu attracted officers who were not from Saga Prefecture, among them Issekikai members Obata Toshishirō, Yamaoka Shigeatsu, and Yamashita Tomoyuki (Tosa-Kōchi Prefecture).[29] As the Sagabatsu transcended the clan clique model that it had long represented, it gathered adherents among the most radical and ultranationalist fringe of the staff officer elite. The irrationalist "young officers movement" found the right-wing ideals of Araki and Mazaki congenial with their own. They respected both Araki and Mazaki highly and applauded Araki's rise to power. In turn, Araki and Mazaki provided the young officers with their most sympathetic audience in the centers of army power.

The ideals of the Sagabatsu were those of the flint-hard Kyushu samurai. *Sakentō* means literally "left shoulder party" and alludes to the Kyushu samurai expression "To stride the wide road of life along a straight and narrow path with one's left shoulder thrust forward," that is, in a position ready for combat. "When touched by a horse, cut down a horse; when touched by a man, cut down a man." Saga was the home of the *Hagakure* school of samurai thought, which considered "the way of the warrior [*bushidō*] as the search for death."[30] This code had been useful in an earlier day to raise samurai children to bear any adversity and every privation. In Utsunomiya and Mutō's Sagabatsu lay the seeds of the turbulent 1930's — the Imperial Way Faction in embryonic form.

External Factors Accelerating Change: The Rice Riots

The changes wrought by World War I not only affected the army in Japan; they also stimulated a reaction among the general populace. The war brought unprecedented prosperity to the modernized nation, but with it there came inflation and a great increase in commodity prices. Steeply rising rice prices in summer 1918 produced Japan's first great outward reaction to the war in the *kome sōdō*, or rice riots, of August and September. There is no evidence of an ideological cause in these riots. They were spontaneous, undirected, and based solely on popular economic concerns.[31]

The Terauchi government had been haphazard in its attention to economic affairs. It had been ineffective and inefficient in doing the things that might have forestalled popular anger and distress over wildly inflating food — especially rice — prices as the Great War neared its conclusion. The cabinet showed considerably more concern for embroiling the Japanese nation in Siberia than for relieving inflation at home. Rice was in short supply in Japan. Imports from Chōsen (Korea) did not alleviate the shortage. The usual suppliers, French Indochina and Burma, the colonies of European combatants, were prohibited from exporting foodstuffs necessary for the embattled "home" countries. As rice supplies dwindled in Japan before the 1918 harvest, prices skyrocketed and the poor people of Japan's urban areas, whose wages had not risen commensurately, began to feel insecure, angry, and oppressed.

The riots began in out-of-the-way Toyama Prefecture, on the west coast of Honshu, where some fishermen's wives of Uozu Town gathered in a "wellside conference" on 22 July to discuss their domestic financial plight. The next day 50 or 60 women met but were dispersed by the police. Day by day frustration and discontent mounted in the town and its environs until a "women's insurrection" broke out in a nearby town on the evening of 3 August,[32] threatening the lives and property of rice retailers. Every day thereafter tensions mounted, and violence spread throughout the prefecture. With the example of Toyama in the news and spiraling rice prices to spur them on, the poor people of urban Japan had set the country aflame with rioting by mid-August. The riots raged through 36 prefectures, 33 cities, and more than 200 towns and villages. It is estimated that 700,000 people vented their frustration and wrath on rice dealers, rice brokers, employers, government officials, and peace officers in an unexampled burst of spontaneous popular discontent.[33]

Faced with unprecedented mass disruption of the peace, the police often found themselves powerless, and harassed civil officials turned in desperation to the army and navy for assistance. Prefectural governors called for troops in 60 instances, including the cities of Kyoto, Osaka, Nagoya, Kobe, Hiroshima, and Ube and the coalfields of Kyushu. Unfortunately, bayonets and live ammunition were used in some cases, and perhaps a score of people died of stab and gunshot wounds. In certain areas the army armed local Reservists Association units, which performed guard duty and other tasks, a use totally out of keeping with the stated objectives of the association.[34] The *kome sōdō* caused the downfall of Terauchi's Chōshū "transcendent" cabinet and brought true party government to Japan for the first time, as Hara Kei's Seiyūkai took control. The rice riots were one more factor alienating the army from the people of the nation. The mobilization of the Reservists Association only added to people's indignation.[35]

The Diet and the People Turn on the Army

The *kome sōdō* were a passing phenomenon; however, new important challenges to state and military authority soon arose, posing far more serious, permanent problems for the military. World War I shattered the polity of Europe and swept away the old concepts of the state and, indeed, the great autocratic imperial structures themselves. Germany capitulated and the Hohenzollern emperor found refuge in Holland as the Weimar Republic replaced the empire. Austria-Hungary, the great multinational state, broke roughly into its constituent national entities as the Hapsburg Empire collapsed. The Russian Empire dissolved in revolution, its royal family murdered and a socialist state proclaimed. The Ottoman Empire, shorn of its Arab possessions and most of its European lands, succumbed shortly after the war.

It is no wonder that imperial Japan viewed the European scene with alarm. Democracy had won a war; socialism, a revolution. The competing, though by no means mutually exclusive, ideologies swept around the world. In China the May 4th Movement began a great national upsurge based on the victorious ideas of democracy and socialism. In Japan the infusion of these ideas did not result in so dramatic a turn, but their influence was unmistakable. Party government appeared in 1918. Japan entered an unprecedented era of parliamentary influence, and political parties flourished. The labor movement blossomed, and socialism became firmly rooted in the intellectual and laboring classes. The Japan Communist Party formed in 1922.

Both these alien but persuasive streams of thought carried the message of peace among nations and peoples even as many of the nations that claimed these ideologies armed to the teeth. After Versailles the League of Nations gave hope to the world that war could be averted through international action. In Japan, as in Europe and America, a strong peace movement was born as a reaction to the horror of the war. As it rose to challenge war as the arbiter of international disputes, proponents of the movement leveled their gaze at the nation's instruments of war, the army and the navy, the militarists who directed the war machinery, and the militarism that powered it. The peace advocates believed that the war of 1914–18 meant an end to war and that armaments were no longer of great utility. It was said that "in today's world armies and things of that sort are like a bed warmer in summer and a mosquito net in winter."[36]

Even as the advocates of arms reduction pressed for cuts in military expenditures, the army and navy sought larger and larger budgets. We recall that the army had added two divisions, the 19th in 1916 and the 20th in 1919, both for the defense of Chōsen (Korea). In 1920 it comprised 21 standing infantry divisions. The navy had embarked on a ruinously expensive expansion program in a futile effort to keep abreast of British and American wartime fleet increases, and in the midst of the postwar aura of peace the three nations continued to build in competition. This naval arms race did not slow until after the Washington Conference of 1921–22. Japan's army budgets increased almost three-fold between 1914 and 1921,[37] the navy's more than ten.[38]

Criticism of the military expenditures mounted among opposition members of the Diet and in newspapers and periodicals. The Siberian Expedition and diplomatic negotiations with China became favorite press and Diet targets. Interpellations from Diet members concerning the Siberian intervention and the independent army position in the negotiations with China were covered widely in the press and added fuel to the argument that Japanese militarism was rampant. The Hara government bore the brunt of criticism of the Siberian adventure for an army over which it could exercise little control. The Nikolaevsk massacre caused great indignation throughout Japan, and much of it came to be directed at the army. These were the days of great speeches in the National Diet. Never before did the Diet ring with such outspoken eloquence. In January 1921 Katō Kōmei, the man who had oppressed China with his Twenty-One Demands, delivered a withering oration from the rostrum of the House of Peers denouncing government policy and army action in Siberia. "Waging a nameless war, they victimize our brave officers and men in vain on the frozen plains of Siberia," he shouted. The press echoed his every word. Katō advocated occupying Sakhalin as reparation for Nikolaevsk, but he demanded complete withdrawal from Siberia. Prime Minister Hara, apparently moved by Katō's words, answered his questions thoughtfully and with measured care.[39] Kokumintō Party leader Inukai Tsuyoshi's punning characterization of the Siberian *shuppei* (expedition) as the Siberian *shippai* (failure, fiasco) in a diplomatic advisory council meeting showed the temper of the opposition.[40]

Soon after the war's end the Japanese economy, which had risen to a pinnacle of prosperity, began to slump badly.[41] The economic strain of a huge military budget and a wasteful expedition in Siberia caused further reaction against the military forces. Japan's wartime prosperity was real, if ephemeral, but the distribution of its fruits was uneven, as the *kome sōdō* attested. After the war, when good times began to disappear, laborers were the first to feel the effect. As production lagged, men were laid off and factories closed. All over the country wages dropped. Taking its cue from the antimilitary attitudes of the intellectuals, labor joined in the criticism of war and the expensive military establishment. In the May Day demonstrations of 1921 one of the Sōdōmei labor federation's slogans was "Reform the Conscription System." In October of that year it resolved to "abolish armaments."[42] Labor joined in demanding withdrawal from Siberia as the Soviet Union emerged as the "first country of socialism."

The Washington Naval Arms Limitation Conference (November 1921 to February 1922) brought immediate benefits by reducing naval expenditures and stabilizing the size of the Japanese fleet, and it was hailed by great numbers of Japanese as a victory for peace and disarmament. With this unprecedented example of cooperative international arms reduction before them, Japanese antimilitarist elements in the Diet and the general population turned their attention to the army.

By the time of the 45th imperial Diet of 1922, the legislature could view Japan's position in the world community with aplomb. Tsarist Russia, Japan's archenemy, had fallen, and the limited power of the new Soviet Union did not yet effectively extend into eastern Siberia. China was weak and divided, posing no threat to Japan. The march to a naval confrontation with the United States had been halted at Washington. No serious external enemy loomed on Japan's horizon. With economic pressures mounting and the public conscious of military costs and resentful of the Siberian waste, the time was propitious to reduce the army. As the 45th Diet got under way, Diet member Ozaki Yukio made an impassioned speech for arms reduction, in which he advocated arming only if the nation was threatened. He warned the country to beware of militarism. This was the day of the Takahashi cabinet (November 1921–June 1922), and Takahashi was no friend to the military. All parties, including Takahashi's Seiyūkai, advanced plans to reduce the army. They had old scores to settle with the military, whose interference in political affairs had delayed the movement of the parties to the front of the political stage. To them, army (and navy) leaders too often appeared as political enemies.[43]

Coming just at that time (February 1922), the death of Yamagata, who had long oppressed the political world as *genrō* and army leader, foreshadowed the decline in military prestige. The political positions of the military, firm ever since the Russo-Japanese War, became the object of free and open criticism. In these circumstances arms reduction came to be a breakwater [for the army] against external criticism.[44]

The Seiyūkai and Kokumintō parties jointly introduced a bill to curtail the army, which they hoped would save the government ¥40,000,000 a year and reduce the time of service for infantry draftees to fourteen months. The Kokumintō presented a bill to abolish the current qualifications for army and navy ministers in order to open the way for civilian service ministers. The Diet even attacked the military's exclusive rights to direct access to the emperor.[45]

The Plight of the Soldier

This complex of factors—the peace mood of the nation, the postwar economic pressures, and the advantageous position of the political parties, intensified by the longtime arrogance of the military, its demands on the nation's human and fiscal resources, and its reckless Siberian adventure—conspired to create an unfortunate reaction against the military men themselves. The younger officers, noncommissioned officers, and enlisted men bore the brunt of this popular feeling, which took a very personal form. If an officer wore spurs on a streetcar, laborers would kick at them. If the handle of his sword or the end of his cape touched another passenger, men swore and women screamed that they were being molested. There were cases of soldiers being beaten by laborers. Inada Masazumi, an army lieutenant at the time, tells of being accosted on the streetcar by laborers who belligerently proclaimed Lenin, not the emperor, to be their boss. In a well-publicized case a streetcar conductor hurled epithets at a lieutenant and an infantry platoon crossing the street in front of his vehicle. Utsunomiya Naokata, who was a second lieutenant at the time, told me of his men's being refused water by farmers while they were on maneuvers in Narashino, Chiba Prefecture.[46] Nishiura Susumu, another subaltern in that period, testified that his instructors at the military academy warned his class to stay out of trouble when they left on Sunday for an outing. It became standard practice for officers living off-post to wear civilian clothes to and from work, while high-ranking officers invited to attend civilian functions donned morning coats for these occasions.[47] Families hesitated to have their daughters marry military men whereas they had been a prime catch a decade earlier. When Inada entered the staff college, he recalls, Maj. Gen. Abe Nobuyuki, representing the commandant, made a welcoming speech to the new class in which he said, "You young officers are all buzzing with the prospect of getting married, but since you won't find brides, study!"[48]

Even the popular songs of the day give us a feeling for the change in the people's attitude. After the Russo-Japanese War the army was twitted good-naturedly, "The officers dissipate, the NCOs go into business, but truly loyal are the privates." In the 1920's the lyrics took a bitter turn. People sang, "There are those fools who volunteer for an army people detest."[49] In this atmosphere conscription, borne by the people dutifully but never loved, became an anathema, and the professional soldier was looked upon as a blackguard or worse.

Naturally, the army reacted defensively as morale sagged under these political, economic, and psychological pressures. Recruitment for military schools fell off sharply. Matsumura Shūitsu writes that of the 300 students chosen for entry into the military academy about 1920, fully 100 changed their plans in order to go to other schools, and the army, with great fanfare, began a recruiting campaign for the military academy.[50] Tanaka Kiyoharu, former Japan Communist Party central committee member and later a successful industrialist, said, "At that time (1919–22) we received the ideas of democracy, and in our school (Hakodate, Hokkaido Middle School) there were almost none who became soldiers. In our class also there was not one person who took the examinations for the military or naval academies."[51] Official statistics show a marked decline in the number of academy graduates after 1918.[52]

Economic pressures and other factors induced many young officers to leave the army.[53] Young officers were quite accustomed to low pay. The famous aphorism *Binbō shōi, yattoko chūi, yarikuri taii* (Second lieutenants penniless, first lieutenants struggling, captains barely making it) predates the 1920's, so the pressures then must have been extreme. A second lieutenant's monthly salary was ¥43 in those days, the rough equivalent of $21.50. Inflation forced a cost-of-living differential of ¥30 to alleviate the young officers' hardship.[54] Matsumura Shūitsu and Nishiura Susumu both recall that while they were military academy cadets, they talked with officers who had graduated a year or two before, and their conversations habitually centered on the difficulty of making ends meet.[55]

Kikkawa Manabu, Araki Sadao's biographer, more flamboyant in his representation of the plight of young officers, describes (without attribution) the scene that confronted Col. Araki Sadao on returning from Siberia to take over the 23rd Infantry Regiment (6th Division) in Kumamoto, Kyushu. "The lower-ranking officers all lived lives of bare subsistence. There were more than a few who lived among the peddlers in back-alley tenements. This is the time, they say, that in Osaka the lives of the officers were so wretched they took pictures of their alley tenements and reported them to Tokyo." When Araki arrived in Kumamoto, he found that the officers talked of nothing but their economic difficulties. The finance officers were the center of attention. "Which stores sell how much cheaper than prices in the city?" "Next time we'll deal directly with the manufacturer and buy meat for so-and-so-much less than downtown prices and divide it among those who go in on it." "Which tailor can we make special arrangements with to get repairs done cheaper?" "Twelve sen for these box lunches is a bit high. Can't we get them for eleven?" Kikkawa goes on to describe the patched uniforms, the tattered condition of chairs, curtains, and rugs in the officers' meeting room (furnished by contributions of the officers themselves), and proposals from officers to obtain money to maintain the meeting room by cutting down a huge camphor tree on the post, traditionally said to have been planted by the feudal lord Katō Kiyomasa (d. 1611). Officers even went so far as to suggest that the regiment sell an immense mirror bought in Germany by General Nogi, which he had donated to the regiment.[56]

According to Kikkawa, not only was morale low, but morals as well. Entering the canteen, Araki found a large poster advertising *Hāto bijin* (Heart Beauty). Puzzled, the new regimental commander asked the manager what in the world the sign was for. He was shocked when the manager explained that it was an advertisement for rubber prophylactic "devices for the protection of health." Soon after Araki reportedly replaced the objectionable advertisement with a placard of his own, which read, *Kakuji no chi o yogosu nakare* (No individual should soil his blood). Thievery in the regiment was so rampant that each company provided a strongbox for the deposit and protection of the men's valuables. In the communal baths there were cords suspended from the ceiling to which the men tied their valuables so that they could watch them even while bathing. The canteen kept its goods in locked compartments, opening them only when a sale was made.[57] Such stories may be exaggerated a bit by the author to demonstrate the remarkable powers of leadership possessed by the future general Araki as he straightened out the mess, but they indicate the kind of real economic hardship and supposed moral laxity that changing times were producing in the army. In part, Araki's view, as reported by Kikkawa, was motivated by his perception of the serious problem of adjustment necessary to meet a rapidly changing situation. Another part may have been merely a Japanese army version of the army's-gone-to-hell syndrome that grips senior officers of any army when they view the shocking conduct of their generational successors.

The Army Reaction

The Japanese officer had been trained to believe that he was a member of an elite. To prepare for death in the service of the emperor was the highest calling for any Japanese subject. The soldier could expect little in return in the way of material reward, but his honorable service entitled him to the respect of those who served the empire in less demanding ways. The people were educated in school to honor and respect him, and, in general, the army's previous conduct seemed to merit the regard of a grateful nation. Now something had gone awry. There were people who refused to believe that the emperor and the nation formed one family and that those who defended the state occupied the posts of greatest honor. To the officers, Western bourgeois democracy fostered not only individualism, which contravened the very nature of their military training, but also the kind of economic competition that led to gross disparities in personal income between certain unscrupulous but privileged businessmen and the broader masses of people. Not very long before, Japanese had considered the commercial class (*shōnin*) the lowest in their feudal society and held the warrior in highest esteem.

The reaction to the "boorish" nouveaux riches, who had made fortunes during the war, was readily apparent. The army passed on stories of conspicuous public consumption while young officers lived in penury. Araki showed great distaste for the *niwaka narikin* (suddenly rich) who vied with their fellows to give the most ostentatious parties at posh geisha restaurants in the great cities. These people asked restaurateurs whether their establishment could furnish meals for ¥5,000 a plate. (A soldier's midday meal cost roughly sixteen sen in 1919.)[58] The *ryōriya* obliged by putting pearls and diamonds in the fishes' eye sockets.[59] General Utsunomiya tells the story of the *narikin* who stuck his car in the mud up to the axles driving illegally through Yoyogi *renpeijo* (the maneuver ground in Tokyo later known to Americans as Washington Heights and still later the site of the 1964 summer Olympic games). He demanded that Utsunomiya's platoon extricate his automobile. Willing to oblige, the soldiers approached, only to find the rich man in the company of three geisha. Outraged, they overturned the car, leaving the *narikin* and his companions stranded in a sea of mud.[60]

Socialist ideology, penetrating the working classes of Japan at about the same time, aroused equal antipathy among the officers. It subverted the very basis of the imperial state and the special privileged position of the emperor's military elite. The Russian army had turned on the tsar and driven him from the throne.[61] The revolutionaries had murdered the royal family. Some Japanese laborers now looked to the internationalist Lenin for leadership rather than to their own sacred emperor, and they insulted his defenders in the streets. Though the army to some extent shared the economic stringencies faced by the urban working classes, the soldiers could not sympathize with their abandonment of Japan's *kokutai* (national polity). They could identify more closely with the attitudes of the rather conservative, tradition-oriented peasants, who contributed most heavily to the army's enlisted base. Though economically oppressed, the stolid farmers still adhered to their belief in the emperor and the nation.

More and more often the army was called on to confront organized labor. Beginning with the rice riots the army faced the workers at Ube and in the coalfields of northern Kyushu. After the war strikes and labor disputes flared, often pitting urban workers against the army. In August 1919 there was a union-led strike of workers at the army arsenals in Tokyo. In 1921, a year of labor unrest, both army and navy troops were called in to control a strike that wracked the Mitsubishi and Kawasaki shipbuilding works in Kobe, where naval vessels were under construction. In both these incidents the disputes involved the production of arms and equipment for the armed services.[62] In the minds of many military officers, such strikes must have smacked of lèse majesté, if not treason.

To the army the solid foundations of the Meiji state seemed to be crumbling. Socialist ideas were dividing the people from the emperor and the army. The political parties, the parvenu elite that had risen on the basis of democratic political ideals, were driving a wedge between the army and the emperor. Political control had fallen into the hands of selfish men who cared so little for the emperor and his defenders that they oppressed the emperor's loyal retainers and endangered the defense of the state, all to satisfy their own lust for money and power.

The army was frustrated and discontented. Most officers grumbled but carried on. Some of the younger men abandoned their calling for economic reasons, a handful for ideological ones. Many of those who remained in service lapsed into reveries of the good old days of Meiji. For a few, like Araki Sadao, the threat was a call to action.[63] But none doubted that they were right and that those who attacked or oppressed them were dangerously wrong. Nishiura Susumu makes this point clear:

As in the army song that went, "In the muddy stream that is the world" — something-something — "it rises steeply to the heights of Ichigaya [the location of the military academy in Tokyo]. The world is a muddy stream, and only we are pure." Those men, in just the same way that the young fellows in today's self-defense forces think that the guys who call them tax robbers are creeps who don't make sense, thought that they were correct, and their belief grew stronger and stronger.[64]

The first army officer to recognize and discuss in print this "social problem" was retired Lt. Gen. Satō Kōjirō, whose *Kokubōjō no shakai mondai* (The social problem from the standpoint of national defense) appeared in 1920. This work connected army-people relations to the necessity of preparing the nation for total war à la Ludendorff and emphasized the socialization of the people in preparation for a total mobilization of the nation's strength.[65]

Satō's later book, *Guntai to shakai mondai* (The military and the social problem), published in 1922, focused on the social problem itself and the deep division between the army (more alienated than the navy) and the people. In it Satō took a liberal attitude toward the intrusion of foreign ideologies. He found nothing new in democracy or socialism. Both ideas, he wrote, have existed in Japanese thought for centuries, and if the Japanese people come fully into contact with them, they will lose their novelty and be placed in proper perspective. He severely censured the army, however, for not allowing the new ideas to enter into the discussion of factors in the alienation of the army from the people. Army officers were not au courant. They could not discuss or refute these ideas in public. The army's problem was its feeling of superiority, its exclusiveness. He blamed the widening gulf between the army and its constituency squarely on its inability to change, its perception of itself in a transcendent role in Japanese society, and its lack of democracy in dealing with the soldiers and the public. The army stamps too many things "secret," he noted. Satō further criticized the army for its narrow system of education and training. Officers and prospective officers should have social training (*shakai kunren*), or else the ordinary citizen could find no bridge to understanding with them. He would, contrary to the admonition of Marshal Terauchi, abolish the military youth schools (*yōnen gakkō*) and select all aspirants to the military academy from regular high school graduates.

On the other hand, Satō did not doubt for one instant that the army's cause was just. Since future wars, like the Great War, would be total wars, Japan must be prepared. Because the people did not understand this situation, the Japanese nation must be militarized while the army was democratized and socialized. Japan must change to an emperor-centered democratic national socialism to ensure the protection, even the survival, of the unique Japanese state in the social-Darwinist–imperialist jungle.

Satō's ideas caused a sensation in Japan. Neither the army nor the civilian objects of his polemic had much good to say about his proposals, but it was not long before reasoning similar to Satō's found wide approval not only in the army but among the people.

The Great Kantō Earthquake and Fire

On 1 September 1923, at two minutes before noon a calamitous event befell Japan, which transformed the position of the army in the eyes of the nation almost overnight. Tokyo and its environs, including the great port city of Yokohama, were struck by a terrible natural disaster, the Kantō *daishinsai*, or great Kantō earthquake and fire. The quake damage was tremendous; the fires and firestorms that raged for three days added countless thousands to the dead, injured, and homeless that the original earth tremor had left. Two-thirds of Yokohama and half of Tokyo burned to cinders. When the holocaust ended, the Japanese nation realized that it had experienced one of the most fearful natural disasters in modern history.

In the capital all semblance of civil order crumbled at the height of the crisis. The army, the one intact instrument of government control, immediately sprang into action to restore a degree of order and to relieve, as best it could, the stricken inhabitants. Under these fortuitous circumstances the army consciously labored to recoup its position of esteem among the Japanese people, and from that time popular treatment of the army took a dramatic turn for the better, not only in the capital but throughout the country.

Kawabe Torashirō, an army captain in 1923, has left us a most graphic illustration of this phenomenon. He was at a staff exercise in Kushiro, Hokkaido, which adjourned hastily when the news of the earthquake arrived. Returning to Tokyo at night a few days after the disaster, he describes the atmosphere:

When I entered the unburned portion of the suburbs [Kamiochiai, near Shinjuku], I could see the movements of men whose shadows were barely reflected flickeringly in the light of candles. These people, peering at my uniformed outline, greeted me twice or three times with "A soldier! Thank you for all you've done." Just a short week before, when I left Tokyo, we in uniform had unpleasant and scornful glances directed toward us in streetcars and other places.[66]

Horike Kazumaro, a young officer in the mid-1920's, later noted complex changes in Japan and the army brought about by the earthquake, but he also detected a pervasive air of pessimism: "The simple, prosperous atmosphere that was the momentum of Meiji, though shaken by influences after the war, changed completely with this [earthquake]." When he entered the staff college (1922), there was still some of the feeling of Meiji left, but about the time of his graduation (1925), "there was a gradual reaction to the influence of the decadent atmosphere of the world after the earthquake disaster." This, then, concludes Horike, was the beginning of political unrest in the army.[67]

The police and fire departments of Tokyo, scattered throughout the disaster area, were simply overwhelmed by the immensity of the catastrophe and ceased for a time to function in a coordinated fashion. The army in Tokyo, concentrated more closely within the confines of certain cantonments, could rally its resources with some degree of rapidity. The troops in the metropolitan area were quickly reinforced by intact units from the hinterlands. In time, units from as far away as Hokkaido and Kyushu were thrown into the relief operation. Many of the units, like the Guards (*konoe*) Division and 1st Division, both stationed in Tokyo, performed no other duty for two and one-half months. Fully 30 regiments of combat troops, 17 battalions of engineers, and thousands of soldiers from supply, signal, and other units helped in rescue, relief, guard duties, and the beginnings of reconstruction by building temporary barracks to shelter the homeless.[68]

The Dark Side of Disaster

Terrible as it was, the horror of the earthquake was compounded by the behavior of its victims. The good citizens of the city panicked, resulting in the death of many more thousands of people. With the breakdown of civil authority, the threat of looting and violence loomed large in people's minds. Neighborhoods sought security in common action, forming vigilante committees (*jikeidan*) for their protection. They cordoned off the streets and formed 24-hour patrols. Armed only with the simplest of weapons—old swords, spears, knives, and the like—and often led by members of the Reservists Association, men with military experience, they attempted to maintain order, but in doing so in certain districts they perpetrated terrible crimes. There is incontrovertible evidence that the army abetted this criminal behavior to some degree in two instances—in the slaughter of Koreans (and some Chinese) and in the murder of political radicals. Whether these actions added to or detracted from the stature of the army in the eyes of the Japanese people is difficult to assess, but because army behavior after the earthquake forms one chapter in its relations with the people, the subject merits some exploration.

By 1923 Tokyo and Yokohama had a considerable Korean population. Virtually all of these people were laborers working at the most menial tasks and living in their adopted homeland in the worst economic and social conditions. The Japanese saw the slums where they congregated as cesspools of crime and violence. The Japanese laboring classes, who lived near the Koreans in similar circumstances, felt threatened by their presence, and in fact the Koreans had at times voiced their frustrations in group protest and violence. The smoldering resentment of working-class Japanese toward these interlopers flared after the earthquake. Rumors of Korean looting and banding together to attack key points in the city spread almost as fast as the fires themselves.[69] Before long, these unfortunate people, many of them living in areas of the city worst hit by the earthquake and fire, were being butchered in the streets by vigilante committees. Reportedly as many as 6,000 were murdered in this way. Koreans were not the only victims of the mass hysteria. Chinese and any Japanese who spoke with a peculiar accent were immediately suspected of Korean background and even some Japanese perished—the victims of mistaken identity.[70] There is ample evidence that the army participated in the slaughter, although it is difficult to assess the extent. Most accounts of the earthquake by army officers indicate that they were quite aware of the spurious nature of the charges against the Koreans and the hysteria that motivated the Koreans' persecutors. There is also evidence that the army and the police took steps to protect these unfortunates in many instances.

The most damning evidence against the army appears in the book *Kantō daishinsai to Chōsenjin*.[71] The editors admit that substantive direct evidence is lacking except for a few military eyewitness accounts, which they cite, but they adduce good circumstantial evidence to support their allegation that the greater part of the slaughter was perpetrated by units of the Guards and 1st Infantry Divisions on 2 and 3 September. These local units sallied forth armed with live ammunition, fixed bayonets, and machine guns. The extant unit orders, reports, and citations prove beyond a doubt that they considered action against "outlaw Koreans," reportedly looting and setting fires, to be a military action. In some areas Koreans were slaughtered in such numbers that it appears beyond the capability of the poorly armed local vigilantes organized by the Reservists Association. Authentic photographs that show army men in battle dress bearing rifles with fixed bayonets, as well as others that direct attention to the gruesome aftermath of mass slaughter, press home their arguments.

On the other hand, Inada Masazumi maintains that the army had nothing to do with the Korean massacre and that it was a product of popular reaction.[72] He cites one instance from his own experience in which the police sheltered Koreans in Shinagawa and were beset by local inhabitants led by Reservists Association members, who resented the police protection afforded these distraught people. His unit aided the police. The police, according to Inada, protected the Koreans wherever they could.

In *Nihon no sōran hyakunen* (A hundred years of disturbances in Japan), writers Itoya Hisao and Inaoka Susumu do not charge the army directly with acts of violence against the Koreans.[73] As anti-establishment authors they probably would have done so were evidence available. They do, however, use quotations from interviews with leftist sources to accuse the home minister in the outgoing Katō cabinet, Mizuno Rentarō, of overreacting to a false charge that Koreans had attacked a customs warehouse in Yokohama on the afternoon of 1 September by ordering the police to form neighborhood vigilante units to protect the entire disaster area from Korean looting. (The Yamamoto cabinet home minister, Gotō Shinpei, did not officially take office until 2 September because of the disruption of the earthquake on the previous day.) They also shed some light on the mysterious broadcasts of the Funabashi Naval Wireless Station heard all over Japan and by ships at sea, which reported Korean rampages quite falsely. It seems that the naval officer in charge was among the first seized by panic on the basis of scant information he had received personally at the home ministry. There is no question that his lapse was harmful and perhaps decisive in unleashing the terrible Korean pogrom.[74]

The small Korean minority was not the sole object of the citizens' fear. There had been much talk of dangerous thoughts in the press and the government since the end of the war. Socialism, anarchism, and communism had taken root in Japan in spite of the disapproval of the authorities. Those on the left had not endeared themselves to the general populace with their fiery speeches, organization of labor for mass action, and talk of revolution. In a nation taught that the national polity and the imperial person were sacrosanct, these very different views were indeed dangerous. In the minds of many citizens the earthquake disaster provided Japanese of "dangerous" tendencies the opportunity they needed to seize power. As a consequence, like the Koreans, known radicals came under attack, and many were murdered. But the radicals found even less protection than the Koreans from Japanese officialdom, which had propagandized and legislated against their activities.

General Tanaka, serving his second term as army minister in the short-lived Yamamoto cabinet, formed only hours before the earthquake, recommended martial law for the stricken area. The cabinet approved unanimously, and martial law was declared on 2 September. The next day Gen. Fukuda Masatarō took office as military governor over the designated disaster area, which grew day by day from Tokyo City and five counties surrounding it to include all of Tokyo Metropolitan Prefecture, Kanagawa Prefecture, and finally Saitama and Chiba Prefectures. The military government had broad police powers, which it delegated to military units, military police, and civilian police officials. These included the right to question any person on the street and to enter and search any premises.[75] On the basis of these powers, the police and military police rounded up and questioned persons of leftist sentiments deemed dangerous to the safety of the city. Some of this activity ended in tragedy.[76]

One of these tragedies had wide repercussions inside and outside the army, tarnishing the new image the military had so assiduously sought through its redemptive works immediately after the disaster. The story involves the murder of the well-known anarchist Ōsugi Sakae by a young army military police (*kenpeitai*) captain, Amakasu Masahiko.[77] It became one of the more sensational in Japan's annals of crime. Ōsugi, the radical feminist Itō Noe, and Ōsugi's nephew (age seven) were brought into the military police substation in Ōtemachi on 16 September, ostensibly for questioning. That night Ōsugi and Itō were strangled to death by Captain Amakasu. The next morning a Sergeant Mori murdered the child when Amakasu's courage failed him. Ōsugi's killing was premeditated, as Amakasu readily admitted at his court-martial. He and his subordinates had waited two days in the neighborhood of Ōsugi's home to apprehend him. The reason for the arrest was to prevent Ōsugi from plotting crimes against the state during the period of the emergency. Actually, by 16 September the anti-Korean, anti-socialist terror had subsided, and there was no excuse for Ōsugi's preventive detention. Ōsugi, who would have liked nothing better than to be a threat to the system he professed to hate, had been immobilized by the earthquake. His small anarchist publishing venture was completely disrupted. He had been spending his days at home or visiting friends and relatives to see whether they had come through the holocaust safely. It was on his return from such an excursion that he was picked up by Amakasu.

His crime discovered and brought to the attention of the press and the government, Amakasu was duly made to stand trial. In the meantime, Army Minister Tanaka, basing his action on the army's investigation of the case, personally reprimanded and removed the commanding general of the *kenpeitai* and the chief of the Tokyo military police unit on 20 September 1923.[78] He forced the resignation of Gen. Fukuda Masatarō as military governor of the Kantō region as the officer directly responsible for the administration of martial law and replaced him with his old crony Yamanashi Hanzō. Tanaka submitted his own resignation also, but it was not accepted.[79]

Not all of the army was so concerned. The chief of the legal section in the army ministry was quoted as likening Amakasu to "a man who attempted to cut away the demoralization of the state."[80] Lt. Gen. Ugaki Kazunari, who had no close official connection with the case, noted in his diary:

Though I can sympathize with his [Amakasu's] motive, I consider his method and timing most regrettable. The actions of the authorities concerned with this are overly rash. They lack composure. By all means, I think it would be good to make the equitable punishments under the law lenient, especially for administrative responsibility. [Appended by Ugaki later] A sacrifice to the existing wishy-washy administrative policies. I sympathize with them greatly.[81]

The trial itself proved a startling indictment of the military police, if not the army itself. The testimony of witnesses, only partially reprinted in the newspapers, revealed strongly prejudiced attitudes among military police leaders against radical elements in civilian society, so prejudiced, in fact, that they condoned Amakasu's heinous act and were willing to cover it up if possible. In a Tokyo *Asahi shinbun* extra edition for 8 October 1923, Maj. Gen. Koizumi Rokuichi, deposed commanding general of the *kenpeitai*, is quoted as having said, "It was truly a courageous act worthy of commendation."[82]

Amakasu insisted that he alone was responsible for the murders, and he probably was. There is no question, however, that the atmosphere within the military police contributed to Amakasu's determination to eradicate dangerous radicals. It may be that only Amakasu had the perverse kind of courage necessary to act on what was a general desire among his colleagues.[83]

The Ōsugi murders are symptomatic of the army's reaction to democratic and socialistic ideas. There is, of course, a certain eagerness in any military or law enforcement agency to come to grips with an enemy that openly seeks the destruction of the structure it has sworn to protect. The *kenpeitai*, imbued with the same spirit of imperial service as the army and in close contact with the internal Japanese movements that openly vowed to overthrow the imperial/capitalist system, naturally felt this urge. Thus, a good deal of support was certain for a man who, though acting illegally and contrary to his instructions, did to the "enemy" what most of them might like to have done. Perhaps it is more surprising that so few of the military police broke discipline in the manner of Amakasu during the unparalleled confusion of the earthquake disaster.

A 1st Infantry Division court-martial board tried Amakasu, Mori, and two other enlisted men on 8 October 1923. It found Amakasu and Mori guilty but acquitted the others. Amakasu received a sentence of ten years, Mori three. This was a light sentence for those days and caused considerable critical press and public comment. In 1923 the public was not yet disposed to accept Amakasu's patriotism as a defense as the court-martial board apparently had done. Although the sentences seemed extraordinarily light at that time, it would be less than a decade before a patriotic political motive could excuse even the murder of a prime minister, as the trials following the May 15th Incident of 1932 proved. The Amakasu affair was the forerunner of the peculiar criminal trials that were held in the 1930's, where high motive became a major factor for clemency or exoneration for terrible deeds.[84]

After the trial an anarchist follower of Ōsugi, Wada Hisatarō, sought desperately to avenge his murder. He first sent General Fukuda a bomb concealed in a package. When the Fukuda family opened it, smoke poured out, but it failed to explode. He tried again for vengeance at the memorial ceremony marking the first anniversary of the great earthquake, shooting Fukuda in the back as he arrived for the ceremony. Fukuda was not seriously hurt, but Wada was seized, speedily tried, and sentenced to life imprisonment. The public again drew an invidious comparison of the treatment accorded Amakasu and the sentence meted out to the anarchist Wada. A popular jingle put it this way:

> For his try, life for Hisa-san
> For his killing, ten years for Ama-san.[85]

As a postscript to the affair it might be noted that Amakasu was a model prisoner and secured parole in three years, which caused a third spate of critical comment in the daily and periodical press. After a two-year sojourn in France, he reappeared in Manchuria, where he served his country as a police official in the Manchurian (Manchukuo) government and later as a respected super-patriot and behind-the-scenes operator. In August 1945 he took his own life with cyanide, allegedly saying, "We have taken a great gamble and lost. That ends the first round."[86]

3

The Changing of the Guard: Ugaki Comes to Power

> There was no way to treat these stoneheads
> other than to replace them.
>
> Itō Masanori

The cry raised in the 45th Diet of 1922 over the size and the expenditures of the imperial army gave notice to its leaders that financial retrenchment was unavoidable and that the army must reckon with the Diet for such prodigious wastes of money as the Siberian Expedition. The Washington Conference had just resulted in trimming naval expenditures and in the promise to leave Siberia. The Diet now turned its full attention to the army. The army could no longer point to a credible hypothetical enemy, and the sharp economic recession made cuts in government expenditures mandatory. The large standing army of more than 300,000 officers and men presented a tempting target for the economy-minded legislature. Long under fire in the Diet for its militarism and its independent position within the state, the army came in for heated criticism for its continuing, fruitless intervention in Siberia and its constant interference in diplomatic relations with China. To the hard-pressed people of Japan, the army and navy suddenly, and not without reason, loomed as *zeikin dorobō* (tax robbers), and popular reaction against them rose.

For the first time the army felt constrained to bow to the popular will. Even Marshal Uehara reluctantly conceded that cuts were unavoidable in the changed international circumstances,[1] and a bit later he ended his opposition to the withdrawal from Siberia.

Postwar legislative activity against the military had begun in the 44th Diet of 1921, where the army and the Hara government weathered blistering attacks. In a prophetic moment at its annual party conference, the

Kokumintō had advocated exchanging militarism for industrialism and proposed to cut the number of army divisions in half and the length of drafted service from three years to one. On the Diet floor Ozaki Yukio introduced a resolution to limit naval expenditures in cooperation with Britain and America and to reduce the army on the basis of the League of Nations Covenant, but his proposal went down to defeat, 285 to 38. Hara's Seiyūkai voted solidly against it, as did almost all of Ozaki's former party colleagues in the Kenseikai.[2]

The Yamanashi Reductions in Army Strength

Politicians began to respond to the change in public opinion. The Washington Conference, called for by the United States in July 1921 to discuss international, political, and military problems in the Pacific basin, aroused expectations in Japan for lasting peace and sharpened criticism of the size and power of the armed forces. Ozaki stumped the nation after the 1921 Diet session and talked to thousands on arms reduction. Postcard responses to his speeches, he said, numbered 31,517 — 92.8 percent favorable to his view.[3] Japan's defense expenditures had risen steadily since the Russo-Japanese War and even more sharply during the Great War. With Seiyūkai support in the Diet, they reached their peak during the tenure of the Hara cabinet,[4] although the 44th Diet did trim the army's budget.[5]

One day after Yamagata died, Seiyūkai Diet member Tsunoda Koreshige, a retired army major general, introduced to the 45th Diet his own bill for army reform and reduction. In addition to financial savings, Tsunoda's farsighted proposals struck heavy blows at the army's privileged status and feudal heritage. Adopting a triangular division organization, Tsunoda's plan called for the abolition of the two brigade headquarters in each division and the elimination of a complete regiment. The remaining regiments would be similarly streamlined, to three battalions of three companies each. The net savings in personnel would amount to the rough equivalent of six divisions.[6] But Tsunoda's proposal went far beyond changes in divisional organization and personnel reductions to include shortening the time of drafted service to fourteen months, abolishing one-year volunteer service and the youth schools, and establishing a system of civilian service ministers, a supreme defense council, and a unified command structure for the army and the navy.[7]

By shortening the time draftees spent in the barracks, the army could draft greater numbers of young men, and the result would be a much larger pool of trained reserves to meet the perceived demands of total war, on the pattern of post–World War I military thought. The establishment of a supreme defense council also served the concept of total war by integrating civilian political, economic, and psychological factors into the overall war planning function, but it struck a blow at the traditional right of the armed services to independent decision in defense matters. In fact, this problem lay at the heart of Tsunoda's plan. To give civilians the portfolios of the service ministries, to unify the command of the army and navy, and even to abolish the army's exclusive system of youth schools for the education and indoctrination of its future officers were all steps that would curb the independent political position enjoyed by the army. Neither the army ministry nor the general staff could be expected to approve such a plan.

Since Yamagata no longer stood as a buffer, the army had to fight its own battle against civilian encroachment. Yamanashi, who had none of the political polish of Tanaka, pressured Prime Minister Takahashi relentlessly until at last he quietly disowned the army reform features of his Seiyūkai colleague's plan,[8] admitting that it was quite unnecessary to revise the qualifications for service ministers or the right of direct access to the emperor.

Tsunoda's bill had one unfortunate feature, which the army was quick to exploit. It proposed the abolition of many garrisons in smaller urban areas by eliminating entire regiments. This, the army pointed out to the Seiyūkai, would cause economic disruption in many areas, which would have political repercussions at election time. This argument cooled the ardor of the Seiyūkai considerably.[9] The ground thus prepared, Yamanashi stepped forward with an army proposal for reduction, a compromise plan that eliminated the features in the Tsunoda proposal objectionable to both the army and the politicians.

The "Yamanashi *gunshuku*" (arms reduction), which was finally adopted by the Diet, made no mention of reform and eliminated the change reducing the length of drafted service that Chief of Staff Uehara found most distressing,[10] but it did cut army strength by 2,268 officers, 57,296 warrant officers and enlisted men, and 13,000 horses. By simply removing one company from the peacetime table of organization of each infantry battalion and one troop from each cavalry regiment, there would be no necessity to close any military installation. The Yamanashi *gunshuku* cut peacetime strength equivalent to five infantry divisions at an annual estimated saving of ¥35,400,000. Although all the major reforms necessary to modernize the army structure were now scrapped, the Yamanashi *gunshuku* did attempt technical modernization on the tactical level. For example, some of the savings were plowed back into the budget to add machine gun units to each infantry regiment and each cavalry brigade, several modernizing readjustments were made in the organization of artillery units, and most important, two air battalions were authorized.[11] More money could have been used in technical improvement had it not been for the earthquake, which obliged the army to spend large sums in disaster relief operations in 1923 and 1924.

In 1923 the Diet again sought reductions in military expenditures, but the impetus to the *gunshuku* movement had begun to slacken, and Yamanashi, now Prime Minister (Admiral) Katō Tomosaburō's army minister, limited concessions to such minor items as the abolition of a railway material facility, two division bands, and the Sendai Youth School. Itō Masanori likens both Yamanashi reductions to "a drop of water on a hot stone."[12]

Uehara and Tanaka at Sword's Point

When Katō Tomosaburō's short-lived cabinet fell in August 1923, the venerable Adm. Yamamoto Gonbei once again took up the reins of government. In the transfer Yamanashi Hanzō, who had served continuously under three prime ministers, stepped down in favor of Tanaka Giichi, whose health had mended. Yamanashi, an unimaginative general of conservative bent, had done very little to solve the multiple problems facing the army. His rise to positions of prominence rested solely on his lifelong association with Tanaka. The redoubtable Uehara Yūsaku had been his opposite as chief of the general staff until he retired in March 1923. The two men presented the government and the Diet with a wall of unbending conservatism, typifying the Colonel Blimp attitude that prevailed among the higher ranks. Using personnel reductions "as a breakwater," they had fought off every executive or legislative attempt to force reform, but in doing so they found the army less and less in harmony with the aspirations and feelings of the Japanese people, and further and further behind in its ability to wage war on a par with the great powers.

Uehara's withdrawal as chief of staff and Tanaka's return to the army ministry heralded change. The Yamamoto cabinet lasted only four months, and for its duration it was preoccupied with the immediate and desperate problems of recuperating from the devastation of the Kantō earthquake. It fell on 27 December 1923, after an attempt on the life of Crown Prince Hirohito (the "Toranomon Incident"), but Tanaka chose as his successor a remarkable general, who had risen in rank and prominence as his protégé. Ugaki Kazunari (often Kazushige) was not from Chōshū but from Okayama; however, he was the type of officer whose talents could not be overlooked. The ambitious Tanaka, recognizing Ugaki's ability, had formed a durable working relationship with him many years before.

In 1911, when Tanaka became chief of the military affairs bureau in the army ministry, Ugaki was assigned as his key assistant, chief of the military affairs section (*gunjika*). Later, when Tanaka became the vice chief of staff, he soon arranged to have Ugaki made chief of the all-important 1st section (operations). Still later, when Tanaka was chosen army minister, according to Ugaki Tanaka purposely left him behind on the general staff to "restrain Uehara and Fukuda" (Fukuda Masatarō, Tanaka's replacement as vice chief of staff).[13] In 1923 Tanaka moved Ugaki in as his vice minister. As a lieutenant general, he stood on the threshold of power.

The early collapse of Yamamoto's cabinet gave Ugaki the opportunity to step from the shadows into the center of army politics, but his elevation to head the army ministry was no easy transition. His appointment became a classic example of a power struggle within the army, and its outcome, in time, came to affect the entire cabinet system. Ugaki was largely a pawn in the struggle to seat him as army minister, although once appointed he seized control with great vigor. The protagonists in the struggle were Uehara Yūsaku and Tanaka Giichi—the last great battle between Satsuma and Chōshū champions.

By 1923 the Chōbatsu, if it still existed, had fallen into a state of decay, in part through indifference and in part through failure to produce prime candidates for high office. There had been a seven-year gap between the time Terauchi Masakata left the army ministry at the zenith of Chōshū power and the time Tanaka took over in 1918. Tanaka showed little interest in maintaining Chōshū clan hegemony even though his reputation as the clique's man relentlessly pursued him.[14] Unlike his predecessors Tanaka did not completely surround himself with officers of Chōshū lineage, although his military affairs bureau chief, Lt. Gen. Sugano Hisaichi, was a Chōshū officer. With one exception, however, his close associates were graduates of the army staff college.[15] He recommended Fukuda (Nagasaki) to succeed him as vice chief of staff and Yamanashi (Kanagawa), who was his vice minister, to follow him as army minister.[16] Yamagata was, of course, consulted, but he voiced no objections. Nevertheless, there were ample cases of favoritism toward Chōshū officers in this period to perpetuate the impression of a still predominant Chōshū *hanbatsu*.

In addition to Sugano there was, for example, Ōi Shigemoto, who displaced a non-Chōshū officer as the commanding general of the 12th

Division just before its dispatch to Siberia.[17] Ōi went on to become the commanding general of the Vladivostok Expeditionary Force. And there was Gen. Oba Jirō, who made his reputation commanding the 3rd Division in Siberia. He later commanded the army in Korea, and then in 1923 he entered the "big three" as the inspector general of military training. There were others. Chōshū still presented a highly visible target for younger officers trying to eradicate the army's roots in the feudal system and transform it into a truly national force.

On the death of Ōyama in 1916, Uehara became the doyen of the Satsuma clique. When Yamagata died, Uehara became *chōrō*, the senior officer on active duty.[18] Willful, egotistical, and jealous of his perquisites, Uehara attempted to assert his seniority in the appointment of men to the army's highest posts, especially since he sensed the threat of a resurgent Chōshū. The army "big three" in December 1923 were Oba Jirō (Chōshū), inspector general of military training; Kawai Misao (Oita — the old province of Bungo, a collateral house to the feudal lords of Chōshū and included in the modern Chōshū clique), chief of staff (Uehara's successor); and Tanaka himself. To Uehara this must have seemed a phalanx of Chōshū strength and a challenge to his own seniority. In order to forestall renewed domination by Chōshū and advance the fortunes of his own followers,[19] Uehara moved to restore the balance and assert his seniority.

When the Yamamoto cabinet resigned, the new prime minister–designate was the well-known peer Kiyoura Keigo. Kiyoura had attempted to form a cabinet in March 1914, but he had been frustrated when, in a celebrated example of obduracy and military interference in the political process, the navy refused to furnish him a minister.[20] If Kiyoura found a shortage of potential service ministers in 1914, in 1923 he was embarrassed with a surplus.

When Uehara learned that his friend and neighbor Kiyoura was a strong candidate for the prime ministership, an item of common gossip about the capital, the marshal decided to pay him a visit. As they discussed Kiyoura's prospects, the conversation naturally turned to the subject of possible cabinet choices. At some point Uehara found the opportunity to recommend Gen. Fukuda Masatarō (Saga) as army minister. Kiyoura, knowing relatively little about the army's internal politics, and possibly caring less, accepted Uehara's recommendation with pleasure.[21] Having planted his minefield, Uehara retreated "in exultation" from Tokyo to his modest country home in Kamakura on the same day, 31 December, to prepare for the New Year's holiday.[22]

On New Year's Day of 1924 Kiyoura received the imperial mandate to form a cabinet. As a member of the House of Peers, he had no party affiliation. His cabinet, to be chosen from the Peers, was to be "transcendent" — that is, divorced, as had been the two preceding admirals' cabinets, from the political parties and the lower house of the Diet. In order to fill his cabinet posts, Kiyoura turned to the House of Peers' Kenkyūkai (Research Association), the most powerful faction in that body.[23] On or about 1 January, Kiyoura's agents went to confer with outgoing army minister Tanaka with the idea that he might stay on in the new cabinet. Tanaka firmly refused but let slip his decision to recommend his vice minister, Ugaki Kazunari, as his replacement. Kiyoura's minions, happy in the knowledge that they would receive an army minister without complicated negotiations, readily accepted Ugaki's name and departed.

Ever since 1913, when the rules governing the qualifications for the appointment of service ministers had been relaxed to include officers of the first and second reserves, the army, as a precaution against the day when some courageous prime minister would attempt to exploit this possibility, had tacitly accepted the principle that the successor to the outgoing minister be chosen by a conference of the "big three" (*sanchōkan kaigi*). The big three would then submit its selection to the marshals and army councillors for their perusal as a matter of courtesy. The system had never really gone into effect, simply because the army minister was in reality chosen in consultation with Marshal Yamagata beforehand and approved by the big three as a matter of course. Since Yamagata's death the agreed-on procedure had not undergone a real test, but the old guard — Uehara, Tanaka, and Yamanashi — had stepped down. According to the formula, Kiyoura, the prime minister–designate, having no real choice in the matter, had only to await the big three's decision.

The version of the affair in Tanaka's biography has it that Tanaka learned about Uehara's recommendation of Fukuda "by another route" and that Kiyoura made no effort to contact the outgoing army minister. In any case, on 2 January Tanaka fired a warning shot by sending a messenger to Kiyoura to remind him that army procedure demanded a conference of the big three to determine his (Tanaka's) successor, but he added that this conference would soon be called and its recommendation forwarded.[24]

Since Kiyoura kept his talk with Uehara to himself, it was not until sometime later, perhaps on 4 January, that Kiyoura and his cabinet makers realized that they had committed themselves to two men for the army ministry. The situation apparently caused considerable confusion in the Kiyoura headquarters. Kiyoura had designated a staff to form his cabinet.

Its members had approached Tanaka in good faith, and Tanaka reciprocated by recommending his successor. On the other hand, Kiyoura could not dismiss lightly his understanding with Uehara, and there was also another complicating factor. One Lt. Gen. Ishimitsu Maomi, then commanding the 1st Division in Tokyo, was a confidant of Kiyoura by virtue of the fact that both of them came from Kumamoto. Ishimitsu was a member of the Uehara/Satsuma clique and stood to be promoted to general if Fukuda became the army minister. He was naturally anxious to see his candidate in office and made a special plea to Kiyoura on Fukuda's behalf, traveling to Kamakura on 2 January to confirm for Kiyoura Uehara's preference for Fukuda.[25]

Friendship with Uehara and fraternal obligation to Ishimitsu notwithstanding, Kiyoura and his staff had no choice but to go along with Tanaka. Tanaka's claim, based on army operating procedures, was far stronger than Uehara's, and in addition, Fukuda as army minister could be a serious political liability for an unpopular transcendent cabinet that was under attack from the enraged political parties even before it was formed. After all, only a few months earlier Tanaka had relieved Fukuda of the command of the Kantō martial law enforcement headquarters as the officer administratively responsible for the Amakasu affair.[26]

Tanaka moved next to check Uehara. He informed Uehara in Kamakura by messenger on 3 January that he (Tanaka) had urged Kiyoura to accept the recommendation of the big three as his army minister, and that Kiyoura had equivocated in his reply.[27] Tanaka apparently had the grace to keep Uehara's line of retreat open, but the marshal chose the course of tight-lipped silence. On the evening of 5 January Lt. Gen. Tsukushi Kumashichi, a Kumamoto officer with close connections to Tanaka, brought Uehara a message from Kiyoura saying that Tanaka had refused to accept the officer Kiyoura had in mind for army minister (Fukuda) and was pressuring the Kenkyūkai leaders to the point where the whole cabinet formation process had reached an impasse. Kiyoura had requested that Tanaka meet Uehara to draw up a list of three mutually acceptable candidates, so that Kiyoura might choose one of them as his army minister. Tanaka had agreed that under the circumstances he should coordinate with Uehara. The question was, would Uehara agree to such a meeting?

Uehara acknowledged that it was perfectly legitimate for Tanaka to have a different opinion from his own on the choice of army minister, but he told Tsukushi to inform Kiyoura that such a meeting would be contrary to his stated principles and quite impossible. He again refused to cooperate[28] or to retreat from his exposed position.

From this point the truth becomes obscure. Every account presents a different picture. Takamiya tells us that Tanaka called a meeting of the big three, presumably on 5 January, and that they chose Ugaki. Tanaka then asked Generals Yamanashi, Ono Minobu, and Machida Keiu to his residence and, as military affairs councillors, had them approve the choice. Machida, a Satsuma clansman, reluctantly ("choking back tears") approved, since he had no other recourse, although he knew of Uehara's intentions and sympathized with the Satsuma position. According to Takamiya, Machida was then chosen to inform Uehara of his defeat.[29] This account lacks a credible basis in the few facts available in primary sources. At best it is oversimplified.

What Tanaka apparently did do was to call a meeting of the big three for the evening of 5 January. No source provides the time of the meeting, but Kiyoura's messenger, Tsukushi, did not arrive in Kamakura until 8:00 P.M. Uehara's refusal to meet Tanaka could not have reached Tanaka's ears until quite late even if Tsukushi used the telephone to make his report to Kiyoura. Of course, Uehara's presence was not mandatory at the meeting and not even desirable from Tanaka's standpoint. He was, after all, establishing the principle that it was the right of the big three to determine his successor, and that keeping the marshals and military affairs councillors informed was a courtesy.[30]

In any case, it is quite clear that the big three chose not a single candidate for army minister but, in accord with Kiyoura's request, a slate of three, Generals Fukuda and Ono and Lieutenant General Ugaki. They were listed in that order, and the order was crucial. Uehara was immediately notified of the result, not by Tanaka in person as some accounts have it,[31] but in a letter carried to Kamakura by Tanaka's military secretary. Uehara received the letter at 2:00 A.M. on 6 January with the request that he give the messenger an immediate reply. The letter read as follows:

As requested by Viscount Kiyoura, the big three and others [indicating that military affairs councillors Yamanashi, Ono, and Machida had attended the conference, or had been consulted separately] have conferred, and as a result we have decided that it is appropriate to recommend as successor to the army minister the following three persons, Generals Fukuda and Ono and Lieutenant General Ugaki. Now we seek your opinion.

Marshal Uehara indicated that he objected to neither the names nor the order in which they were listed except that he thought the third person listed was too young to trust with the administration of the army and therefore disadvantageous under current changing conditions.[32]

While Tanaka's secretary was journeying to Kamakura, Tanaka reported the big three decision to Kiyoura, apparently without awaiting a reply from Uehara.[33] According to Tanaka's biographers Tanaka, when asked, assured the viscount that Ugaki was a man of great talent, a fine military administrator, and nothing more.[34] Others, such as Imamura Hitoshi, an officer close to Uehara, say that Tanaka reversed the list so that he presented the big three recommendation in the order of Ugaki, Ono, Fukuda, and that Kiyoura approved the first choice.[35] The Uehara biography states that the marshal returned to Tokyo on 6 January to pay his New Year's respects to the emperor. He was met at the station by General Machida, with whom he discussed the progress of selecting the army minister, but he did not learn until he visited Kiyoura hours later, at 3:00 P.M., that Kiyoura had chosen Ugaki.[36] This account contradicts Takamiya's contention that the big three chose the army minister and Machida was rather cruelly assigned to break the news to Uehara.

It is evident then that Kiyoura himself selected his army minister from a list given him by Tanaka. Barring unrecorded persuasion and advice from Tanaka at the time, Kiyoura and his advisers chose their army minister freely from a short list that read Fukuda, Ono, Ugaki — or Ugaki, Ono, Fukuda. There is no direct evidence to confirm either, but several circumstances argue against the latter list even though it later became entrenched in the popular version of the affair. First, Tanaka was too sophisticated a politician to engage in such a crude deception. Second, there was no need for him to do so. Kiyoura's advisers had probably already persuaded the prime minister–designate to abandon Fukuda because of his political vulnerability and the hostility his selection would create among powerful forces in and out of the army. Third, if the list had indeed been reversed, Uehara would have known of it and charged Tanaka with duplicity. Uehara's biographers strongly criticize Tanaka for his conduct in this instance, but they do not accuse him of having reversed the list.

If this reasoning establishes the sequence of Fukuda, Ono, Ugaki as the likely one presented to Kiyoura, what then happened to Ono? Ono was not only the second choice of the big three, but a military affairs councillor as well. He was one of the army's ranking officers, privy to top level discussions on the selection problem. In addition, he was not squarely in Tanaka's camp as Takamiya says,[37] but a member of Uehara's Satsuma clique.[38] His Satsuma affiliation is why Uehara suggested his name to Kiyoura in the first place. The answer probably lies in the fact that Ono looked forward to retirement and did not want the position, as indicated in the Tanaka biography.[39] It seems, also, that Tanaka knew this, but

Uehara did not. Furthermore, Tanaka knew it when he sent the priority list to Uehara, but he did not inform Uehara. Uehara was duped, but not in the way Imamura states. Tanaka did not reverse the list. He just managed to eliminate the top two choices before presenting it to Kiyoura.

On the morning of 6 January Kiyoura visited Ugaki to offer him the army portfolio. That evening Ugaki accepted. On the following day Kiyoura presented his cabinet to the emperor and officially took office.[40]

Apart from any clan rivalry, Tanaka was seeking a clear determination of the process for selecting the army minister in the absence of the stabilizing force of Yamagata. He wanted the outgoing army minister to select his own successor with the unanimous concurrence of the chief of staff and the inspector general of military training and the general understanding of the army's senior officers "in order to prevent men who play up to the political parties from being made army minister." Uehara disagreed, saying that such a narrow method would prevent the harmonious exercise of government policy, giving rise in turn to discord between the army and the people and inviting their advocacy of civilian service ministers.[41] In truth, Uehara would have liked to step into Yamagata's shoes. Had Tanaka and Uehara's positions been reversed, the two might have switched arguments. In any case, Tanaka wielded the real power in this instance and, as a consequence, won the battle.

Unfortunately, this unseemly and petty squabble led to more than petty results. Uehara, incensed at Tanaka's perfidy in reaction to his own knavery,[42] refused henceforth to have anything to do with Tanaka except, for form's sake, at public functions. After this incident Tanaka and Uehara never mixed socially. Tanaka apparently made some attempts at reconciliation and Oba Jirō went to great lengths to bring the two men together, but to no avail. They remained estranged until death removed Tanaka in 1929.[43]

If this defeat angered Uehara, one can only imagine the effect on Fukuda. Forced to resign for his purely administrative responsibility in the Amakasu affair, of which he had neither knowledge nor control, General Fukuda was in a desperate situation. If he did not recover quickly, his military career was at an end. Tanaka had been ruthless in his treatment of Fukuda after the Amakasu affair, and even Ugaki had sympathized with him in that instance.[44] Now Tanaka struck his career another devastating blow, pitilessly destroying Fukuda's one last chance. Fukuda saw the entire episode as a plot to ruin his career. His plight elicited sympathy from many of the army's highest-ranking officers including, of course, Machida, Ono, and all the members of Uehara's Satsubatsu. Chōbatsu officers, though perhaps personally sympathetic to Fukuda's position, probably tended to rationalize Tanaka's action on the basis of the principle involved. Fukuda was the unfortunate victim. However, the incident drew clear lines once more between the retainers of Satsuma and Chōshū. The upper levels of the army were again divided into two camps, but on the basis of new hostility. Tanaka and Fukuda met only once after the affair. Relations between them then ruptured completely, Fukuda declaring, "I will oppose Tanaka in everything he does."[45]

For younger officers of field grade rank who were already filled with resentment at the feudalistic personnel management practices perpetuated by Chōshū's stranglehold on the army's personnel system, this example of Tanaka's high-handedness brought into focus even more sharply the drastic need for reform. The story that Tanaka had reversed the lists became current gossip among them, and it may be no coincidence that the movement to exclude Chōshū men from the staff college reached its peak at this very time.[46] Chōshū again held all the big three positions; personal sympathy for Fukuda turned him into a reform candidate and Uehara's cause, the cause of reform. A "concerned instructor" at the army staff college wrote:

The despotism of the Satsuma clan in the navy, the so-called *Satsu no kaigun* [Satsuma navy], has ended. Nevertheless, in the army the domination of Chōshū continues as before. We must, by all means, stop its pollution of the national army with its private army personnel practices. But if even the power of Marshal Uehara cannot bring about this reform, as a last resort there is nothing left for us but to see that there are no successors among Chōshū soldiers for the army's central organs [i.e., army staff college graduates]. Having schemed unfairly to place many of their young clansmen in schools right up to the staff college, it will be necessary for us concerned instructors to reverse this [practice] by banding together and devising ways to make them ineligible. This [situation] can be compared to the expression, "When the priest was hated, even his stole was an abomination." It is an inhumane thing to blame children for the sins of their parents and elder brothers, but there is no other way to straighten out the army.[47]

This unfortunate incident, handled so irresponsibly by both Uehara and Tanaka, gave new impetus to the attacks on Chōshū. Although Tanaka could count himself the winner, it was a Pyrrhic victory. The younger, reform-minded officers redoubled their call for change, many of them paradoxically rallying round Uehara, the army's most conservative element. Very soon Tanaka's position in the army became untenable, and he escaped into the world of politics, leaving the battered remnant of the once proud Chōbatsu to fend for itself in a hostile environment. It did not survive.

The whole affair was a needless personal tragedy for Tanaka, Fukuda, and even Uehara and another blow to unity in the army. One lasting, baleful result for all the Japanese political world was the firm establishment of Tanaka's system for picking the army minister's successor. In effect, it reestablished the active duty qualification for the army minister, and it soon became a bludgeon used by a more highly politicized army to control the selection of entire cabinets.[48] The prime minister became dependent on the big three in selecting his army minister, effectively removing the post from his area of choice.[49] Ironically, this system was used against Ugaki when he tried to form a cabinet in 1937.

Ugaki Takes Control of the Army

In spite of these inauspicious beginnings, the emergence of Ugaki as the army minister began a new era in army politics. Ugaki Kazunari soon became so powerful that he could cut four more divisions from army strength, institute a vigorous though unsuccessful program of modernization, and crush the remaining strength of the clan cliques. His personal following developed to the extent that the next seven years of army history — to the Manchurian Incident — can be called the Ugaki era.

Army Minister Ugaki was the military giant of his day. Proud, self-assured, independent, and dictatorial, he ran the army personnel apparatus with an iron hand, gradually adopting for the use of his own followers the methods he deplored in the hands of the Chōbatsu. For years Ugaki was Tanaka's trusted lieutenant. His step-by-step ascent to the pinnacle of army leadership was as a member of the Tanaka/Chōshū clique. When he entered the cabinet as Kiyoura's army minister, it was assumed by both his friends and his enemies that it was as a member of a resurgent Chōbatsu. Nothing could have been further from the truth.

According to notations in Ugaki's diary, Ugaki considered that the relationship between him and Tanaka had always been exploitative. When Tanaka was chief of the general affairs bureau in the army ministry, he made Ugaki head of the military affairs section only because there was no suitable Chōbatsu man available, but later, recognizing Ugaki's abilities, he brought Ugaki in as his chief of operations when he became vice chief of staff, in order to help him advertise his own (Tanaka's) talents to the world at large. When Tanaka became army minister, he left Ugaki behind in the general staff headquarters, expecting him to act as a check on Uehara and Fukuda (then vice chief of staff). When Tanaka's friend Yamanashi took over with his "policy of repressing men of ability," Ugaki was consigned to the countryside as a division commander with Tanaka's concurrence. Tanaka never lost his thirst for power and, as Ugaki goes on to say, when he emerged once again as army minister, he brought Ugaki back as his vice minister in the expectation that Ugaki would work again on his behalf. At last, stepping down from the army ministry, Tanaka planned to maintain his own position within the army by choosing Ugaki, "on whom he could rely for sustenance," as his successor to block the intrusion of Uehara and his faction.[50]

If this passage marks Ugaki as an ingrate, it also allows us some understanding of the character of the man and the system within which he rose. Ugaki was the first to believe in his own ability. From Ugaki's viewpoint Tanaka merely used him as a tool. There seems to be no question in Ugaki's mind that he would have risen just as fast and gone just as far without Tanaka's patronage had the system allowed him to progress on his own merit. One can feel Ugaki's resentment at having to work for years in relative obscurity to further the career of a man of towering ambition who stood in the spotlight as heir apparent to the Chōbatsu and later in the glare of public attention. The weakness of the army personnel system, based as it was on personal loyalties, the carryover of a recent feudal past, then becomes vividly apparent. The stresses and strains of this anachronistic system of personnel management is reflected in Ugaki's attitude toward a man he neither trusted nor admired, but on whom he depended for recognition and advancement.

Ugaki also reveals the divisive character of the army's professional staff system, borrowed in the days of Katsura Tarō from the Germans. Graduates of the army staff college, like Ugaki, saw themselves as an elite. He had little but contempt for his enforced service as a division commander, which took him from the center of army activity and prevented him from exercising his abilities in the most advantageous manner.[51] This attitude is opposite to that of, say, Ugaki's British counterpart, to whom the command of his home regiment would be the greatest honor, or to an American general, who would consider the command of a division the fulfillment of his life's work. To Ugaki, the troops, the battalions, and the divisions were the toys of staff officers. The commander of troops was not a commander, but a rubber stamp for the decisions of bright young graduates of the *rikudai* on his staff. The positions of power and influence, Ugaki knew, lay in the top positions of the army ministry and the general staff. There were, of course, regulations requiring professional staff officers to serve in command assignments, but the assignment of a lieutenant general of general staff background to command a division often signaled that he was no longer on the inside track to the highest ranks and most influential assignments and that his career might soon be coming to its close.

At other times, usually when angered by certain conditions or circumstances, Ugaki commented in his diary on his senior contemporaries. Ōshima Ken'ichi, Yamanashi Hanzō, and Fukuda Masatarō come in for criticism,[52] but Ugaki saved his sharpest barbs for Uehara, about whom he wrote quite frequently. When Uehara finally retired as chief of staff in March 1923, a large farewell celebration accompanied the occasion. During the course of the evening Uehara gave an address, from which Ugaki quoted from memory in his diary — "Through the nearly eight years I've held this position, I've come to the present day without serious error" — to which Ugaki rejoined:

Does he really believe that to be true, or was it just a kind of pleasantry? Even the rank and file like myself think of ourselves in the present situation as having in recent years considerably reduced and liquidated the vision that the efforts of the previous emperor and our forebears had made clear as crystal, and furthermore, as unconsciously having caused the death of contemporaries whom we martyred in extending the national fortunes. We feel deeply that our efforts and measures have been so ineffective and therefore stand ashamed. From his remarks one sincerely wonders whether or not he has any feeling of responsibility in this regard.

Uehara continued, "Though I leave my current post, as a marshal I will still maintain my connection with the army. As long as my body or, at any rate, my mind and spirit remain sound, I will work on as before without change. Listen to me well in this, for I'm going to show you." Ugaki then added that it would be all right if the emperor were to ask him to continue to work (as the Meiji emperor had asked Yamagata and Ōyama Iwao), but failing that it would be most magnanimous if Uehara just left things up to his successors.[53] Even when Uehara died in 1933 at the age of 78, Ugaki had nothing good to say about him.

I would not hesitate to say that his existence was all but useless, no, destructive to the state and the army. This man roundly criticized Viscount Yamamoto [Gonbei], saying that he was despicable, like somebody the palace maids corrupted, implacable like a snake. I don't know enough about the viscount as a man, but just the fact that this criticism fits the marshal to perfection shows that it takes one to know one.[54]

Ugaki singled out Uehara and Fukuda for special criticism as a result of their vehement opposition to his appointment as army minister. He complimented Kawai, Oba, and Yamanashi for standing by resolutely, and he defended the process by which he was chosen, but he lashed out at the people "among my seniors who forget the issues, who forget the necessity to maintain the honor of the military and act blindly, adhering to their own individual position and advantage. A terrible pity. [Because they act this way] there are many instances when they hurt the image of the army and diminish respect for it."[55]

There was little elation in Ugaki's appointment. He took no pleasure from Tanaka's victory on his behalf, nor from the fact that he was entering an anachronistic transcendent cabinet in an era of party dominance. Only force of circumstances — the cabinet could not be completed without his participation — and persistent encouragement from Kawai and Oba, at last, after a long day's hesitation, brought him around to accepting. "I agreed to join the cabinet that evening [6 January], resolving on a spirit of sacrifice."[56]

Few army ministers assumed office under more trying circumstances than Ugaki. Tokyo and the Kantō region had not yet begun to recover from the disastrous earthquake and fire of September, and the army still carried the heavy responsibility for rehabilitation and the construction of temporary housing in the miserable winter that followed. The earthquake had merely added to the economic plight of the country. New retrenchments in government expenditures were inevitable, and everyone knew that the army would be called on for a sizable contribution.

Internally, the army faced critical problems in its only partially recognized need to modernize both its weapons and its organization. Thanks to Uehara and Yamanashi, there had been little progress in technical modernization, almost no progress in reorganization except at the lowest tactical levels, and no progress whatsoever in planning for the integration of the civilian political and economic structure with the military for the prosecution of total war. Last but not least, the army's central organs were rent by factionalism. The hostility Uehara, Fukuda, and the Kyushu factions felt for Tanaka and his Chōbatsu was willy-nilly transferred to Ugaki. Ugaki's every move was made in the teeth of tenacious opposition from Uehara and his growing Ueharabatsu.[57] This bitter hostility became apparent very quickly when the Kiyoura cabinet fell in June 1924. Katō Kōmei, leader of a three-party coalition, was designated to form a cabinet, and he asked Ugaki to continue in office. Ugaki wrote in his diary that he wanted to retire, but he feared that the serious work of army administrative reform would be impossible under a man like Fukuda, who was obsessed with becoming army minister. He accepted Katō's offer only after learning that General Ono and Marshal Uehara had approached Katō and his associates on Fukuda's behalf.

Katō's was a reform cabinet, the first party cabinet since Takahashi's Seiyūkai government withdrew in 1922. Katō promised the people universal suffrage for all male citizens over twenty, reform of the House of Peers, and retrenchment in government administration and finance in the aftermath of the earthquake disaster. This cabinet meant business; the parties were in control again, and Ugaki, realizing that change and sacrifice were in the wind, did not wish to entrust the important task of army reorganization to anyone but himself,[58] least of all to his enemies. As vice minister under Tanaka, Ugaki had acted as chairman of the military systems investigation committee.[59] Now, as army minister, he ordered the work already started to continue under his new vice minister, Lt. Gen. Tsuno Kazusuke.[60] This committee soon recommended a third army reduction and reorganization, to be carried out in 1925.

Faced with serious internal political opposition to any program he might propose, Ugaki moved deliberately to consolidate his hold on the army's personnel system to ensure that the officers friendly to him were in the most effective positions to uphold his programs. Coming as he did from Okayama, a prefecture whose numbers in the army officer corps were not large, there was no way he could have built an "Okayama *hanbatsu*" of talented home province officers. Instead, Ugaki had another device in mind. He had said that he disliked the grandstanding personnel policies of Tanaka, Ōshima, and Yamanashi, and he promised to purge the army of their practices when he had the opportunity, in order to restore discipline.[61]

Ugaki's method was to surround himself with men of ability regardless of geographic background. Freed of clan ties, he turned to his military academy classmates of the first graduating class for support, "firmly gripping hands with" Lt. Gen. Suzuki Sōroku (Niigata) and Lt. Gen. Shirakawa Yoshinori (Ehime). Through these two men he extended his hold to younger officers. Suzuki brought in Kanaya Hanzō (Oita, 5th class), Minami Jirō (Oita, 6th class), and Tatekawa Yoshitsugu (Niigata, 13th class); Shirakawa added Kawashima Yoshiyuki (Ehime, 10th class). Through his long-term connections with Tanaka and the Chōbatsu, Ugaki also received the support of the remnants of that clique, primarily Sugano Hisaichi (2nd class) and Tsuno Kazusuke (5th class). His own protégés included Hata Eitarō (Fukushima, 7th class) and Hata's younger brother, Shunroku (12th class), Abe Nobuyuki (Ishikawa, 9th class), and Matsui Iwane (Aichi, 9th class). To this group we should add three classmates of Hata

Shunroku—Ninomiya Masashige (Okayama), Sugiyama Hajime (or Gen) (Fukuoka), and Koiso Kuniaki (Yamagata), and one classmate of Tatekawa's, Hayashi Katsura (Wakayama).[62]

Ugaki soon brought several of these close associates into key positions in the army's central organs. In addition to Vice Minister Tsuno, Hata Eitarō was already in position as chief of the military affairs bureau. Hata followed Tsuno as vice minister in 1926, and Abe Nobuyuki replaced him as chief of the military affairs bureau. Suzuki Sōroku became chief of staff in 1926, Kanaya Hanzō vice chief of staff in 1925, and Matsui Iwane chief of the second (intelligence) division in the general staff headquarters in the same year.[63]

Uehara's retirement from the chief of staff post and Ugaki's strong grip on the army ministry began to redress the balance between the administrative and operational organs of the army. Kawai, Uehara's successor, ranked Ugaki and at times opposed him, but he never dominated him. Kawai's successor, Suzuki, was a pillar of the Ugakibatsu, and his successor, Kanaya, during Ugaki's last army ministry (1929–31), was completely dominated by Ugaki.[64] Thus, Ugaki built the first of the modern *gunbatsu*, based on talent as well as personal leadership. Since all seventeen members of his clique were graduates of the staff college, it must be classified as a clique within the staff college elite.[65] Later, in April 1927, when Tanaka Giichi became prime minister as head of a revived Seiyūkai, Ugaki stepped down and turned the army ministry over to his classmate Shirakawa. By that time the Ugakibatsu was such a well-oiled machine that it continued to dominate the top positions in the army until 1931.[66]

Ugaki used one more fortunate circumstance to consolidate further his hold on army leadership. In April 1925, on the eve of the massive reform, now in its final planning stage, Tanaka Giichi presented Ugaki with a golden opportunity to rid himself of many of his highest-ranking opponents. Tanaka's interest in army politics had gradually dimmed. He had accomplished everything he could within the structure of that institution, and his current position as a military affairs councillor offered him no challenge. His recent battle with Uehara had estranged him from many of his army contemporaries, and cries against Chōbatsu despotism could be clearly heard in the ranks of the younger officers. It was time for Tanaka to seek an alternative outlet for his ambition.

The possibility of Tanaka's entering politics had been discussed as early as August 1923.[67] His connections with the Seiyūkai in Hara's day made him an attractive candidate to lead that party, now in disarray. Early in April 1925 Takahashi Korekiyo, the current party head and Tanaka's bête noire in the days of the Hara cabinet, began serious negotiations with him. Within a few days Takahashi offered, and Tanaka accepted, the presidency of the Seiyūkai with the concurrence of the party's leaders.

As a general on active duty, however, Tanaka could not formally embark on a political career; therefore, he immediately petitioned the emperor through Army Minister Ugaki for release from active duty. With imperial approval Tanaka entered the reserve and the world of Japanese politics on 9 April 1925. On 13 April, at the age of 62, he was installed as president of the Seiyūkai.[68]

With Tanaka making the first move, Ugaki found it opportune to add to the list of retirees eleven more generals and senior lieutenant generals, many of them men in Uehara's camp and opposed to Ugaki's army reform plans. The generals were all military affairs councillors: Fukuda Masatarō, Machida Keiu, Ono Minobu, and Yamanashi Hanzō. The first three could be counted on to uphold Uehara and oppose Ugaki. Of the seven lieutenant generals Ishimitsu Maomi, Fukuda's partisan, and two others certainly counted as members of the Uehara clique.[69] After 1 May 1925, when these eleven retirements became effective, Ugaki suddenly ranked very high on the army list. Only the two marshals Oku and Uehara, Chief of Staff Kawai and Inspector General of Military Training Oba, Generals Kikuchi Shinnosuke and Nara Takeji, and Ugaki's two classmates and supporters Suzuki and Shirakawa ranked above him.[70] Only Uehara could be counted on to oppose him. Not only had Ugaki established his own position firmly, but he had destroyed Uehara's support in the upper ranks. In August the army promoted Ugaki to general.

4

Reduction and Modernization: The Ugaki Era

> I tried to seize the initiative, but the tendency of the army was to go in the opposite direction. Resisted by my juniors, everything I wished to do came to naught.
>
> Ugaki Kazunari

Beginning in May 1925 the army launched its one bold attempt to modernize. This effort, known as the Ugaki *gunshuku*, had far-reaching effects inside and outside the army in the years to come. Ugaki considered his plan not a *shukushōan* (reduction plan) but a *seirian* (consolidation plan).[1] He wished to use it to satisfy the public demand for reducing military spending by decreasing the size of the army as part of general government retrenchment after the earthquake, but the money saved was to be plowed back into research and the hardware for modernization. In the welter of ideas on what to do about the army, among the active duty officers only Ugaki came forward with a clear-cut, reasonable, and well-designed plan for change. But, as we shall see, the results were disappointing if not disastrous. Ugaki himself said years later, "The tendency of the army was to go in the opposite direction."[2] Perhaps at another time and in other circumstances Ugaki's proposals might have transformed the army into a relatively modern, rationally based military force, but the internal stress and tension in the officer corps had progressed so far by Ugaki's day that his reforms only aggravated the political situation within the army, and a significant number of officers rose to thwart his effort. The imperial army was apparently unwilling to face the monumental difficulties of a rational solution to the nation's defense problems.

Japan had entered the Great War under the terms of the Anglo-Japanese Alliance, but within the army a substantial core of sympathy for

Germany remained. The Japanese constitutional and governmental system owed much to the example of Germany in the Meiji era, particularly in the army, where the very staff and command system rested firmly on a German base. The army sent officers to Europe for various purposes, a large proportion of them to Germany,[3] and there is little question that army officers in general considered the German imperial structure more congenial to the Japanese ideal than the structure of other European nations. In the democracies of Europe and America, the apparent victors in the war, a Japanese officer was likely to find little of political relevance or inspiration. As a consequence, after the war the army showed more interest in the German defeat than the Allied victory. How could a nation with the finest army in Europe, more akin to the ideals and spirit of the Japanese army than any other, led by a dedicated and loyal officer corps, at the head of a highly motivated well-trained soldiery, fall into defeat? The answer must lie in the changed nature of warfare and the German nation's response to it as explained by General Erich Ludendorff.[4] The *Reichswehr* was not defeated. It had been "stabbed in the back" by the German government and people, who collapsed under the strain of a protracted war. There was a fatal gap between this splendid army and the civilians of the nation, who had not allowed the still intact army to carry on in the face of an unexpectedly long and arduous war.

The fate of the Russian monarchy revealed even more sharply the dangers to an imperial state if the army and the people were not one. The impact of the wholesale destruction of Europe's great monarchies was traumatic. Japanese officers, like the articulate retired Lieutenant General Satō Kōjirō, were driven to serious reflection on the situation in Japan after the war when they faced a reaction to Japanese militarism. War could no longer be considered a mere extension of politics, but future military considerations must undergird the political, economic, and psychological attitudes of the empire and its people if the nation was to survive. Having seen the great empires of continental Europe precipitately disappear with the war, the army, dedicated to an imperial system and indoctrinated in its service, began to distinguish between the national polity of European empires and that of Japan, coming to the highly irrational conclusion that the Japanese Empire was indestructible.[5] Japan's unique insular civilization and the perpetuation of its imperial line for ages eternal became cardinal, sacred, and mystical virtues to the Japanese army. It came to view with alarm the insidious foreign tenets of pacifism, socialism, and democracy that, for various reasons, were subverting the imperial system and the military forces that supported it.

Anxiety over external world political changes, the rising popularity of powerful foreign political ideologies, and the growing discord between the people and the army were matched within the army by its perception of the defensive role it must play, the means at its disposal, and the power of its enemies. The view was discouraging. Military planners are by the nature of their work a pessimistic lot. Since they must plan for every contingency and be prepared for the worst possible case, their estimates are frequently disturbing. Among the Japanese military the situation was probably aggravated by the fact that they planned in virtual isolation without the ameliorating or restraining influences of other government agencies.

There was, moreover, much for army planners to fret over. The Great War had completely changed the character of war. Total war not only encompassed the political, economic, industrial, social, and psychological factors of the civilian community in far greater measure than ever before, but there were quantitative and qualitative changes in the armies engaged. Even small European countries had trained and fielded huge armies. Problems in control required a pyramid of headquarters above the division level — in corps, armies, and army groups.

A great technological leap provided revolutionary armaments delivering fast, accurate, and incredibly heavy fire. The airplane had established its importance as a reconnaissance vehicle and showed promise as a tactical and strategic weapon. The tank might prove effective as a way to break the stalemate of trench warfare. Artillery had been revolutionized during the war. No longer a vulnerable, direct-fire weapon, it provided devastating, accurate, high-angle fire from concealed positions far behind friendly lines.

The Germans had introduced poison gas into warfare with disastrous effects. Smaller tactical weapons proved equally important. The trench mortar and the machine gun were the twin scourges of the western front. The mortar provided front-line infantry with high-angle-fire weapons capable of killing men protected in trenches. The light machine gun gave mobile direct firepower to small infantry units. Both weapons tremendously increased the effectiveness of infantry firepower.

In addition, a revolution in mobility took place as the internal combustion engine came into its own. Not only tanks and airplanes but more prosaic cargo trucks supplemented the railway as a means of supply and released armies from their dependence on the railway networks, reducing the railroad's tactical and strategic importance.

The requirement for huge masses of infantry meant sweeping changes in training methods. Troops must be instructed quickly and efficiently. A shorter time in the barracks meant a much larger reserve. Technical training now applied to a wider range of soldiers. Officer training, too, changed character. With masses of men under arms and thousands of situations simultaneously requiring instant decisions on the battlefield, commanders must rely on junior officers on the spot. Junior officers, and noncommissioned officers as well, were required to take the initiative, opening the possibilities for individual action. Training emphasis veered sharply away from blind discipline toward thoughtful individual action.

Among Europeans and Americans, two general theories of modern warfare were gradually evolving. The first required a relatively small modern standing army to absorb the shock of an initial assault in order to give the nation time to muster its large reserves and total resources for a protracted war. The second theory sought to avoid protracted war through a large standing army and a readily mobilizable reserve in order to strike a crushing initial blow before the enemy could mobilize for a second defense. The British and the Americans tended to accept the former type of defense; the German military, whose recent defeat could be rationalized as the result of a long war, later opted for the second — the *Blitzkrieg*. The Japanese army, knowing the nation's economic weakness in comparison to the other great powers and harboring somewhat paranoid suspicions of psychological weaknesses in its people, was attracted to the German approach.[6]

As in other nations, the new view of warfare among military men was paralleled in Japan by a contradictory civilian impulse toward pacifism and internationalism. Both were reactions to the experience of the war. One was the anguished cry of decimated populations — a movement to realize the Wilsonian ideal of a war that would end war. The other was the response of professionals who were attempting to confine war within the bounds of sanity by ensuring the survival of the all-important nation-state by rationally adapting their organization and tactics to scientific and technological changes. In Japan the Yamanashi and Ugaki arms reduction plans exemplified the clash. The Yamanashi *gunshuku* was an almost total victory for militant pacifism with little or no concession to the needs of the military who, among themselves, had responded in traditional terms, having no clear vision of what changes must take place in the military system to effect its modernization. The Ugaki *gunshuku* symbolized the reversal of the position that was hostile to the military. Cuts were necessary for economic rather than emotional reasons. Compromise was possible to allow for military modernization, and Ugaki knew what he wanted for the army.

It was one thing, of course, to have military attachés in European capitals and observers in the Allied trenches to report and interpret the course of the war and the manifold changes occurring on and over the battlefields, and quite another to convince army leadership that change was necessary. It took time for an army that had hardly participated in the massive four-year conflict to absorb its lessons. As might be expected, the greatest impact the European war observers made on the army was not among senior officers, for the young attachés and observers were at a psychological disadvantage with them. The older men in the army had fought in the Russo-Japanese War, and their feeling for war was for that war. They were proud of what they had done and the way they had done it. Older, more set in their ways, they were unlikely to be swayed by the importunities of their juniors. On the other hand, young field grade officers with no experience in the Russo-Japanese War, fresh from Europe, were often assigned as instructors at the staff college or branch schools. There they had ample time and occasion to capture the imagination of the uncluttered young minds of lieutenants and captains.[7]

Kobayashi Jun'ichirō was such a man. An artillery officer who spoke French, Kobayashi had observed and mastered French artillery technique in 1916 and 1917, before and during the war. He brought back a panoramic sight, the instrument that made indirect artillery fire possible, and lectured at the staff college on the European use of artillery. In 1922 he became an instructor at the field artillery school,[8] preaching the doctrine of massed indirect artillery fire so eloquently that he came to be known as *hōhei no kamisama* (god of the artillery). Sakai Kōji, who performed a somewhat analogous function for aeronautics, taught at the staff college from 1923 to 1925 and later.[9] Ishida Morimasa, whose nine-volume *Ōshū taisenshi no kenkyū* (A historical study of the Great War in Europe) won him just acclaim, received his European training in Switzerland and Germany in the early postwar period. He taught the history of the war at the staff college from 1925 until 1932.[10] Ishiwara Kanji arrived at his rather idiosyncratic theories of modern warfare as a student in postwar Germany, where he met regularly with officers of the defunct German imperial army general staff. Ishiwara taught at the staff college from 1925 until 1928.[11] Itō Masanori writes:

The rapid progress in all kinds of weaponry and the tactical revolution that accompanied it in World War I left the Japanese army far behind. . . . When the Dentsū and Kokusai news agencies received the news of the appearance of tanks [on the Somme front in September 1915], they had not the faintest idea what they were. When the word *tanks* was used, the correspondents, who knew only of gas tanks, had no way to translate it. They ran to the army ministry to ask, but there were no officers there who knew.

This is just one of several new weapons about which the Japanese army and public had little or no knowledge. "It was what was called the era of scientific warfare and a great revolution that transformed the Japanese army into a 'nonscientific army.'"[12] Malcolm Kennedy, a British military attaché in Japan, observed:

The War . . . brought out new and hitherto almost un-thought-of inventions, the possession of which has now come to be regarded as a *sine qua non* for any army which may be called upon to take the field against that of a first-class power. . . .

In most of these matters the Japanese Army is still some way behind its European and American counterparts. This is, of course, partly due to the fact that these other nations were able to develop them throughout the War by virtue of practical experience in the field, whereas the Japanese, being far removed from the seat of war, had to depend mainly on second-hand information, and, moreover, as is always the case in peace-time, in all countries, money for experimental work in Japan was necessarily restricted.[13]

By 1925 the army had, in truth, made little progress to prepare itself or the nation for the rigors of total war; it had become a second-rate army or worse. Itō Masanori notes:

In the Russo-Japanese War they had fought a first-class war, but half the reason for victory lay in the intrepidity of the generals and the valor of the soldiers. This [spirit] came to be a belief in certain victory, and many's the time they fell back on their vigorous fighting spirit. [After the Great War] they were nearly blind to the spectacle of newly produced weapons and an abundance of ammunition dominating the power to make war.[14]

If not blind to the problems, the army certainly faced a formidable array of technical obstacles and tactical changes before it could rank again with the armies of the great powers. The number one problem was probably the machine gun. The army had them. They were in use during the Russo-Japanese War, but World War I had seen both quantitative and qualitative changes in that terrifying piece of equipment. European armies had four heavy machine guns per infantry battalion. The imperial army had no machine guns at the battalion level. In addition, European armies had organized the lowest-echelon tactical group (the squad) around the light machine gun, which could be carried with the infantry in an attack. The Japanese squad carried only rifles, there being no light machine gun in the tactical weapons arsenal.[15] Japanese infantry still advanced as a line of skirmishers, as they had in the Russo-Japanese War. This type of formation was disastrous in the face of coordinated direct fire from machine guns, mortars, and artillery. As Horike Kazumaro puts it:

Up till this time [post–World War I] the core of our tactics was close combat relying on the bayonet. This became the decisive force in battle, and since what was called the "close combat principle" of tactics was traditional after the Russo-Japanese War, they weren't able to switch easily to these new tactics based mainly on firepower. Worse yet, they continued [to use] the close combat tactical principle right up to World War II.[16]

The artillery presented the second great problem. The Japanese still insisted on the use of flat-trajectory, direct-fire field artillery pieces, whereas the European armies had replaced them with new indirect-fire weapons with an arched trajectory, primarily the howitzer. Replacing all this hardware and developing a tactical system to accompany the changes would be a very costly and time-consuming process that did not even bring into consideration the really expensive development of weapons of the future like the tank and the airplane. The army had no tanks, no fighter aircraft, no bombers, no poison gas, and, as a consequence, no chance against an army that did have them.

Itō Masanori estimates that Japan's 21 divisions were the equivalent of no more than 5 to 7 European divisions, of use only against Manchurian banditti but an embarrassment as the army of a first-class country.[17] Tanaka Ryūkichi, also exaggerating, deems the Japanese divisions inferior to Chinese mercenaries.[18] Finally, the mobilization strength of the imperial army remained very small for a country with so large a population. Thanks to Uehara's adamant opposition, the term of service for drafted infantry soldiers remained three years. At this leisurely pace there had been no need to improve the efficiency of training and no significant enlargement in the mobilizable reserve, which remained at about a million men.

Fujiwara Akira considers all these deficiencies merely superficial problems stemming from a lack of experience in the war. Since it had not been necessary for the army to reform, there had been no accompanying change in financial and industrial institutions or technical know-how, and tactics remained strictly bound to a conservative tradition. Beyond this he sees a more serious problem based on contradictions between the intrinsic characteristics of Japanese society and the army. For him the imperial army was the class army of the emperor system, not a popular army. It was established in the early Meiji period as a weapon for class suppression, but by forming a police force and transferring internal security duties to it, by fulfilling the role of a military force overseas in the Sino- and Russo-Japanese Wars, and by basing the conscription system on "all the people of the nation soldiers," the army took on the outward appearance of a popular army for a time. This image shattered in the rice riots of 1918, when the army bared its class character to suppress the people. The unpopular Siberian Expedition deepened the cleavage, and the extreme unpopularity of the army after the war was in large part due to this revelation.[19]

Fujiwara's Marxist analysis does not take into account the fact that the army was perhaps as popular as any army ever is for most of its existence, nor does his explanation tell us why military service in "classless" societies is often no more welcome than it is in those supposedly rent by class contradictions, but it is useful to show the impact of the rice riots and the Siberian Expedition on army-to-people relations. The army's role in the rice riots was probably unavoidable. Every government uses its army as a reinforcement for the police. When police power breaks down under extreme stress, the army is routinely called in. In the case of the rice riots, as in the case of the Kantō earthquake, the army tended to use unreasonable and excessive force. Its overreaction, not its intervention, caused the intense bitterness.

The Siberian Expedition was another matter. In that case, by voluntarily entering and stubbornly pursuing a course of action for four years under an obdurate and powerful chief of staff, the army tended to alienate foreign governments and peoples as well as the people of Japan. It squandered millions of yen, of which at least a part might have been used for military modernization. When Ugaki criticized Uehara's declamatory farewell speech, he undoubtedly had such wanton acts in mind.[20]

For an army whose objective was the ability to survive and win a total war, the imperial army was indeed in a poor position. It did not have the equipment, organization, or tactical system to fight such a war, nor did it have the financial, industrial, and technical backing to make necessary changes even if it could overcome the strong internal resistance to change. The Kantō earthquake, following the financial waste in Siberia, compounded the problem by absorbing any monies that might have been used for immediate military modernization and by lowering still further Japan's overall industrial and technical standard.[21] Above all, as Fujiwara Akira observes, "For the prosecution of a total war, which requires as its indispensable basis the ideological and political solidarity of the nation, the estrangement and mutual distrust between the army and the people was the greatest contradiction."[22]

The Circumstances of Ugaki's Reform

The growing political consciousness at all levels of society, which had leavened Western civilization since the beginning of the nineteenth century, soon entered Japan and worked analogous changes there. By the first quarter of the twentieth century the Japanese were thinking in bewilderingly diverse and new social categories, many of them uninteresting, incomprehensible, or threatening to an army officered by men trained together in a narrow and conservative sphere of thought and action.[23]

Some officers, like Ugaki, recognized the problem of handling modernization and public relations together in the face of inexorable pressure on the army to spend less money rather than more. The Yamanashi *gunshuku* had failed to address the modernization problem squarely and in fact had rejected excellent suggestions. Yamanashi had skirted the public relations problem. Yet Ugaki, Yamanashi, and virtually all army officers could agree that — no matter what new ideas had penetrated the Japanese people, ideas tending to discredit or render the army superfluous, and no matter what mistakes the leaders had made in the past to damage the army's public image — their analysis of the world situation and the dangers it presented to Japan and the imperial system were correct. For the army the preservation of emperor and state was still the highest value, and perceived internal or external threats must be opposed with all the resources at its disposal.

The Ugaki and Yamanashi reductions were not only different in character; they were also very different in circumstance. Much had taken place in and about Japan to alter the atmosphere in which the Ugaki *gunshuku* would be executed. In 1925 the army was not being singled out for discriminatory reductions but was being called on to do its part in the general financial retrenchment of an economically depressed nation. There was no longer any clamor against militarists and no cry for arms reduction in the name of pacifism and international brotherhood. Certainly it was the great earthquake that made new arms cuts unavoidable, but it had also brought compensations. There was now little hostility toward the army and its personnel. Since the disaster there was a new feeling of mutual trust and community between army and people, even though perhaps it was diminished in some circles by the Amakasu and Kameido incidents. Ugaki was very quick to recognize the change in atmosphere and judge its effect on the army. About 19 September 1923, he entered the following in his diary:

The people of the country except gross ingrates, at least all classes of people who feel the direct influence of the recent calamity, have a feeling of gratitude for the actions of the army. Moreover, the idea of cursing the military and the advocacy of arms reduction will perhaps change somewhat as a result of [their] appreciation. However, for we who spend our lives in the military, considering appreciation and current ideas and doctrines as two different things, it is necessary to manage our own affairs. Though it is not beyond the realm of possibility that the past will be swept aside on the strength of this popular wave of gratitude, it would be a mistake to place great expectations in it. We must continue at our discretion to devise appropriate measures against these aforesaid ideas and doctrines.[24]

The army quickly took advantage of this change in attitude. Army Minister Tanaka sought to cancel the deactivation of four battalions of the Manchuria garrison, among the last scheduled reductions under the Yamanashi *gunshuku*, because there might be mistaken judgments about the authority of the empire there owing to the converging circumstances of the earthquake in Tokyo and the civil war between Zhang Zuolin (Chang Tso-lin) and Wu Peifu (Wu P'ei-fu) in North China. At the same time he proposed that the Diet increase the strength of units in Korea "because of conditions in the border region."[25] In China there had been a ground swell of reaction against Japanese imperialism. The Chinese had already regained sovereignty in Shandong, and in 1923 a strong popular movement arose for the return of Dairen (Dalian) and Ryojun (Port Arthur), the Guandong (Kwantung) Leasehold.

In the midst of the psychological and economic depression that followed the earthquake, the United States struck a stunning blow to Japanese pride by passing the Immigration Act of 1924, which permanently barred Japanese immigration to the United States. In Tokyo on 1 July 1924, National Humiliation Day marked the event with mass meetings in which a "hate America" theme predominated. The immigration act, institutionalizing theories of Asian racial inferiority in the United States, completely negated the goodwill engendered by generous American relief aid following the earthquake, but more important, it killed the concept of Japanese-U.S. harmony and cooperation on which government foreign policy had been based since Hara's day. Much of the argument for arms reduction and disarmament was based on this cooperation, which had led to Japanese concessions at the Washington Conference and to the Yamanashi *gunshuku* itself. Now the Japanese, more than ever, felt they had been duped and cheated at Washington,[26] and the navy view since the fall of imperial Russia that the United States was Japan's prime hypothetical enemy found further acceptance among the general population.

On one more domestic development, civil governments (party and nonparty) and the army could agree — the danger foreign revolutionary ideologies posed to the state. If further proof was needed, the official attitude toward radicals quickly came to the surface as one by-product of the earthquake. The communist youth Nanba Daisuke's attempt on the life of Crown Prince Hirohito in December 1923 shocked all of Japan.[27] It brought down Yamamoto's nonparty government and created a new perception of danger from the left. When the 49th Diet passed the Katō Kōmei government's bill for universal male suffrage in summer 1924, it also enacted the notorious peace preservation law, which abridged political freedom for the followers of "nonconforming ideologies." In the same year, in spite of other budget austerities, Ugaki received authority for the army to increase the size of the military police in Japan proper,[28] and from this year the army classified and removed much material routinely provided in the army ministry annual statistical report.

Arms reduction in 1925 was an economic necessity, but no longer the consequence of broad public pressure against the military establishment and its still noticeable tendency toward militarism. The primary target for the Katō cabinet, under whose leadership the 1925 *gunshuku* bill passed the Diet, was not the army, but the political power of the House of Peers, as represented by the previous Kiyoura cabinet.[29]

Ugaki's task would have been far simpler had he led a unified army, but he did not. Some people opposed him as a surrogate of Tanaka and the Chōbatsu. Underlying their arguments against his proposals was a determination to oppose him in anything he undertook. Among the older officers there was considerable inertia regarding change of any kind. Many officers who were not motivated by political opposition to Ugaki and his personal *gunbatsu* joined those who were, purely on the basis of a reluctance to change the military system. The older officers found unprecedented political support from the formerly apolitical younger officers who formed the lower stratum of the army elite as graduates of the staff college. Some of the younger men, conscious of the need for modernization, gave priority to internal personnel reform, which involved them in anti-Chōshū, anti-Ugaki activities. All in all, between those who opposed Ugaki politically and those "stoneheads" who resisted change,[30] Ugaki faced strong opposition in his own camp.

The Ugaki *Gunshuku*

In recognition of the fact that great changes were taking place in military equipment, organization, and tactics during the war, the army ministry formed the temporary military affairs investigation committee in 1915. This committee continued to function until it was abolished for no good reason in March 1922 upon the completion of plans for the Yamanashi *gunshuku*. Its effect on army modernization was negligible except to apprise the army of the problem. In late 1923, when Army Minister Tanaka, realizing that new adjustments in the army must be made after the earthquake, appointed Ugaki to form the military systems investigation committee, there began "fundamental planning for army reform and the adjustment of armaments on a scientific basis."[31] The committee, expanded to include members from the general staff headquarters, continued under Ugaki's indirect leadership when he became army minister in January 1924, establishing the parameters of his *gunshuku* on the "scientific basis" prescribed. As the joint committee began its work, Ugaki told the members:

To provide for a basic renovation of the military system will necessitate large expenditures. But in looking at our nation's current financial situation, gasping in the postwar financial doldrums and just recovering from the wounds of the great Kantō earthquake, there has been a tremendous burden on the national treasury, so in renewing armaments we cannot very well seek to spend more than at present. Accordingly, the expenditures needed for reform must all be obtained from within the department.[32]

Ugaki tells us through his diary that he had three objectives in mind as he formulated his readjustment plan: (1) to promote improvement in the national defense, using public demand for further army reductions as a lever; (2) to arouse people to consciousness of the connection between army reduction and the welfare of the countryside; and (3) to take the first steps toward a conciliatory, integrated national defense, uniting the army and the people.[33]

In other words, Ugaki schemed from the beginning to use the money saved through troop reductions to modernize the army. In the name of *gunshuku* (arms reduction) he would have *seiri* (consolidation) while seeming to acquiesce to public feeling and the spirit of government retrenchment. Ugaki's subterfuge supported the army's value structure, which had nothing to do with the army as an institution to serve the people. Since what he did was for the emperor and the state, there was no conflict of conscience.

Point two, Ugaki admits, was designed to teach people an economic lesson. The army, more than any government institution, contributed to the economic well-being of all of Japan by spreading large numbers of its paid personnel throughout the country instead of concentrating them in the capital. To close army camps outside the large cities would throw an immediately noticeable burden of unemployment and economic distress on smaller urban communities throughout Japan. People in the hinterland would think twice before supporting further reduction of the army.

Ugaki's third point involved the narrow, self-righteous worldview of the army officer. If the ideas of the people and the army had drifted apart, even if the estrangement was in part the army's fault, the army's view was the correct one. It was the duty of the army to make its view prevail once again for the sake of the imperial system and national survival. As Ugaki himself wrote:

The greatest single cause for the German collapse was a lack of conciliation and unity between the people and the army. In total war, even for a highly efficient army, if it does not maintain the cooperation of the nation, glorious victory in battle is equivalent to daydreaming of roses. There is no need to follow the mistaken ideas of the people. We must take the lead to correct them. It is no good to reject these popular ideas, which we have to tolerate, by sticking to history and tradition. We must accept them with an open heart and seek unity and conciliation between the army and the people in them. The true meaning of the consolidation also rests on this premise.[34]

A part of Ugaki's plan was to place in schools throughout the nation a large number of professional officers whose services in units would no longer be needed owing to deactivations. Thus, Ugaki planned the first concerted effort to mobilize civilian support for the army since Tanaka formed the Reservists Association in 1909 under Terauchi.[35]

As the work in the military systems investigation committee went forward, it became clear that the initiative for the consolidation plan came from the army ministry, and the opposition from the general staff, including Chief of Staff Kawai and Vice Chief Mutō. Only the strenuous efforts of Army Vice Minister Tsuno and Hata Eitarō, the military affairs bureau chief, finally brought the general staff into line.[36] In July an agreed-upon draft was ready. On 13, 16, and 26 August the army ministry met with the military affairs council, the senior officers of the army, to seek its approval. The voting went along straight factional lines. Fukuda led the fight against the plan and found his support in Uehara, Machida, and Ono, the Uehara-Satsuma clique; Tanaka, Yamanashi, and Oba supported Ugaki. To break the impasse after three bitter sessions, Ugaki pressured Marshal Oku, the aged council chairman, and in the end he received approval for his plan by the barest margin, five to four.[37]

In order to coordinate the placement of active duty officers in the schools, the army worked closely with Education Minister Okada Ryōhei, who cooperated fully in the enterprise.[38] With cabinet approval the Ugaki consolidation plan went to the Diet in April 1925, where it carried in both houses without difficulty.[39] As Itō Masanori points out, this was the high point in cooperation between party government and the army, with military training in the schools the quid pro quo for a sizable army reduction.[40]

The heart of the Ugaki *gunshuku*, which went into effect on 1 May 1925, was the reduction in army strength by four complete infantry divisions, the 13th (Takada, Niigata Prefecture), the 15th (Toyohashi, Aiichi Prefecture), the 17th (Okayama — Ugaki's birthplace), and the 18th (Kurume, Fukuoka Prefecture). The deactivation of these divisions abolished sixteen regimental area headquarters, and in addition the army cut other small units and headquarters. The total reduction in personnel was 33,890 officers and men,[41] and the annual saving more than ¥28.5 million.[42] With this money the army had authorization to activate a small experimental tank unit, two regiments of antiaircraft artillery, and the Taiwan Mountain Artillery Battalion. It could now expand the two aircraft battalions into two air regiments as aviation became a new, separate branch of the army. It could also expand heavy machine gun and motor transport units, develop a light machine gun, and improve wireless communication equipment, all top priority items for modernization.

The most controversial portion of the *gunshuku* package was the assignment of 2,000 active duty officers to secondary schools and colleges as military instructors.[43] Although criticized and to some extent resisted for a short time, this system became an accepted feature of Japanese public schooling within a few years. Its stated object was "to temper the minds and bodies of the students, to foster collective belief and by this means to improve the quality and character of those who are the mainstay of our people, and concurrently to advance our national defense capability."[44] It became, as Ugaki planned, a tool for inculcating the army worldview in young people and a first step toward bringing the people and the army back into one harmonious whole.[45] In the following year the army instituted the next phase of the Ugaki plan in cooperation with the education ministry. The result was a four-year part-time system of military training for young men between the ages of sixteen and twenty who would not go on to higher schooling.[46]

This program, administered by the public school system, used members of the Reservists Association as instructors, who taught from materials provided by the army in order to "uplift young men and prepare them for the day they will enter the army through the draft." Filled by volunteers until 1940, when entry became compulsory, this system gradually expanded into formal schools that trained young women as well as young men.[47] By these means the army gradually gained a substantial foothold in Japan's public education system.

During the years of its great unpopularity, the army had been troubled because the number of volunteers for its officer and noncommissioned officer programs had dwindled dangerously and the quality of the applicants had fallen off. The new system of training within the schools anticipated stimulating interest in military affairs and military careers. The army would create the opportunity to recruit for the military academy and build the large pool of reserve officers necessary for a nation preparing for modern, total warfare.[48] Providing positions for officers in the schools had the secondary effect of absorbing some of the shock to army morale by reducing the number of young officers dropped from the rolls. As Itō Masanori tells us:

The three-point platform of the Katō cabinet was universal suffrage, reform of the House of Peers, and administrative consolidation. Since it was necessary to retrench the national budget, both for operating expenses to recover from the Kantō earthquake and fire and as a depression policy, each ministry, without exception, resolved to consolidate. Even the army, which had reduced twice already, was not permitted to stand as an exception. Rather than try to avoid it, Ugaki seized the initiative to launch a crushing blow. He, who had watched the decisive victory of the Goken Sanpa (the three factions for the protection of the Constitution — Katō's coalition) quietly as Kiyoura's army minister, now realized that the age of party government had clearly emerged and also recognized that the popular demand for arms reduction was pressing. In addition, he believed that it was to the army's advantage to get along by listening to these voices and responding realistically to the demands of the people. He reached the conclusion that, having entered the era of party government, cooperation with the party platform and gaining party trust would be an advantage to the army for the future progress of army administration. The conceited ideas that one hates political parties and dislikes party members and that only soldiers are patriots were old-fashioned and a self-deception.

Thus, there was something heroic in the figure of Ugaki, who rose to grapple with arms reduction. One evening in April 1925, on an occasion when I had the opportunity to meet Katō, Wakatsuki [Reijirō], and Hamaguchi [Osachi (Yūkō)] at Katō's residence, I heard Katō say that Ugaki was a splendid man and that if there were that kind of men in the army, there was nothing to worry about. The other two added their agreement in chorus as I remember.[49]

The public appreciated Ugaki's altruism. "The newspapers, too, wrote, 'The greatest earthquake since the army began,' and showered him with public favor, saying, 'To think, the army has such men.'"[50] Obviously pleased, for a short time Ugaki was able to enjoy a feeling of success. He reported to his diary in early June 1925 that the soldiers coming home from the army seemed to be welcome in companies, stores, and factories. He had the feeling that the period when people shunned men returning from the service had passed. On 10 June he confided:

It is a superficial view to think of this military consolidation simply as material adjustment, which exchanges men and horses for machine power. We can realize through it a firm belief in the certain victory of the army and the people, a concilia-tory unification of the ideas of the army and the people, an awakening of the spirit and the stabilization of officers' positions by the management of personnel. In other words, this is a spiritual consolidation. Reform in the spiritual realm has special meaning. By the very accomplishment of consolidation in both its material and its spiritual aspects, we should find perfection.[51]

The Ugaki plan did not stop with the reduction of four divisions from the standing army and the insertion of military training into the schools. These were but the first steps. Ugaki, as we have seen, also took measures to remove many of the older, more recalcitrant officers who opposed his changes. In an effort to reach the people, he quickly expanded the role and function of the Reservists Association after 1925, when it became active not only in the youth training program, but in other fields.[52]

On 1 October 1926 Ugaki reorganized his ministry with the object of preparing the army and the nation for total war. One of the major changes was the formalization of a structure for modernization and mobilization in a new *seibikyoku* (bureau of supplies and equipment). One of its divi-sions was the *dōinka* (mobilization section), headed by brilliant young Lt. Col. Nagata Tetsuzan and, after March 1928, by Lt. Col. Tōjō Hideki. During this period the army began a coordinated effort to work with other ministries of the government to plan for the wartime mobilization of all of Japan's resources.[53] In 1928 the army ministry mobilization section pub-lished its first general mobilization plan.[54]

In January 1927 a completely new draft law (*heiekihō*) replaced the old *chōheirei*, which had been in effect for more than fifty years. Among other major changes this new law reduced the active duty time for con-scripts from three years to two, abolished the one-year volunteer service system, and established an officer candidate school system for training reserve officers. In December of the same year, after Ugaki had left the post of army minister, the training regulations changed to reflect the reforms in the draft law.[55] These new training regulations, with their further emphasis on spiritual training, show the beginnings of the internal reaction to the progressive aspects of Ugaki's consolidation plan.

The Reaction to Ugaki's Reforms

But the reaction against Ugaki was already in motion before the *gunshuku* was fairly under way. On 1 May 1925, there was an extraordinary ceremony at Shintenpu, the Meiji emperor's storehouse for war trophies at the Fukiage Gardens within the Imperial Palace compound.[56] On that day most of the regimental commanders of the sixteen disbanded infantry regiments returned their regimental standards to the emperor, from whom they had received them many years before. The scene was charged with emotion.

For an army like that of the United States, in which there is comparatively little geographical and, hence, emotional significance to unit designations, the deactivation of a unit is a mere inconvenience, so to many people the spectacle is hard to convey. In the Japanese army a regiment, especially a country regiment, was a proud symbol of the area in which it was stationed. The enlisted men and some of the officers were the sons and brothers of local people. The regiment and the camp that had housed it for as long as fifty years were a part of the community, a mark of distinction, an emblem of the awesome presence of the emperor among his people. The deactivated regiments, like all the others, had glorious histories from the Russo-Japanese War and earlier. The fathers, uncles, and even grandfathers of their enlisted men had served in these regiments in earlier campaigns. Those who lived remembered their service with pride, if not with pleasure. To the members and former members of these regiments, "the battle flag was the sign of life. To return it was tantamount to an act of death in which you hold your funeral while still alive."[57]

The army, reflecting the general preference of Japanese society for close-knit, vertically structured social units, which afford little opportunity for lateral mobility or communication, found the deactivation of entire regiments very difficult to accept. The young officers felt the loss most keenly. They had been assigned to a *botai* (mother unit) as cadets in the military academy. That regiment was to be their home for the rest of their army lives. Except for the chosen few among them who became staff officers, they would seldom serve anywhere else. To have these ties broken was like losing home and parents or, as some described it, a living death. Deactivation of sixteen *botai* sundered the irreplaceable emotional ties to unit and comrades that were an integral and sustaining feature of Japanese army life.

The affected young officers were not stoics. Yamaguchi Ichitarō, imprisoned for life for his part in the February 26th Incident of 1936, later expressed his deep disappointment in the following words:

My beloved 53rd Infantry Regiment of Nara had been deactivated. Its battle flag, under whose honorable banner we had pledged to die, had been returned to the Imperial Palace. A final salute to that flag was carried out at the Nara parade ground in the gently falling summer rain. The regimental commander at that time was [Col.] Etō Genkurō [a native of Nara]. All the people cried. If we weakened our national defenses so, what would happen? Though the Powers had maintained huge armies since the Great War, why was it that Japan alone disarmed? Moreover, on the streets were not the crowds of war profiteers blowing their noses on hundred-yen notes? The young officers were fed up with all this.[58]

Koiso Kuniaki, later prime minister of Japan but then an army colonel, happened to be assigned as the regimental commander of the 51st Infantry Regiment at Hisai in Mie Prefecture. On 27 March 1925, he received word that his regiment was scheduled for deactivation. His division headquarters (3rd, Nagoya) informed him that his camp would come under the command of the 33rd Infantry as of 1 May. His officers were to be reassigned to several regiments nearby, and half his noncommissioned officers would be separated from the service, the other half joining the 33rd Infantry. Koiso, as one of the pioneers in Japanese aviation, sympathized with Ugaki's aims, but he felt keenly the disappointment and chagrin of his officers and men. The townspeople of Hisai and Tsu, the prefectural capital of Mie, caught by surprise, reacted strongly against the deactivation, but nothing could be done.

On 30 April dignitaries from all the cities and towns of the prefecture, led by the governor, attended a tearful farewell ceremony centered on the regimental colors. In the afternoon the entire regiment marched the colors to the station at Aikogi, five kilometers away, through lines of country folk and the families of regimental officers and men. As the train bearing the color guard left for Nagoya, the standard bearer, on Koiso's order, thrust the colors from the car window. Koiso noted that he saw no man in the assembled regiment who was not in tears. When Koiso delivered his colors to the commanding general of the 3rd Division in Nagoya, as he entered the general's office, that officer snapped to attention and saluted the dying colors of the 51st Infantry.[59]

On the first day of May four senior generals — Fukuda, Yamanashi,

Ono, and Machida — several generals of lower rank, about five hundred other officers,[60] and thousands of noncommissioned officers entered a waiting list or were separated from the service. Two thousand other officers were assigned to unfamiliar and, to most, uninspiring work in schools across the nation. Hundreds upon hundreds of junior officers were transferred from deactivated home regiments to new regiments, where they were treated coldly as outsiders.[61]

Most of the officers dismissed or transferred were not the elite graduates of the staff college, but the *muten* group,[62] those who did not wear the badge of the staff officer — in other words, *taizuki shōkō*, or unit officers. The men affected were younger officers, under 30 years of age, who had been raised in the post–Russo-Japanese War atmosphere in which the army was respected, even revered.[63] They joined the army with high hopes and great expectations as youngsters out of high school or, in the case of those who attended the youth schools, at the age of twelve. Their lives as young officers had been an unending economic struggle. Now this new blow enveloped them in bitterness. The army that had offered so much to talented youth a few years before had emptied their young lives of hope and meaning.

For those who remained untouched directly by the *gunshuku*, there were indirect effects, the uncertainty of change, the sight of famous units dropped from the rolls, and friends and classmates dismissed or relegated to positions where their careers could not prosper. A pall of anxiety seemed to lower over the army,[64] and morale sagged badly. The cumulative effect of two large personnel cuts clogged the personnel system so that promotions came slowly. The lack of interest in and need for more officers for the standing army shrank the size of military academy classes to the lowest level since 1895. The graduating classes for the four years 1928–31 averaged 225 men, about one-third the average for the years 1897–1918. This drop in officer graduates caused a chronic shortage of seasoned company and field grade officers for the army in the China Incident and the Pacific War.[65]

The officer corps soon heaped its resentment on the men who caused them this anxiety. Ugaki became the target, not openly at first, of a broad range of ill-feeling from dislike to hatred as the man responsible for the ruin of four divisions, sixteen regiments, and the lives of thousands of their fellows. He had touched the life of nearly every professional soldier in the army in a way that aroused in them little but antipathy and fear.[66] Ugaki soon became aware of the problem:

On 16 June, on the occasion of the [annual] division commanders conference, I held a meeting of [active and retired] flag officers residing in the Tokyo region. In a normal year the number of guests does not exceed about 300, but this year there were more than 400. The reason is not that the number of retired persons increased appreciably because of the consolidation, but it would not miss the mark to see in it a tendency for dissatisfied elements to stand by with bated breath — a tendency to feel impending change.[67]

Subsequent developments brought him in closer contact with the ground swell of discontent in the lower ranks of the officers. Tanaka Ryūkichi writes:

[The transferred] officers had to content themselves until further notice with an alien existence in the units to which they were newly assigned. Young people are sentimental. Most of them displayed dissatisfaction with the present state of affairs and sought an outlet for their discontent. One manifestation was to anathematize Army Minister Ugaki, who had caused the dissolution of their home units in the name of military consolidation. Another was for the disgruntled to fall easily into the habit of ideological pilgrimages.

The Ugaki *gunshuku* then fed directly into the stream of discontentment that gave rise to the "young officers movement" of the 1930's. Personal discomfiture led these men into ideological experiments in which the degeneration of society and politics became the prime target for their indignation.[68] The politicians who argued for arms reduction claimed victory over the army in 1925 and attributed the cutbacks to their own efforts. Most officers believed that Ugaki and the army had bowed to the despised politicians,[69] an unforgivable sin to an officer corps taught since the days of Yamagata that the army, standing above politics, must not be swayed by the changing winds of public opinion.[70]

As the economic depression of the late 1920's deepened, the young officers, in close contact with the soldiers at the unit level, knew all too well the desperate economic plight of the soldiers' families, since the draftees came largely from among the poor farmers and workers who made up the vast majority of the nation's population. Both their own situation and the situation of the enlisted men's families could, through facile analysis, be attributed to the ineptitude, greed, and lack of conscience of parvenu politicians, the very men to whom Ugaki pandered. To the young officers the world had gone awry, and they came rapidly to the conclusion that only radical action could restore Japan to the equilibrium of the past. Ugaki's supposed transgression was never forgotten. In 1937, when Ugaki attempted unsuccessfully to form a cabinet, he faced a stone wall in the army. Tanaka Ryūkichi describes the feeling:

In spring 1937, when Anami Korechika was vice minister of the army, his secretary, Ono, cursed Ugaki in a loud voice. I was near him and asked him why. He answered, "No reason! He reduced the army in a conspiracy with the political parties, and he broke up my assigned infantry regiment, the 66th from Utsunomiya. That's why!"

Ono was an outstanding student at the staff college; he had a fine mind. If this man could say such a thing, one can guess what others said.[71]

The officers assigned to the schools, a bit older than most of those transferred directly to other units, also had a disturbing experience. In addition to the trauma of assignment to duties in an unfamiliar atmosphere, the actions of the students caught their eye. They were shocked at the indiscipline and attitude of self-indulgence that accompanied the individual freedom of the 1920's. Some students had turned to Marxism; others embraced the libertarian ideas of Western democracy. Looking at them from the straitlaced viewpoint of military men, they could not help feeling that this generation was completely unconcerned about the fate of the country.[72]

The Relative Importance of Military Spirit

Another matter that became a topic of serious discussion as a result of the Ugaki *gunshuku* was the relative importance of morale, or *seishin*, in modern warfare. The question was not whether good morale and moral training were still important factors in war, because their importance was indisputable, but whether an army with excellent morale could, without the latest weapons, prevail over a materially superior enemy. Japan faced an uphill fight in modernizing. It was weak financially and unprepared industrially and technologically to bring the army level with those of Europe and America. Could *seishin* close this gap? Many officers, especially those of a more conservative bent, thought that it could. But morale now had a new dimension. In a modern total war the morale of the army must be matched by the morale of the people. Again the German example floated like a specter before the army, as a passage by Kennedy illustrates:

In regard to the fighting qualities of the Japanese army, a conversation I had about this time with a subaltern whom I met in the train is perhaps pertinent. . . . The subject itself cropped up while discussing the fighting qualities of the Germans. He asked me what I thought of them as fighters, and amongst other things I had replied to the effect that they were very good so long as they felt that they were winning, but that they had not sufficient stamina to pull themselves together again once they were on the run. Much to my surprise he said, "Yes, and that is just where we Japanese fail too. We are too cocksure of ourselves because we have never been defeated, and the result will be that a reaction will set in if we ever run up against a stronger nation than ourselves, and irretrievable disaster may result."

. . . From what other Japanese officers have told me at different times, it seems true that there is a very considerable feeling of anxiety amongst the military in Japan that even the army may not be entirely free from such failings if ever they should be faced with certain defeat. It is largely owing to this fact that so much attention is paid to raising the *moral* of the army by constant application of *seishin kyōiku*, . . . "spiritual training."[73]

The positive response to the dilemma posed by the importance of total *seishin* in total war is reflected in Ugaki's plans for military education in the schools and the whole train of popular indoctrination outside the framework of the military establishment that they set in motion over the next two decades. But within the army a negative argument arose, which held that *seishin* was of paramount importance in an army without modern weapons. As time went on and modernization failed to attain its objectives, this argument gathered momentum, until *seishin* became the army's substitute for weapons.

Later the arguments for a redoubled emphasis on *seishin* formed the core of the attack on Ugaki and the Ugaki *gunshuku*. Araki Sadao, Mazaki Jinzaburō, and the Sagabatsu officers, whose military philosophy was based on the *Hagakure* and Kyushu samurai tradition, which strongly inclined them toward spiritual and moral solutions to military problems, argued fiercely against all the materialistic aspects of Ugaki's consolidation plans. The reorganization of the army ministry to include a separate supply and equipment bureau and a mobilization section, and the coordination of army and civilian bureaucrats in the *naikaku shigenkyoku* (cabinet resources bureau) for the total mobilization of national resources for war were danger signals that presaged a stress on despised European materialism and neglect of the Japanese spirit.[74] Opposition to Nagata Tetsuzan's 1928 general mobilization plan soon came to the surface.

No European or American observer of the Japanese army in action ever denied that the soldiers fought with great bravery and courage even in desperate conditions. The imperial army had a superior system for inculcating young men with a spirit of devotion and sacrifice. This had been amply demonstrated on numerous occasions, including the Sino-Japanese and Russo-Japanese Wars and even on the Siberian Expedition. The Russo-Japanese War stood as a primary example of what sheer tenacity and courage — what high morale — could do in fighting a superior enemy.

Marshal Prince Yamagata Aritomo, the father of the Imperial Japanese Army.

Marshal Count Terauchi Masakata, army minister, 1902–11.

Marshal Viscount Uehara Yūsaku, chief of the general staff, 1915–22.

General Baron Tanaka Giichi, prime minister, 1927–29.

General Ugaki Kazunari, army minister, 1924–27, 1929–31.

General Baron Araki Sadao, army minister, 1931–34.

General Okamura Yasuji,
commanding general,
China Expeditionary Army,
1944–45. A founding member
of Futabakai.

General Tōjō Hideki,
prime minister, 1941–44.
Futabakai/Issekikai member.
(Courtesy of the U.S. Army)

Seishin seemed to have won that war for Japan. The army of the 1920's was officered by men steeped directly or indirectly in the experience. It would not be easy for army officers to question the importance of *seishin* when considering a war against an enemy with tanks, massed machine guns, and artillery firing barrages, because most Japanese officers had no experience with these awesome weapons. One illustration of this attitude from *Daihon'ei rikugunbu* should suffice:

About 1923 or 1924 discussions to decide on the manual of combat principles were held in the general staff headquarters. Representatives from the staff college, the army ministry, and the inspectorate general of military training gathered to debate. On that occasion a certain Colonel X, who had observed World War I in Europe and had personal experience with the signal technical progress of modern warfare, argued fiercely to the effect that our country could not hope to win in any future war against the Powers with its existing organization and weaponry. The strategy emphasized in this manual [he said] is probably unworkable. If we do not provide the weapons effective for modern war, it is clear we will not rank with but drop behind the Powers. . . .

But the consensus was that this was defeatism. This was making light of the moral requisites. The belief in ultimate victory was in itself the basis for victory in battle, eclipsing material military strength. Ever afterward faith in ultimate victory was the army's belief; in the end it was looked on as a creed. . . . In the Manchuria and China incidents [the army] fought the poorly equipped Chinese army, ultimately strengthening their belief in unending victory.[75]

At the time of the Ugaki *gunshuku*, the earthquake and the depression made the hope for modern weapons to match "the Powers'" even more forlorn. Ugaki's step toward modernization turned out to be a first step and nothing more. The Great Powers were moving forward so quickly that the gap between them and Japan continued to widen. In the imperial army, infantry and artillery firepower did increase; more machine guns and a light machine gun entered the army arsenal, but never in numbers to match the firepower of a European infantry division. There was some progress toward mechanization, but tanks remained an experimental item. Only aircraft, whose development was left to civil industry, progressed to any satisfactory degree. The ratio of artillery to infantry remained low, and Japanese artillery weapons and tactics lagged far behind their Western counterparts. Basically, the infantry branch had to continue to depend on the rifle and the bayonet[76] — and *seishin*. As one lecturer from the army ministry frankly told the students of the 40th class at the staff college (graduated 1928), "At Japan's current national strength, if we were to arm the army with modern weapons, it would be of about thirteen divisions."[77] As Horike Kazumaro indicates, this may have been an optimistic estimate:

We made studies, but putting it bluntly, Japan's industrial capacity at that time could not carry out all these things we've spoken of, like mechanization of the army, the development of tanks, and the use of aircraft in group formations. If we overstrained in trying to do it, it would have entailed a third and a fourth force reduction, and the army would have been broken up.[78]

With other nations, especially the Soviet Union, progressing rapidly and Japan completely unable to overtake them, the frustrated army knew what must be done but could not do it. It saw only one alternative—reliance on *seishin*. As Horike expressed it, "If against tanks you have no anti-tank guns, you can't very well stand idle in full knowledge of the circumstances. It becomes a matter of using human bullets. It isn't that one necessarily thinks this is good, but . . . if you have nothing else, there's no other solution."[79]

For the army *seishin* came to mean more than ultimate sacrifice under desperate circumstances. It was easy, given the army's historical experience, to construe *seishin* as more than a substitute for materiel, as a higher value, which transcended the necessity for modern scientific weapons almost entirely. "In poverty-stricken Japan the discussion of military techniques became intertwined with the advocacy of *seishin*, and those who adopted science and recommended rationality were apt to be called cowards."[80] As Itō Masanori points out, it was possible to a certain extent to rely on courage when weapons were lacking, but the imperial army carried things to extremes. The worst one could say was that it was an antiscientific army; the best was that its men were brave, but that gave them no license to belittle the weapons they could not have. Since the country was poor, they turned to *seishin*. In justice to them Itō could say that it was the kind of army one would expect from Japan, the product of the country and its people. However, the navy would not settle for this total reliance on *seishin*, so by pouring out its heart's blood, navy leadership added research to artifice and reached first-class rank with respect to weaponry. The army, on the other hand, made do by depending on inexpensive men, rather than expensive weapons.[81]

In a sense, the whole problem was self-generated by the military view of Japan's place in the world. If one accepts the fact that a hypothetical enemy is indeed an enemy, then the construction of a large fleet is justified to protect Japan and its possessions from an American threat. If one assumes that Japan's continental position is vital to the survival of the nation, as the army did, and that China, Russia, and other nations threaten this position, then a large modern army or, failing that, an army imbued with a do-or-die spirit is essential.

In sum, a confrontation arose within the army between those who held the realistic attitude toward warfare that came from the West and those who believed in a traditional Japanese view of the supremacy of *seishin*.[82] At first confined to the rational discussion of military problems such as the modernization of weapons, organization, strategy, and tactics, later it took the form of the traditional, majority view, turning *seishin* into a form of political or religious belief. Ugaki, the apparent champion of the rational, minority view with his debilitating sacrifice of the army to the "false gods of modernization," became the object of criticism and attack. The Ugaki *gunshuku* could be counted as only partially successful, but there was a great reaction against it, owing to the temper of the army, the nature of the reduction, and the accumulating failures in modernization. The one really lasting success, if it can be so counted, was the army's penetration of the school system — and its direct access to young people. Ugaki's plans failed in the areas where large sums of money were required and where the army's conservative elements were in a position to block his reforms.

At the end of 1928 Ugaki entered in his diary an assessment of his successes:

For more than three years after receiving this important position from the emperor, I resolutely executed a consolidation of military arms, and I carried out the practical application of science and the establishment of scientific research and investigation in the army. To impart the belief in ultimate victory to the people and the army and to fulfill [the requirements of] military preparedness, I applied [military] education and training to the schools and to the youths, and I planned for soundness of heart and mind among the people. At the same time, by encouraging unity and conciliation between the people and the army, I worked to secure the position of the army as the pillar of the nation and took the first step toward a general mobilization of the state. Though a trifling matter, I responded to the changes of the times to improve the treatment of officers and men, and using the latent power accumulated over many years, with one blow I forced through a complete reform of the conscription law, that statute so important for delineating rights and duties, without treading the mistaken road of my predecessors with respect to the publications law and the labor law.[83]

It is difficult to detect any dissatisfaction with his own performance through the cloak of Ugaki's considerable ego, but by this time the strongman had stepped down, and army discontent could manifest itself more openly. When Ugaki once again resumed the post of army minister, in

1929, the circumstances had changed and his approach to the mounting problems he faced was totally different.

Ugaki's Opposition

Since Ugaki had come to power through a bitter factional struggle between Tanaka and Uehara, he faced a ready-made opposition from the defeated Ueharabatsu. Whether he liked it or not, he represented Chōshū not only to senior officers but also to the field grade officers who were attempting to destroy the shell of Chōshū hegemony. Ugaki found himself in the peculiar position of having to join battle with an opposition others had created, but which opposed him at every turn. Uehara's opposition came quickly to the surface when the Kiyoura cabinet fell and Katō sought to keep Ugaki on as army minister, and again when Ugaki fought for army acceptance of his consolidation plan. Uehara stood behind the opposition in both battles. In the latter case, however, Uehara's cause was popular among the large number of conservative older officers in the army, and with the Saga clique in the fore they began to rally to the marshal's standard. Uehara picked for his point of opposition the modernization of the artillery, clinging to the outmoded direct-fire system of the Russo-Japanese War. For Ugaki it was an exasperating experience, and the impasse between the two sides transcended reason to become a confrontation of emotions,[84] unbecoming to the men involved and debilitating for the army.

Ugaki responded by moving against his opposition through his hold on the personnel system. As noted earlier, he retired generals and lieutenant generals in large numbers in May 1925 and had himself promoted to general in August. To consolidate his position further, at the time of the retirement of the generals he transferred the troublesome vice chief of staff Mutō Nobuyoshi, symbolic head of the Sagabatsu, who had sided with Uehara in opposing the consolidation plan. In July 1926 he appointed Mutō commanding general of the Guandong Army, removing him from Japan entirely. In March 1926 he retired Chief of Staff Gen. Kawai Misao, who had supported him in his rise to army minister but opposed his *gunshuku*. Ugaki replaced him with his friend and classmate Gen. Suzuki Sōroku, as he had replaced Mutō with another of his followers, Lt. Gen. Kanaya Hanzō. Other transfers were not so advantageous. In May 1925 Maj. Gen. Matsui Iwane, another Ugaki man, came in as chief of intelligence (second division, general staff), but his classmate, the outspoken and erratic Maj. Gen. Araki Sadao, took over as chief of operations (first division, general staff).[85]

Ugaki may also have kept pressure on Uehara and his followers in other, less orthodox ways. According to Imamura Hitoshi, a military police captain, Kotake Shinji, paid a call on Marshal Uehara one day to tell him that he had received orders to place the marshal's house under surveillance and to watch those who came to visit him. He reported the fact to Uehara because he considered it peculiar to keep the army's highest-ranking officer under observation. Imamura attributes the order to Vice Minister X of Chōshū, a very thinly veiled reference to Tsuno Kazusuke. The perceptive Captain Kotake, deploring the way the cliques were dividing the army, appealed to Uehara (of all people) to do something about it and announced his intention to resign from "this corruption-ridden army." In reply, Imamura quotes the marshal (probably after the fashion of Thucydides) as saying:

Is that so? Former army minister Tanaka's acts were unjust at that time [when Uehara and Tanaka argued over Ugaki's appointment], but I know nothing about Minister Ugaki. After seeing his order of appointment, I apologized to the emperor for any damage to the unity of the army because of this problem. As for Uehara, he will never lead you astray. Furthermore, in order to allay the oversensitivity of the army ministry, I will inform them before the fact of Uehara's actions. I want you to rest assured of that. As long as there are wild men like that in the central headquarters, there will be a particular need for military policemen like yourself.[86]

There is justification for Uehara's charge of oversensitivity in the army ministry, and this is confirmed by a basically friendly source. At the time Major General Matsui and Major General Araki entered general staff headquarters, Col. Koiso Kuniaki received an assignment to head the organization and mobilization section (*hensei dōinka*) on the general staff. In this capacity Koiso did staff work on a proposal by Ugaki to shorten the length of drafted service for graduates of the school and youth training programs from two years to eighteen months. Completely opposed to this step for his own reasons, Koiso circulated his objections among the staff sections and wrote an article for the *Kaikōsha kiji* (the army's professional journal) that came to the attention of the army ministry. A day or two later Vice Minister Tsuno called Koiso to his office to ask him why he had written what he had. After Koiso defended himself by saying that he had written only what he believed, Tsuno asked him, "Didn't you get the outline from Uehara and write it?" This, Koiso denied hotly, saying that he had no idea what the marshal thought about the subject, nor did he know whether Uehara had even expressed an opinion contrary to the army minister's. Tsuno, apparently satisfied, dismissed him,[87] but Koiso continued to oppose the readjustment on the basis of his personal experience as a regimental commander. In the long run he was overruled. It may be as a result of this difference of opinion, which angered Ugaki, that Koiso's promotion to major general was delayed until December 1926, five months after most of his classmates who were promoted received theirs.[88]

If Koiso disagreed with the army minister's policy on this one occasion, Major General Araki disagreed with the entire program and the philosophy behind it. Guided by principles of extreme nationalism, Araki rejected the idea that Japan should continue to follow the West. Typical of the romantic idealism that permeated the thinking of the officer corps, Araki felt that Japan should place its faith in an independent, spiritually suitable Japanese war philosophy.[89] In his former positions as provost marshal general (*kenpei shireikan*) and section chief in the general staff headquarters, Araki had already met and embarked on more or less close relationships with the civilian nationalists Inoue Nisshō, Michikawa Kametarō, Yasuoka Seitoku, Kita Ikki, and Ōkawa Shūmei before the ideas of these men became the general intellectual currency of army officers. He was a director of Baron Hiranuma Kiichirō's ultranationalist Kokuhonsha (the Basis of the State Society, in which Ugaki also held membership).[90] Araki came to the key position of chief of operations with well-formed ideas about the direction Japanese army training and operations should take from his experience with the Russian army in Europe (1915–18), in Siberia and Manchuria (1918–19), and as a regimental commander in Kyushu (1919–21).

Under Araki's direction the operations division began work to rewrite the *Tōsui kōryō* (The general principles of strategic command), which had been last revised by Ugaki in 1918. The result was the *Kōgun no hongi* (Basic principles of the imperial army), which particularly emphasized spirit or morale as superior to materiel in combat, in recognition of Japan's "insufficient numbers of troops and scant resources." Here we also see the beginning of the official use of the term *kōgun*, or emperor's army, to indicate that the army is the emperor's, not the people's.[91] Araki also arranged to have "surrender," "retreat," and "defense" removed from the language of the manual, words with a negative connotation that, to him, impinged psychologically upon morale.[92] After March 1928 the new *Tōsui kōryō* became the official doctrine of the "imperial" army and remained so until 1945. Araki's efforts ensured the priority of morale over equipment. The acceptance of the abstract concept of *seishin* as superior to concrete materiel, an untestable hypothesis without combat and irremediable, if wrong, once combat was joined, proved a total disaster for Japan in the Pacific War. From this first step the new emphasis on *seishin* permeated the army field manuals and training material; it became an integral part of the school and youth training programs and, later, part of the army's general propaganda to the Japanese people. Later the same year the inspectorate general of military training issued *Seishin kyōiku no sankō* (A guide to spiritual training), and in 1930 the two-volume *Bujin no tokusō* (The morality of military men).[93] In the 1930's a stream of writing on *seishin* and spiritual training, official- and civilian-sponsored, flooded the country. Before many years Araki, Mazaki, and leaders of the resurgent opposition to the Ugaki *gunbatsu* called the former army minister "Ugaki the traitor" for having sacrificed army units and morale to the less important purpose of modernization.[94]

In sum, Ugaki's consolidation failed in its first objective (to modernize the equipment, organization, and tactical deployment of the army) and succeeded in its second (to make the people aware of the close connection between the army and the economic well-being of people in the countryside), only to cause a lasting, violent reaction to the *gunshuku* among the army's officers and noncommissioned officers. Its only lasting success was to expose the schools and young people of Japan to army indoctrination. It was the great chance to bring the rigid ideas held commonly in the army into harmony with the ideas of the people of Japan, on the army's terms. The road to the militarization of all of Japan lay open.

But the overall internal effect of the Ugaki *gunshuku* was to factionalize the army further. It gave the dissatisfied younger officers a target for their growing sense of insecurity and provided a rallying point for senior officers like Uehara, Mutō, Araki, and Mazaki, who opposed Ugaki. Uehara, distressed at the treatment accorded him as *daichōrō*, or senior officer, had his conservative sensibilities further wounded by the consolidation that he opposed. It was natural for him to find support in Mutō and the Sagabatsu. Uehara and the Sagabatsu together could manage a loosely articulated opposition supported by younger officers of middle and lower ranks on the twin bases of antagonism toward a perceived resurrection of a Chōshū clique, personified in Ugaki, and reaction against a consolidation that they regarded as army submission to venal and corrupt political parties. The total effect was to divide the army as never before in its history — a division that boded ill for its future and for the future of the country.

5

The Growth of Dissidence

Unions based on private interest for self-protection are
factions. There is but one faction; there are no others.

Nagata Tetsuzan

Army factional strife after Yamagata's passing largely cleansed the army
of the old, *hanbatsu*-type military cliques based on clan background and
feudal loyalties, only to replace them with a new factional structure. Even
the still identifiable geographic cliques such as Chōshū, Satsuma, and Saga
no longer retained undiluted their provincial character. Roughly from the
middle of the Taishō era all army cliques and factions, whether geographic, personal, or politically motivated, had a new common basis in
the graduates of the army staff college. In the early years of Shōwa these
new *gakubatsu*, or school cliques, came into their own.

The staff college had opened its doors in April 1883 (Meiji 16) to train
staff officers and potential general officers. During the Meiji period the
number of staff college graduates remained small, and those who attained
high rank were not overly conspicuous in comparison to nongraduates in
positions of authority. Year by year the ratio of staff college general officers increased, however, until by the end of the Taishō and the beginning
of the Shōwa eras "one could count on ten fingers" the generals and
lieutenant generals, other than technical service officers, who were not
graduates of the staff college.[1] By the second decade of Shōwa (1936) staff
college graduates occupied virtually all important positions related to the
army's combat function.

A situation like this had to cause resentment among the vast majority
of the army's officers who were not members of this elite. Discrimination
in favor of less than 10 percent of the officer corps was not restricted to
elevation to flag rank, but it permeated all aspects of the officers' military
life. During their years as field grade officers the difference in promotion
time between staff college graduates and nongraduates averaged about

one rank. When they attained the rank of general, the gap between men of the same military academy class widened to as much as two steps in rank. Further resentment arose when staff college graduates of later military academy classes came to command units in which graduates of earlier classes held more modest positions. Similar preferential treatment was accorded staff college graduates in the matter of assignments. The non-staff college, or *taizuki* (unit), officers spent their military lives in peacetime in the dull but arduous routine of the training field and maneuver ground, while the staff officers served in more prestigious and meaningful positions in the major headquarters.

There is no question that the staff college graduates represented the cream of the officer corps, but in actuality their superiority was relative, not absolute. There were incompetents among them as well as superior officers among the *taizuki* majority, but the inflexibilities and ingrained prejudices of the staff college graduates, who managed personnel promotions and assignments for the army, made the distinctions between the two groups nearly absolute. *Taizuki* officers with outstanding records and qualifications could not expect treatment equal to that of even the poorest staff officer.

For the most part this dangerous dichotomy received little outward recognition. The *taizuki* officers kept their feelings to themselves as members of a highly disciplined military force that was inculcated with deep loyalty to the emperor and trained to respond to all orders from superiors as though they were from the emperor himself. Outstanding graduates of army branch schools, who were all unit officers, constituted a more serious opposition to the hegemony of the staff college clique, demanding recognition for their own outstanding performances. As Matsushita points out, however, this was not like competition between Mitsukoshi and Takashimaya (Macy's and Gimbels'), but more like competition between Mitsukoshi and a kitchenware dealer on the outskirts of town.[2] Matsushita takes a very serious view of the effect of the smoldering resentment among the majority of officers:

Graduates of the army staff college originally were given a graduation insignia — it was the same for naval staff college graduates. The shape of this insignia was similar to a *Tenpōsen* [large coin of the late Tokugawa era], so they called *rikudai* graduates the *Tenpōsen gumi* [Tenpōsen group] and nongraduates the *muten gumi* [no-insignia group]. The confrontation between the *Tenpōsen gumi* and the *muten gumi* was the greatest [source of] antagonism in the army, and it was a cancer from the standpoint of control. If one does not understand the circumstances of their confrontation, one cannot hope to know the truth about the army.[3]

How serious the relationship between line and staff really was is difficult to determine, but there is no question that it added to the feeling of malaise and stagnation that already burdened the troop units of the army, and it stimulated the young officers to active opposition, not only to the status quo in the army and the nation, but also to cooperation with like-minded staff officers.

There was never an open clash between the staff officers and the line officers, unless the February 26th Incident of 1936 is so considered, but until Japan went to war in 1937, changing the relations between the two groups markedly, the army paid an exorbitant price in esprit and morale for an elite staff organization whose members reserved all the privileges of rank and assignment for themselves while quarreling for the positions of greatest power. The "young officers movement" soon became a dissident element among the unit officers. It rejected the staff college elite and its attitudes, but it received little more than varying degrees of sympathy and support from older line officers.

The Formation of the Issekikai

The internal power struggle, which marked the politics of the army from the death of Yamagata Aritomo to the early Shōwa era, reflects a reaction to the hold Chōshū had maintained on the personnel system for decades. Among protagonists such as Uehara, Tanaka, Fukuda, and Ugaki, professional ideals were to some degree subordinated to ambition, jealousy, and greed for power.[4] The concurrent opposition to Chōshū rising among young staff officers was the product of more idealistic motives, at least in its beginnings. Like the general officers, the field and company grade officers of staff and line soon found other reasons for discontent in the atrophy of the army — among them, public and party opposition, forced reductions, and the growing corruption in the parties and their governments, the new "illicit union of money and power" formed between the parties and the great capitalist plutocrats,[5] the increasingly stringent economic situation, which hurt the majority classes whose sons filled the army's ranks, and the perception of Japan's faltering position in Manchuria.[6]

The organization of field grade officers that resulted from the meeting of the "three crows" at Baden-Baden in 1921 continued to expand slowly throughout the decade of the 1920's, adding to its ranks field grade officer graduates of the staff college who had spent their company grade years in an army dominated by the Chōshū and Satsuma cliques. Their original common bond was a hatred of the *hanbatsu* personnel system, which stifled the advancement of talented men on the irrational basis of feudal clan background. Their one remarkable overt activity had been the movement to deny men of Chōshū birth entry into the staff college. Members of the group certainly participated in that movement and may have directed it, but the evidence is purely circumstantial.

Since the regular haunt of its members was a French restaurant in Shibuya called Futabatei, the name Futabakai (Futaba Club) came into use among them. Futabakai membership did not exceed eighteen or nineteen; it included graduates of only the 15th through 18th classes of the military academy.[7] Though the club was small in numbers, its influence began to be felt as its members, at work in the very sensitive centers where decisions were made, rose in rank within the military hierarchy.

Following the example of the Futabakai, Suzuki Teiichi of the 22nd class began recruiting for an association of younger staff officers in or about September 1927.[8] Suzuki's group held its first meeting of nine officers in Tokyo at the Kaikōsha (the army officers association building located at Kudanzaka in Tokyo) on Thursday, 3 November 1927, "to discuss national policy." The Mumeikai (Unnamed Club), Kokusaku Kenkyūkai (National Policy Research Club), or Mokuyōkai (Thursday Club, as it is consistently referred to in Okamura Yasuji's diary) included primarily officers of the 20th to 25th graduating classes of the military academy. They later invited to their discussions two more senior officers, Nagata Tetsuzan and Tōjō Hideki of the Futabakai, who were treated as members of the group. Okamura Yasuji and Itagaki Seishirō of the Futabakai also dropped in from time to time, but they were not considered members.[9] So from its very beginning the Mokuyōkai had close ties to the Futabakai. Membership of the Mokuyōkai eventually grew to 25.

Suzuki Teiichi tells us that the focus of the Mokuyōkai was on the backward state of army weapons and equipment. However, the members' research and discussions led them quickly into such matters as the effects of the Ugaki *gunshuku*, Japan's population problem, and the increasing danger to Japan's position on the Asian continent as Russia recovered from its revolution and China threatened to unify under Chiang Kaishek.[10] Unlike the Futabakai, the Mokuyōkai was neither action-oriented nor motivated by any particular anti-Chōshū bias. Its members were young enough to remain unmoved by any threat of Chōshū domination of the personnel system that had so disturbed their seniors in the Futabakai.[11]

As the army's apprehension over conditions on the continent quickened to crisis with the Guomindang's northern expedition to unify China, the Jinan incidents, and the withdrawal from Beijing and subsequent assassination of Zhang Zuolin, the Manchurian warlord, both the Futabakai and the Mokuyōkai concentrated more and more of their attention on the Manchuria situation. Then on 19 May 1929, the two organizations came together to form the Issekikai, for the urgent purpose of finding a solution to what they called the *Manmō* (Manchuria-Mongolia) problem.[12] The new, larger organization included officers of all classes from the 15th through the 25th with one exception, the 19th. The Issekikai numbered more than 40 officers. However, the older Futabakai continued its separate concurrent existence.[13]

The ultimate power and influence of the men of the Issekikai must not be underestimated. They provided Japan with 1 prime minister (Tōjō Hideki), 2 ministers of state (Obata Toshishirō and Suzuki Teiichi), 6 (full) generals (Tōjō, Itagaki Seishirō, Doihara Kenji, Okamura Yasuji, Okabe Naosaburō, and Yamashita Tomoyuki), 30 lieutenant generals (including Nagata Tetsuzan, who was appointed posthumously), 8 area army commanding generals, and 14 army commanding generals. Five (Tōjō, Itagaki, Okada Tasuku, Mutō Akira, and Yamashita) died as war criminals, and 4 others were imprisoned for war crimes. Four remained war prisoners of the Russians or Chinese until they died.[14]

At first glance it might seem merely coincidental that no members of the 19th class belonged to the Issekikai. Only a handful of persons from each of the other classes participated in any case, but this omission serves to illustrate another subtle form of discrimination within the army structure. Two facts about the 19th class stand out. First, it was the largest class ever to graduate from the military academy. The size was dictated by the need for officers in the Russo-Japanese War, which led to an expansion of the military academy. The 17th class had 353 graduates; the 18th, 910; the 19th, 1,058; and the 20th, 276. The 18th and 19th classes were thus extraordinarily large, with the 19th the larger of the two.

This brings us to its second and more important distinction. The 19th class was the only one up to this time that, except for a handful of holdovers, had no youth school (*yōnen gakkō*) graduates in its ranks. The class consisted almost entirely of graduates of civilian high schools. As explained earlier, the military academy drew its students from two primary sources, the army youth schools specifically designed for that purpose and civilian high schools. All other graduating classes of the military academy had a mixture of young men from both sources. In the rigidly hierarchical and elitist structure of the army, we have already seen that graduation from the staff college conferred elite status. Graduation from the youth schools was another filter for entrance into the mainstream to power. Until the youth schools were abolished, military academy students always divided into two broad camps, with the youth school cadets lording it over cadets from the high schools. After graduation from the military academy, the superior class status of the youth school graduate and his supercilious attitude toward his classmates with high school backgrounds continued throughout his career.[15]

The 19th class, then, was a class left out as far as the predominant youth school graduates were concerned, because it had no "elite" element built into it. Ten percent of most classes went on to the staff college. Less than 6 percent of the 19th class attended. Of the 19th class officers who did graduate from the staff college, 60 percent became flag officers. In the 20th class more than 13 percent of the class went on to the staff college, and of them more than 75 percent became general officers. A member of the 20th class had almost a three times better chance to become a general than officers one year senior to him. This leads to another salient point in the development of the officers' political movement from Baden-Baden to the Issekikai. It was dominated by men who received their early training and indoctrination in the youth school system. Of the 37 officers in the Issekikai on whom I have found firm data, 31 were definitely *yōnen gakkō* graduates; only 6 may not have been. Takahashi Masae tells us that only 3 of them were not.[16]

Ugaki may have abolished the regional youth schools in part to rid the army of this type of discrimination, but he transferred the means to indoctrinate the youngsters of Japan to the public school system and the youth training program at the same time. The result was that the narrow view of army officers spread throughout Japan with no broadening of outlook within the army itself, since it still chose officer candidates and cadets for the military academy from among the most highly indoctrinated stratum of Japan's youth. As Matsushita makes clear, "at the center of the rising staff college cliques within the army, there was a strong youth school clique."[17]

By 1929 the sub-rosa movement of staff officers had reached a new stage of boldness and heightened activity. In 1921 at Baden-Baden the "three crows" had set the objectives of the movement: personnel reform by destroying the Chōbatsu, and qualitative improvement in Japan's ability to wage total war by improving the capability of the army and setting the people and the army in harmony once again. The method selected was a conspiratorial association of like-minded young staff college graduates who would use their collective influence to further the objectives of the movement. The crude beginning was the action taken to prevent the sons of Chōshū from entering the staff college. In 1928 and 1929, as the members advanced in rank, status, and position in the central organs of the army, their objectives became more directly attainable.

Okamura's diary, the only source that gives us any idea of how the Futabakai actually went about its business, provides us a tantalizingly sparse outline. The group met informally on a more or less regular basis. Those who happened to be in Tokyo attended; the rest probably kept in touch through correspondence with friends or occasional visits with other members. The form of the meeting was discussion. Hard and fast decisions do not seem to have been the rule; the sense of the meeting prevailed. The implementation of any program was apparently just as haphazard and informal. This was an amorphous conspiracy directed against a formless enemy. Until the emergence of the Issekikai, it remained self-contained, relying on the membership for its ideas and its leadership. But there were certain unmistakable directions in which the members headed.

First, they attempted to seize control of the personnel management system, the traditional key to army power. When the Issekikai was founded, it is supposed to have adopted as one of its objectives "the forceful pursuit of various policies to reform the army personnel system."[18] This included the placement of members in key staff positions to effect such changes. The policy was an extension of the anti-Chōshū movement, but it naturally tended to favor Issekikai members. It goes without saying that it also perpetuated the exclusive staff college monopoly at the army's centers of power. Okamura, for example, headed the assignments branch in the personnel bureau of the army ministry beginning in August 1929. Another Futabakai member, Isogai Rensuke, replaced him in 1931. Entries in Okamura's diary and the records of the Mokuyōkai show a continuing intense Futabakai, Mokuyōkai, and Issekikai interest in personnel affairs.[19]

The second trend was toward recognizing the central position of Manchuria in the future of the Japanese Empire. The danger to the imperial position on the continent became an increasing concern of the army after the Washington Conference. By 1927, when Tanaka Giichi formed his cabinet as head of the Seiyūkai, the solution of the *Manmō* problem was the top priority issue for his government. The army, delighted with Tanaka's selection of priorities, showed similar concern, as did the officers of the Futabakai and Mokuyōkai, several of whose members were the army's leading young "China experts."[20] In fact, in June 1928 one of the Futabakai's most ardent members committed premeditated murder on the outskirts of Mukden in the hope that it would precipitate the Japanese seizure of all of Manchuria. Kōmoto Daisaku's assassination plot against Zhang Zuolin not only destroyed Tanaka but also led to the breakdown of discipline within the army, which in turn opened the door for the Manchurian Incident outside Japan and the destruction of party government within. In the ensuing period of increasing army factionalism, the era of the Shōwa *gunbatsu*, no faction ever opposed an aggressive policy in Manchuria or the solution of the *Manmō* problem by force of arms, if necessary.

A third direction for the activity of the staff officer movement, begun after the formation of the larger Issekikai, involved membership participation in high-level army politics by supporting general officers whose attitudes and actions appealed to them. The outspoken Araki Sadao, who was chief of operations (first division), general staff headquarters, beginning in May 1925 and commandant of the staff college from August 1928 until August 1929, influenced the Issekikai greatly; Araki's friend and classmate, and fellow member of the Sagabatsu, Mazaki Jinzaburō; and Araki's predecessor at the staff college, Hayashi Senjūrō[21] — all radical conservatives opposing the Ugakibatsu — were the generals admired and supported by the group.[22]

The activity of younger officers in army politics, virtually nonexistent in the days of Yamagata and only tentative in the late Taishō period, now began to burgeon. The activities of the Issekikai in the first years of Shōwa form the single most important aspect of this movement. Issekikai political action had two very significant consequences. First, it led to contact with civilian radical ultranationalist elements.[23] Second and more important, the contact with the Araki-Mazaki (Saga) faction caused a split in the Issekikai in 1931 after the October Incident (a failed coup attempt by young army officers), influencing media recognition of two primary Shōwa *gunbatsu* factions — the Kōdōha (Imperial Way Faction), which followed Araki, and Nagata's independent Tōseiha (Control Faction). The competition between the two became increasingly bitter. After the February 26th Incident, which Kōdōha officers viewed with great sympathy, the increasingly powerful Tōseiha engineered the final downfall of its rival, ensuring the emergence of officers identified with the Tōseiha cause as the power in the army.[24]

Soon after Araki became chief of operations, Ogawa Tsunesaburō, a man in sympathy with but not a member of the Futabakai, was assigned (March 1926) as Araki's most important section chief (operations). Ogawa maintained close contact with the Futabakai, and Araki's nationalistic philosophy of the supremacy of *seishin* may have begun its penetration of the Futabakai at this time. In December 1926 Obata Toshishirō, a founding member of the Futabakai, replaced Ogawa. Araki and the Futabakai came into direct contact as Obata became more and more a follower of Araki.[25] Together with Yamaoka Shigeatsu and Yamashita Tomoyuki, the Tosa group within the Futabakai, and others among the younger members of the Issekikai, Obata eventually became identified with the Kōdōha. Nagata, still the driving force of the Futabakai-Issekikai, was far too independent a man to follow anyone for long. He and later Tōjō came to oppose Kōdōha emotionalism, indiscipline, and extremism, and hence became central figures in the Tōseiha.

The Issekikai, like the Futabakai, remained until the Manchurian Incident in 1931 an organization more interested in army reform and Japan's continental position than in domestic social and political reform. A creature of staff officers, it did not readily identify with the depressing poverty that beset the common people of Japan. In spite of later Kōdōha pronouncements on domestic reform issues, the Issekikai itself never advocated the use of army power for revolutionary change within Japan.[26]

New Dissidence: The "Young Officers Movement"

Young field grade officers do not remain young forever. By 1929 the officers of the Baden-Baden group were all colonels. In 1931 Yamaoka became the first general from the Futabakai-Issekikai. After that, the number of generals among this group rose steadily. But discontent in the army was not confined to the 16th class of the military academy and its allies nor to the staff college elite from which the Issekikai was formed.

At the end of the Taishō period a new storm center of dissident activity was already gathering among cadets of the military academy and young commissioned officers, many of them twenty years junior to the men of the Futabakai. The activities of these relative youngsters constitute most of what has been termed the "young officers movement." The younger men were of another generation, and though their dissatisfaction derived from somewhat similar sources as that of their older fellows, their interpretation of this discontentment and its expression in action were far different. In the first place, these young officers were not a part of the staff college elite. When they turned to dissidence, they were still too young to have been chosen for study in the staff college. Few of them, talented as they were, ever entered that institution.[27] They were for the most part *taizuki shōkō*, or unit officers, products of the youth school–military academy system. As the authors of *Kokkashugi undō* write:

Without knowledge of the real world they entered the *yōnen gakkō,* and from that time on they were separated from society. Receiving rigorous military training, they graduated from army schools. Bearing personal responsibility as the pillars of the nation, they left the military academy and for the first time entered the real world. For these young officers, encountering this era of military reductions and postwar nouveaux riches, these were incomprehensible things that roused their indignation.[28]

In the second place, the membership was far less well defined than that of the Futabakai-Issekikai coalition. The names of a few men can be traced from the beginning of the movement until its tragic end in February 1936, but many of them were in and out. The "young officers movement" was as amorphous in its membership as it was diverse in its activities, beliefs, and goals. It never had the kind of day-to-day coherence that kept the Futabakai-Issekikai intact. We can, of course, detect a strong element of irrationality in the Issekikai. Its later split into Kōdō and Tōsei factions reflected a divergence between emotionalism and pragmatism among its members, but the young officers inclined far more to the irrational, and in later years they displayed this preference by their general sympathy toward the less rationally inclined Kōdōha. The "young officers movement," though completely sympathetic to Japanese expansionary goals, concentrated far more of its energy on domestic affairs, embracing revolutionary change and extreme methods for attaining often disparate goals.

The "young officers movement" centered on the men who graduated in the 37th class of the military academy. It was no coincidence that their year of graduation (1925) corresponded to the year of the Ugaki *gunshuku,* a time of great stress and lowered morale. These young unit officers had no tough-minded, independent individual like Nagata Tetsuzan to lead them, but there was one man above all others who in the beginning acted as an ideological focal point for the movement. This man was Nishida Mitsugi (popularly but incorrectly read Zei; also sometimes Mitsugu).

As a youngster, Nishida attended the Hiroshima youth school, where he graduated first in his class. He went on to the military academy located at Ichigayadai in Tokyo, graduating in the 34th class (1922),[29] and shortly afterward received his commission as a second lieutenant of cavalry. During his years at Ichigayadai he became acquainted with the *Manmō* problem and the civilian "greater East Asia" movement through his association with the civilian ultranationalists Kita Ikki and Michikawa Kametarō, then active with Ōkawa Shūmei in an organization called the Yūzonsha, an ultranationalist propaganda organization.[30] He also read about and came to believe in the program outlined in Kita Ikki's *Nihon kaizō hōan taikō*, a plan for reorganizing Japan on a national-socialist basis while retaining the imperial structure.[31]

A confirmed renovationist as well as an ultranationalist, Nishida went on to cavalry unit duties first in Korea, then in Hiroshima.[32] But his promising military career was destined to end abruptly. In Hiroshima he contracted pleurisy, a disease from which he suffered chronically, and in May 1925 the army retired him to the reserve.[33] Released from active duty, he made his way back to the capital, where he entered Ōkawa's new ultranationalist society, the Gyōchisha (Society for Action), to serve as the editor of its house organ, *Nippon*, which had the army, especially the general staff headquarters, as one of its prime propaganda targets. Ōkawa had formed the Gyōchisha in February 1925 from the wreckage of the Yūzonsha, which collapsed in 1923 as the result of quarrels between Kita and Ōkawa.[34] As a concurrent duty Nishida taught "military science" at Ōkawa's Daigakuryō, a private nationalist academy that held classes at an abandoned weather station on the Imperial Palace grounds. Among the visitors to the Daigakuryō were young army and navy officers and cadets of the military academy, some of them contemporaries of Nishida, others younger.[35] Expounding Kita's facile radical solution to Japan's domestic social ills, Nishida developed a following, especially among the cadets of the military academy.[36]

One of these cadets, Suematsu Tahei, a survivor of the February 26th Incident, later wrote of his experiences with Nishida. They first met in October 1925, just as Suematsu was entering the military academy regular course (*honka*). Between graduation from the military academy preparatory course (*yoka*) and entry into the regular course, Suematsu had served as an officer candidate with the 5th Infantry Regiment in Aomori, which was to be his home unit. There he had fallen in with a group of disgruntled young officers recently transferred from the 52nd Infantry Regiment, deactivated in the Ugaki *gunshuku*. On Suematsu's return to Tokyo one of these young men, an admirer of Nishida, took Suematsu to meet him during a trip to Tokyo.[37] As for many other young men, this meeting was his introduction to the ultranationalist movement. Again quoting *Kokkashugi undō*, "The military academy cadets and the young officers who were worried greatly over the enthusiasm for arms reduction, the tendency to insult the military, and the ideological and social unrest suddenly developed close relations, seeking a solution from Nishida Mitsugi, who shouted for them to bring about reform under new leadership and to hurl themselves into the maelstrom of the social movement."[38] On Sundays and holidays and during trips to Tokyo, Nishida's lodgings became the focus of activities for young officers and cadets.

In 1926 new discord—an endemic condition in these unstable right-wing groupings—arose within the Gyōchisha, and Nishida left to throw in his ideological lot with Kita. Soon after, Ōkawa's ally, Imperial Household Minister Makino Nobuaki, widened the rift between Ōkawa and Kita and Nishida by contriving to have the latter two arrested for threats to himself. Makino had sold some imperial property in Hokkaido to a private group, provoking Kita to write a scurrilous pamphlet (*kaibunsho*) denouncing Makino. Makino's retaliation put both Kita and Nishida in jail for a time, and half the Gyōchisha membership left the organization to protest this vindictive act, shattering the nationalist movement.[39] Setting up his own establishment in Yoyogi, which he called the Shiriusō, Nishida provided a gathering place for radical young army officers. This was the first reformist group, albeit loosely constructed, consisting primarily of young officers. In this year Nishida, with Kita's approval, published two editions of the *Nihon kaizō hōan taikō*.

In the following year Nishida attempted a more ambitious project—the foundation of an organization he called the Tenkentō (Party of Heavenly Swords). In July Nishida sent his young associates, mainly army officers but also some navy men and civilians, mimeographed copies of a tract entitled *Tenkentō kiyaku* (The Tenkentō covenant).[40] The manifesto was radical and revolutionary in tone, embodying the outline of Kita's work. At the end, Nishida appended the names of 70 men throughout Japan who purportedly subscribed to the covenant, the very men to whom he had sent copies. The military police quickly became aware of the document's existence, and since any one copy revealed the names and whereabouts of all the so-called members, it was a simple matter to launch an investigation. Suematsu Tahei received his copy in the mail at the 5th Infantry Regiment in Aomori, where he was a probationary officer. Busy, he laid it aside, but a few days later, returning exhausted from a four-day, three-night training exercise and march, he found the military police awaiting him. Awkward sessions in military police interrogation rooms followed for Suematsu and most of the others named on Nishida's roster until the military police were satisfied that the *Tenkentō* was little more than a figment of Nishida's fertile imagination, a dream of heavenly swords rather than a reality.[41]

For many years the *Tenkentō* has been accepted as a genuine coales-

cence of the "young officers movement," and writers have dated the beginning of the movement from it. But as Suematsu has said, "[the *Tenkentō*]
was just mimeographed scraps of paper strewn about the country."[42] Nishida's widow has testified that in the Tenkentō, "there were Nishida,
myself, and the dog."[43] As far as Suematsu is concerned, the Tenkentō
incident was a setback for the "young officers movement" and a personal
"minus" for Nishida. After all, he had used the names of some 70 people
without their permission, causing them considerable inconvenience and
embarrassment, and he had shown a rather tactless disregard for their
positions and their sensibilities, needlessly exposing their lives to military
police suspicion and scrutiny. For example, Morimoto Takeo, a classmate
and friend of Suematsu's, very active in the "young officers movement" up
to that time, severed all ties with Nishida and never again participated in
any enterprise with which he was connected, a wise decision as it turned
out. Suematsu, too, cut his contacts temporarily.[44]

The *Tenkentō* was not, then, a takeoff point for the "young officers
movement," but a setback in its development. The important thing, however, was that the movement withstood the shock of military police surveillance and investigation and, in time, emerged stronger than ever.
Nishida, to some degree, recovered his role in holding the movement
together and Kita Ikki, who had now greatly curtailed his own activities, apparently maintained contact with his ardent disciple Nishida and
through him with the young officers themselves. After the Ketsumeidan
(Blood Brotherhood) assassinated the head of the house of Mitsui, Baron
Dan Takuma, in March 1932, Mitsui began regular subsidies to Kita (who
had no connection with the killing) in the amount of ¥20,000 per annum
to forestall any repetition of the attack.[45] There is evidence that Kita
used a portion of this money to support Nishida and the "young officers
movement."

In any case, the movement among unit officers could boast no overt
activity after the *Tenkentō* incident of 1927 until 1930. In that year a
storm of controversy arose in both the army and navy after the London
Naval Conference. This was the renowned *tōsuiken mondai* (the right-to-
command problem), in which army, navy, and civilian ultranationalists
claimed that the chief of the naval general staff had been denied his right to
command when the naval treaty was signed by the conference delegation
in the face of his adamant disapproval. They contended that, as a result,
the government and the London delegation (which included the navy
minister) endangered the existence of the empire.

During the controversy 1st Lt. Ōkishi Yoriyoshi (35th class), then on duty in Sendai at the leadership school, seized the opportunity to publish secretly and distribute to fellow ultranationalists throughout the army two issues of a magazine he called *Heika* (Soldier's fire). The issue dated 29 April (the emperor's birthday) criticized in scathing invective the Hamaguchi cabinet's obstruction of the right to command and the right to access to the emperor and called on like-minded patriots to resist political encroachment on military prerogatives. A second issue, printed and distributed soon after, was a cry for revolution — a coup d'état by the military and civilian nationalists — to sweep away "injustice and crime, the imperial household ministry, the aristocracy, political parties, the *zaibatsu* [monopoly capitalists], the school cliques, and red traitors."[46] The *Heika* incident caused new military police investigations, which must have revealed that the radical movement among the young unit officers was still alive. Thus, in the early years of Shōwa two distinct dissident movements had emerged within the imperial army, one among the staff officer elite, one among the unit officers, centering in two groups of officers 10 to 25 years apart in age. These two movements never could merge. There was a gulf between them even wider than the difference in their ages that could not be bridged, a schism in the army inherent in the separate elite general staff system.

The word *taizuki* was the term the unit officers applied to themselves; Miyakezaka, the site of the army central headquarters in Tokyo, was their word for the staff.[47] Miyakezaka was "they," distant, inaccessible, the source of change and perturbation, the higher-ups who coldly and impersonally controlled their lives. Young staff officers, the unit officers' military academy classmates who went to the staff college, severed ties with the units, joined Miyakezaka, and were seldom seen again except when they imposed themselves on the units as battalion commanders and later when, on the threshold of success, they returned for a short stint as regimental commanders. They were the "dragon's children," no longer a part of unit life, its special perceptions and special problems. And yet, in the long run, these men would return to command brigades and divisions, reaping the rewards of a successful career, when many of their line officer classmates were being retired as lieutenant colonels and colonels with only small pensions.

To the unit officers Miyakezaka was the army counterpart of slick, modern, urban life while they represented the real army, rooted in the solid traditions of rural premodern Japan. The *taizuki* officers exalted the feudal rural values of frugality, loyalty, integrity, and obligation. They saw these values reflected in the peasant and small-town boys who made up the majority of their enlisted men. Their direct contact with rural Japan attuned them to the more traditional aspects of Japanese life and tended to breed mistrust of the city, its people, and, within the army, the staff. They thought in terms of *heinō ittai* (soldier and farmer, one body), who shared a mystical bond of understanding. The tribulations of the countryside were reflected in the soldiers since they were one and the same. That only the *taizuki* officers understood the peasants was an article of faith.[48] They felt authorized to represent them and articulate their woes.

The *taizuki* officers tended to romanticism in dealing with Japan's rural past and irrationality in their perception of the emperor and his place in the imperial state. They believed in the emperor as a godhead. This belief overrode considerations of modern science and rationality. The unit officers cared little for modernizing organization and weapons; loyalty and *seishin* were far more important. The army leaders and staff officers who tended to espouse these ideas were more acceptable to the *taizuki* officers; the leaders who minimized or neglected the importance of such things were rejected. The leading figures of the "young officers movement," though many of them were talented, even brilliant, were almost invariably products of the narrow education of the youth schools and the military academy. They had none of the leavening that the staff college imparted. *Taizuki* officers did not go overseas for study; they did not serve as attachés in foreign capitals, nor did they share the experiences of the staff officers who had that opportunity. Among the unit officers an undiluted parochial viewpoint prevailed.

The unit officers were also acutely aware that it was they and the farm boys they led who would die for emperor and country in combat, not the staff officers who made the plans and directed the officers and men of the units to their graves. They were proud to make this sacrifice if called on, but in the meantime they felt themselves entitled to the respect of their peers. The unit officers and the men they led needed a secure base from which to fight. With that assured, death could be as light as a feather.

Fukoku kyōhei, a prosperous country and a strong army, had been the goal of the empire since the restoration. The unit officers of the 1920's needed only to look about them to see that the requirements of a prosperous nation were not being satisfied when the farmers were impoverished and the relinquishment of a son to the army was likely to mean financial disaster for an entire family. How could the contradiction be resolved? How could the ideal be realized under the present circumstances? For one thing, the unit officers looked at the modern sector of the Japanese economy as a burden on the virtuous traditional sector, which was being neglected — nay, oppressed — for the benefit of the new. Release the farmer from his burdens, allow him to give his sons to the army and the emperor, secure his livelihood, and the emperor and the state would stand forever. For the unit officers, greedy politicians, monopolistic capitalists, false advisers to the throne, and the carriers of traitorous foreign ideologies must be swept away to return to the simple stability of a people in arms protecting state and emperor. The "young officers movement" represented these values in extreme form, but their activism was not representative of the unit officers as a group.

Although some activist staff officers believed as the young officers did, they could not co-opt their movement. In 1930, as the result of the London Naval Conference, a movement began among the staff officers that stressed internal reform. When they formed the Sakurakai, which was restricted to officers of the rank of lieutenant colonel and below, a few of the younger Issekikai officers joined.[49] Some *taizuki* officers showed initial interest, but by the second meeting those who had not graduated from the staff college numbered no more than one or two.[50] In October 1931, when certain Sakurakai officers attempted to stage the second of two abortive coups (the "October Incident") whose objective was to seize control of the army and the government, they solicited the aid of the young officers, but with no success. Neither Nishida nor Inoue Nisshō gave anything more than vague promises of support.[51] They disliked each other and detested Ōkawa Shūmei, who was heavily involved with the Sakurakai staff officers. The young officers generally viewed this elite coup as "staff fascism" and divorced themselves from it entirely.[52] As for the Futabakai men, they not only gave little support to Sakurakai efforts, but they were instrumental in quashing both the March (1931) and October coups.[53]

As early as 1928 all the elements of dissidence in the army were well developed, and it took only a worsening situation and indecision at the highest levels of the army structure to provide the opportunity for this discontent to burst forth in the 1930's in attempted coups d'état, assassinations, and internal crises in Japan and aggression overseas. The lines of the struggles were already clear-cut. Ultranationalist dissidence among the staff officers received much of its outside stimulus from Ōkawa Shūmei, who, compared to other civilian superpatriots, placed greater emphasis on overseas expansion than on internal revolution. Ōkawa later encouraged the army to seize the leadership of the state, but he had little interest in Kita's kind of state socialism.

The loosely articulated "young officers movement" of unit officers was divided radically in its beliefs. Most of its adherents dreamed of a new

Japan within the general framework of Kita's *Nihon kaizō hōan taikō*, but relatively few of them accepted it without varying degrees of modification. They generally advocated foreign expansion, through war if necessary, and internal reform based on an idealized emperor system. Some, perhaps even more radical, sought to establish a self-governing society of family farm villages under direct imperial rule, a physiocracy that would do away with the corruption of urban civilization entirely.[54] They were influenced by the thought and writings of men like Gondō Seikei and Tachibana Kozaburō. Some others compounded nationalistic Nichiren Buddhism into their ideological mix, finding the teachings and preachings of the Nichiren priest Inoue Nisshō congenial. It is not surprising then that devastating factional turmoil raged within the army as an accompaniment to the struggle for reform at home.

It is astonishing how few real activists there were in the plots and conspiracies that followed in quick succession from 1930 to 1936. Though difficult to count accurately, they probably never numbered more than 200 or 250 and at most times considerably fewer. That these men, in groups rent by petty factionalism based on intellectual hairsplitting and the demands of personal loyalty, could cause so much havoc to civil government and military discipline in Japan and send army divisions into action overseas, showed not so much the weakness of army leadership (weak as it was) as a certain basic level of unanimity of ideas within the army. High motives excused despicable acts because everyone in the army from top to bottom understood the patriotic basis for dissident action, even though they might not approve of the method or even of the goals.

Most officers agreed that radical reactionary changes were necessary for Japan, and they could empathize with those, no matter how misguided, who were willing to take their careers and their lives in their hands to bring them about. It is significant that, between 1928 and 1936, no officer who engaged in a criminal act based on an overzealous regard for the emperor and the state suffered the punishment usual for his crime. It is amazing how the same names appear as participants in plot after plot between 1931 and 1936. Perhaps it is going too far to say that had Kōmoto Daisaku and his underlings been quickly and appropriately punished for the assassination of Marshal Zhang Zuolin, the period of undisciplined turbulence among the young officers in the early and mid-1930's could have been avoided. Certainly, had the Sakurakai officers and civilian plotters of the March Incident of 1931, the first of its kind, been brought to justice, much future anguish and bloodshed would have been avoided, but the army leadership seemed immobilized and feckless in the face of such cabals. It was easier to force Prime Minister Tanaka Giichi to flout the emperor's expressed wishes than it was to try Colonel Kōmoto for murder.

In the meantime, economic conditions in Japan grew even worse. In 1929 the world depression struck, and in October government employees, including officers of the military services above the rank of second lieutenant, received a 10 percent cut in pay.[55] Although no outward reaction to the pay reduction was possible among military men who served the emperor out of patriotism, not for economic gain, there is no question that the army acted later against the conditions that made the retrenchment unavoidable. Protest against the pay cut was muted, but the officers translated their personal economic discontent into fear for the defense of the nation, hatred toward politicians and rich men who, in the officers' perception, brought on and exacerbated lopsided economic distribution, and sympathy for the masses in straits similar to their own.

Army Politics Fan the Flames of Factionalism

It soon became apparent that the real power was moving out of the hands of the men at the top of the military pyramid to the younger officers of middle rank who held the key staff positions in the army's central organs. The new Shōwa cliques also revealed a tendency to accept certain influences from outside the army in the name of unity of people and army.[56] But even though the unit officers in the "young officers movement" were a dissentious, factious group and the most radical expression of discontent within the army, they never seriously threatened the position of the staff college elite, even in February 1936.

By 1928 Ugaki had stepped down in favor of his friend and classmate, Shirakawa Yoshinori. At the time of Ugaki's withdrawal (20 April 1927) Uehara successfully forced the acceptance of the Sagabatsu leader Mutō Nobuyoshi, whom Ugaki had "exiled" to the Guandong Army, as the new inspector general of military training.[57] The post of inspector general was not a glamorous one, but Mutō was now a member of the "big three," and his tenure did not depend upon the winds of politics and the lives of cabinets as did the army minister's.[58] Mutō remained in that post from August 1927 until May 1932, long enough to see other men of the Sagabatsu in top posts.

Uehara, still burning with resentment against Ugaki and supported by a powerful faction in the active army, had one more hand to play. Ugaki's classmate and supporter, Gen. Suzuki Sōroku, had been chief of staff since March 1926. Not long after Ugaki resumed the post of army minister in the Hamaguchi cabinet (July 1929), Suzuki was forced into retirement, having reached the statutory age limit. Uehara seized the opportunity to renew his battle with Ugaki by proposing that Mutō be appointed chief of staff. Mutō was certainly well qualified for the job. His record of service was impeccable. He was much admired by all who knew him in and out of the service and, in spite of his position as titular head of the Sagabatsu, he did not seem to dabble in factional intrigues or throw undue support to his own faction.

Ugaki, knowing where Mutō's backing came from, refused to entertain his candidacy, choosing instead his cohort Kanaya Hanzō, a problem drinker, to replace Suzuki. However, in order to force the decision in favor of Mutō, the Sagabatsu — Araki Sadao, Mazaki Jinzaburō, and others — mounted an unprecedented campaign, not unlike an election campaign, to rally support in the army for their candidate, and Uehara himself let it be known to the emperor through his contact with Prince Kan'in and the emperor's aide, Gen. Nara Takeji, that Mutō was the best-qualified person for the position. The affair enraged Ugaki, who saw the army's senior officer threatening the good order and discipline of the army (already shaken by the Zhang Zuolin assassination incident) and usurping his own ministerial prerogative to deal directly with the throne on army personnel matters. As a result, Ugaki forced through his own decision against all opposition, and Kanaya became the new chief of staff in February 1930.[59]

This was the end of the line for Uehara. He ceased to be active in army politics from this time, but Mutō's supporters within the army headquarters were united after their campaign as never before. In less than two years Uehara's and Mutō's Sagabatsu supporters emerged into the army's seats of power as the Kōdōha under the leadership of Army Minister Araki Sadao.

6

—

The *Manmō* Problem and
Tanaka's Positive Solution

> For Japan, afflicted with domestic instability, the only way out
> is to solve the *Manmō* problem.
>
> Ishiwara Kanji, *Guandong Army Plan for*
> *the Seizure of the* Manmō *Region*

Politics in the Japanese army, stimulated early by the structural inequities within it and affected later by the domestic problems facing the nation, became more and more concerned with external affairs during the 1920's, until Japan's foreign relations acquired overwhelming importance for the army about 1930. Since Russia retained its leading position as the army's hypothetical enemy, it is not peculiar that continental affairs and Japan's continental position formed the underlying basis for the army's interest. China's weakness had made it the pawn in Russo-Japanese rivalry since the time of the Sino-Japanese War. Just as instability in China and the collapse of Russia had inspired the army to dream of a permanent solution to Japan's continental problems during and immediately following the Great War, the specter of a resurgent Russia and a unified China aroused almost pathological fear for Japan's position on the continent by the late 1920's. Given the army's social-Darwinist view of international relations and the importance of Japan's continental position, carved from the flesh of army men in two brutal wars, it was easy for the army to translate Japan's survival on the continent to the preservation of the empire itself.

The linchpin of Japan's continental position was, of course, Manchuria (including portions of eastern Inner Mongolia), where Japan, at the expense of China and Russia, had acquired extensive political and economic privileges, centering in the Guandong Leasehold, the civilian port of Dairen (Dalian), and the military base at Ryojun (Lushun, or Port Arthur), and in the South Manchurian Railway system extending from the

Guandong Leased Territory at the tip of the Liaodong Peninsula deep into the heart of the vast Manchurian plains. The army, which created, controlled, and defended this vulnerable frontier, was aware not only of the tremendous economic potential of this rich and underpopulated territory, long isolated from China proper as a reservation for the Manchu people, but also of its strategic position at the convergence of Japanese, Russian, and Chinese power and ambition. The army in Ugaki's day, obsessed by the vision of total war, believed that resource-poor Japan could only survive with the natural wealth of Manchuria at her command.

The essence of army strategic planning since the Russo-Japanese War had been to defend the Japanese Manchurian frontier against all rivals, but principally Russia. As part of that defense the army was to develop the area economically to the advantage of the empire and extend military, economic, and political control beyond the narrow confines of the leased area and the railroad right-of-way. As time went on, the technological progress in warfare, the theories of total war, and the apparent necessity for a massive integrated economic base for the successful prosecution of and survival in an environment of total warfare heightened the army's perception of the necessity for Japan to develop Manchuria as the empire's lifeline. The acquisition of Manchuria ceased to be only for the greater glory of Japan and became the key to national survival.

These aspirations involved the army deeply in Chinese affairs and led to the development of extensive intelligence, advisory, and diplomatic functions paralleling, often rivaling, and sometimes overbearing those of Japan's civilian government. The effect of this "dual diplomacy" is not of central concern here, but the internal political struggle in the army for control of the military input into Sino-Japanese relations was an important factor in the development and direction of army politics in the period 1918–28.

Japanese Army Activity in China, 1915–25

Early in the Great War the Japanese government sought to take advantage of the Powers' preoccupation in Europe to strengthen its position in China through the "Twenty-One Demands." The resulting treaty (25 May 1915) gave Japan new concessions in Manchuria and a substantial foothold in Shandong Province.[1] In 1922 in Washington, Japan agreed to relinquish the Shandong position, but there was virtually no retreat on Manchuria.[2] The military had comparatively little direct influence on the government policy that prompted the Twenty-One Demands, nor did the army, then in partial political eclipse, exercise any great authority at the negotiations in Washington. However, the army had become involved in the conduct of Japan's continental affairs even before its representatives assisted Zhang Zuolin to power[3] and aided rebellious Chinese in upsetting Yuan Shikai's schedule for founding his own dynasty in spring 1916.[4] These and earlier activities were all prompted by the army's desire to detach Manchuria from China. Army initiative in such actions increased noticeably after Uehara and Tanaka joined forces in the general staff headquarters in fall 1915. During his trip to China Tanaka personally turned his attention to Zhang Xun's abortive attempt to restore the Manchu imperium, using the army's already extensive apparatus in China to influence Zhang's decision to desist.[5]

Under the Terauchi government such intrusions continued, generally in cooperation with the foreign ministry. The effort to draw China into the war, the loans to purchase Japanese weapons to make the weapons systems of the two countries compatible, the reinstatement of Duan Qirui as prime minister, and the Sino-Japanese Military Agreement of May 1918 all fall into this category.[6] In 1920, during the war between the Anhui and Zhili cliques, the army secretly helped to support the losing Anhui cause in spite of the government policy of noninterference.[7]

With regard to Russia, during the Siberian Expedition all negotiation with local or regional Russian governments of whatever political hue was conducted by military officers or by foreign ministry negotiators under their careful scrutiny. In Siberia we see for the first time army diplomatic and military activity, often controlled by the general staff, diverging from the position of the government and even the army minister.[8]

In the heyday of Diet and popular anti-militarism following the war, the army position on the continent suffered severe blows. In accepting the Nine Power Treaty at the Washington Conference, Japan made concessions to the United States (and China) with respect to Chinese sovereignty. Although the treaty was not a renunciation of established rights, it did restrict future activity. In separate negotiations with the Chinese, the Japanese government not only renounced in effect all rights to the German holdings in Shandong Province but also agreed to withdraw army troops from Qingdao, Hankou, and northern Manchuria. The notorious Group 5 of the Twenty-One Demands, postponed in the 1915 negotiations, was dropped, and the Japanese government withdrew its right to priority in providing advice with respect to Manchuria to the Chinese government and in furnishing loans for the extension of the railways. All other Japanese rights in Manchuria remained intact.

Army leaders apparently smarted under these humiliating concessions, but there was little they could do. As Ugaki lamented to his diary:

The removal of troops from Shandong, the evacuation of Hankou, and now the withdrawal from Siberia have become realities. Those independent actions of the empire have all come to nothing. Nay, as in the case of our stationing troops in Shandong, which was our right by treaty, there is the tendency to relinquish the great proportion of our special rights and withdraw. Thus we further contract our noticeably diminished national prestige and national rights. The realization, flashing before our eyes, that the Japanese government is abandoning its responsibilities in China is truly unbearable.[9]

In China the army still maintained its intelligence and advisory apparatus, however, and under new conditions of instability and civil war in that country the army's representatives felt disposed to act.

In the first Mukden-Zhili War (1922) between the warlord forces of Wu Peifu and Cao Kun on the one hand and Zhang Zuolin's Manchurian troops on the other, Japanese army advisers and foreign officials on the spot called for the support of Zhang. The foreign ministry and the government had all they could do to enforce a noninterference policy on their representatives in the field,[10] but even in the face of strict instructions to the contrary, the Japanese advisers to Zhang Zuolin helped Prime Minister Duan Qirui to escape Beijing.[11]

On the recommendation of Marshal Uehara, shortly after the end of the first Mukden-Zhili War the army posted Maj. Gen. Hayashi Yasakichi to the Japanese legation in Beijing as attaché. Hayashi apparently had secret orders from the general staff headquarters concerning the protection of Japanese interests in Manchuria in the event of renewed warfare in North China.[12] When the second Mukden-Zhili War broke out in September 1924, again threatening Zhang Zuolin's autonomy and, by extension, Japan's position in Manchuria, the army was prepared to act. The Katō (Kōmei) cabinet and Foreign Minister Shidehara Kijūrō announced a strict noninterference policy for Japan. Nevertheless, Hayashi and army advisers to warlords Zhang Zuolin and Feng Yuxiang successfully engineered the defection of Feng from Wu Peifu. Feng's betrayal caused Wu's defeat and the collapse of his control over Beijing, temporarily relieving the pressure on Zhang Zuolin. In this instance the army representatives again acted in direct violation of stated government policy with the apparent knowledge of Army Minister Ugaki.[13] In November 1925, when Zhang Zuolin faced the rebellion of his subordinate Guo Songling, the Guandong Army intervened on Zhang's behalf, once again defying Foreign Minister Shidehara's official policy.[14] Interference in China in contravention of specific official restraints was one indication of growing army mistrust of the government's policy of cooperation with the United States and Great Britain, a consistent theme in Japan's policy since Hara's day.

Japanese Opinion Toward China Hardens

Japanese public opinion favored a conciliatory attitude toward China during the period of reaction against militarism in 1920 and 1921. Press and popular feeling applauded the concessions made to China in Washington, and there seemed to be a genuine hope in Japan that China would soon unify and that relations between the two neighbors would improve. But when China took the initiative in demanding further concessions from Japan and events revealed that Anglo-American Far Eastern policy was self-serving and oppressive to Japanese interests, and as the Japanese internal economic situation deteriorated, the army view that the empire's stake in Manchuria was vital to the well-being if not the existence of the nation became increasingly attractive. The press and the Diet reflected this disillusionment in open criticism of Foreign Minister Uchida's policies and, later, Shidehara's. It is in this period that the *Manmō* (Manchuria-Mongolia) problem emerged as an issue in Japanese politics.[15] Its reflection in army politics particularly concerns us here.

Early in 1923 a popular movement began in China, agitating for the return of Dairen and Port Arthur. In March, in response to anti-Japanese feeling, the Chinese government, still smarting under its failure to remove the basic inequalities in relations between China and the Powers and especially resentful over its treatment at the hands of the Japanese, unilaterally denounced the Sino-Japanese Treaty of 1915, the one forced on China as a result of the Twenty-One Demands. When Japan refused to recognize this act, the Chinese began a nationwide boycott of Japanese goods. In reaction, Japanese public opinion began to change. Uchida's "weak diplomacy" came under fire in both houses of the Diet and even the prestigious *Asahi shinbun* criticized the Chinese for "digging their own graves."[16] In an atmosphere more congenial to its position, the army gradually added its own objections to the official China policy to the mounting chorus of criticism, and it grew bolder in its activities in China. Imai Seiichi wrote in a perceptive article that appeared in the magazine *Shisō* in 1957:

What lent strength to their assertions was the reality of the fighting in China, which continued unabated. Because of this internal strife, even the rights returned by the Washington Conference had not yet been realized. It was argued that China must first tend to itself before looking abroad. This change in public opinion not only disclosed the importance that the *Manmō* rights occupied in popular sentiment, but it also revealed that the hope for a new China had lost force. This became a lever for the revival of army power. . . .

At this point we should note the character of the so-called Shidehara diplomacy. Shidehara diplomacy advocated respect for the rational position of China, defense of the rational viewpoints of Japan, and noninterference in China's internal politics. A rational position meant complete acceptance of already existing treaties and already established interests. . . . That the Chinese side was opening fire on the line on which this [Shidehara diplomacy] depended was clear in, for example, the negotiations on tariff regulations after the establishment of the Guomindang government. But even this mildly concessionary diplomatic policy drew heavy opposition from the privy council, the House of Peers and, of course, the army. The protection of our rights in Manchuria and Mongolia became for them a handy slogan. Our special interests centering on Manchuria and Mongolia and our poorly secured loans based on the Nishihara loans were, in a sense, a cancer to cooperative diplomacy with China, and one might say that they blocked any fresh start in Japanese diplomacy.[17]

Another factor in Sino-Japanese relations adding a sense of urgency to the conservative and military point of view was the reemergence of Russia in diplomacy with China. The Soviet government signed its first official diplomatic agreements with the Chinese government in Beijing in May 1924.[18] Apparently conciliatory documents negotiated more or less on the basis of sovereign equality, they signified only a temporary rapprochement between Russia and China, but they shook to its foundations the Japanese army policy of Sino-Japanese military cooperation against Communist Russia.[19] As C. Walter Young, a contemporary authority on Manchurian affairs, observed: "According to a second agreement on the CER signed the same day, Russia recognized Chinese sovereignty in the Chinese Eastern Railway zone and agreed that China might redeem the line with 'Chinese capital,' that the fate of the line would be determined by China and Russia to the exclusion of third parties, and that management of the road would be a joint Russo-Chinese concern."[20] This was in striking contrast to Japanese exclusive rights in managing the South Manchurian Railway. Another blow to Japan's position in South Manchuria came in September 1924 when the Russians made another agreement directly with Zhang Zuolin, which again recognized the principle of joint management of the CER.[21] Needless to say, Russian diplomacy raised Chinese public opinion to new heights of anti-imperialist and anti-Japanese fervor.

The Japanese government (Kiyoura cabinet) reacted sharply to the prospect of the Sino-Soviet agreement by devising new guidelines for Japan's China policy with army participation. According to this *Tai-Shi seisaku kōryō* (Outline for a policy toward China), Japan would henceforth work to prevent the penetration of foreign influence, uphold the position of Japan, work for Sino-Japanese harmony, develop China's rich resources, and extend Japan's economic power. Japan would base her actions on the Washington treaty system but act autonomously. The document noted the special position of the Manchuria-Mongolia region in "the defense of Japan and the survival of its people." The plan "settled on a policy calling for 'clearing anew the path to the North Manchuria region,' in which Japan's facilities had been hitherto limited."[22]

The CER joint management agreement between Zhang Zuolin and the Soviet Union had an immediate effect on the Japanese army. Revised war plans for 1923 extended the region for opening hostilities with Russia from Harbin northwest toward Qiqihar (Tsitsihar), but the plan depended on the cooperation or benevolent neutrality of the Chinese army in Manchuria. If Japan were to face an allied Sino-Soviet army, the army would find itself opening hostilities against the Chinese in southern Manchuria.[23] The maintenance of adequate guards along the Japanese-controlled SMR system became more important than ever.

On 3 June 1924, directly after the Sino-Soviet agreement was signed, general staff headquarters' estimates of the situation predicted that the Chinese would soon demand the withdrawal of Japanese troops from Manchuria, that to underline these demands the anti-Japanese movement would further intensify, and that there was danger the Sino-Japanese dispute would broaden into an international problem. The Japanese government had agreed in 1905 to withdraw its railway guards from the SMR if and when the Russians did, and in Washington, under the terms of the Nine Power Agreement, it further agreed to investigate and report jointly with the Chinese any disputes arising from the presence of Japanese troops on Chinese territory. The general staff reasoned that the Zhili faction in Beijing would soon demand the withdrawal of Japanese troops in order to put pressure on Zhang Zuolin, and that if Japan refused, it would intensify the anti-Japanese movement in the name of recovering Chinese rights. Japan should be understanding of Zhang in this predicament and support him while resolutely opposing the anti-Japanese movement. If the problem became an international one, the United States would probably support China. In this event Japan must steadfastly maintain its position and brazen it out.[24]

These fears were never realized. After more than a year and a half of intermittent negotiations in which the overtones of a covert imperialist struggle over their respective Manchurian interests played a significant role,[25] Japan and Russia restored diplomatic relations in January 1925. As a part of the negotiations the Japanese army agreed to withdraw the North Sakhalin Expeditionary Force, the only foreign troops remaining in Soviet territory.

Only a short time later relations between the Soviet Union and the various factions in China substantially worsened. Zhang Zuolin displaced the more pro-Soviet Feng Yuxiang in Beijing in 1926. In April 1927 Zhang staged his famous raid on the Soviet legation in Beijing. In spring and summer 1927 the Guomindang purged the Chinese Communist Party members from its ranks and expelled all Soviet advisers. In November 1925 the Japanese general staff headquarters, perceiving a rising competition between the Soviet Union and Japan for the control of Manchurian railroads, presented a plan "to prevent the penetration of other nations' influence into the *Manmō* region." The plan recognized the advantage of having all new railway construction done by China, and it sought to exclude Soviet capital and influence from trunk lines and stave off the use of capital from any power other than Japan, China, or the Soviet Union. Finally, it listed seven railways the Japanese should seek to have the Chinese construct and the priority for their construction.[26] This plan was the forerunner of a 1927 scheme for negotiations with Zhang Zuolin on the construction of railways, and it "revealed clearly the basic methodology for the execution of the army's plans vis-à-vis Zhang Zuolin." It was part of this plan, of course, to hide the strategic military nature of these railways by having them built by the Chinese for ostensible economic and commercial reasons.[27]

The *Manmō* Problem Quickens to Crisis

For Japan all the foregoing was merely preliminary to the crisis in the *Manmō* problem. The fear of communist ideology and Comintern agitation in Japan that spawned the passage of the peace preservation law in 1924; the popular perception of danger to the empire from "Red" Russia and the renewed sense of importance now accorded the Japanese position on the continent, especially in Manchuria; the desperate economic fears at home, heightened by terrible losses in the great earthquake; and the feeling of diplomatic isolation after the Washington Conference — all these came to focus in the prospect of a unified, revolutionary China apparently bent on sweeping Japan from Manchuria. To make matters worse, the

Chinese revolutionary movement under Guomindang leadership appeared at first to have strong links to the hated Soviet Union. Japan, having recently retreated from Siberia, Shandong, and Sakhalin, now felt a sense of desperation about her continental position and seemed determined to oppose any further weakening of it. The army, which was at once the agent for the creation of Japanese continental rights and their defender, became a spokesman for this point of view. Soon it was leading criticism of government policy perceived detrimental not just to maintaining the status quo but to expanding continental power — a viewpoint of increasing validity to growing numbers of Japanese.[28]

In July 1926 the Guomindang (Nationalist) army under Chiang Kaishek began the Northern Expedition from Canton to unify all of China. Accompanied by Russian advisers and Chinese Communist Party members, it had advanced in two broad columns north to the approximate line of the Yangzi River by the end of 1926, sweeping demoralized warlord armies before it. In northern China Zhang Zuolin, now in control in Beijing, banded together most of the warlords in loose alliance to repel the invading southerners. These stirring events engaged the rapt attention of the Japanese, who were conscious more than ever of their stake in the Manchurian region.

As the Nationalists' revolutionary army entered cities along the Yangzi, a series of incidents occurred that involved foreigners and foreign interests. In January 1927 Nationalist troops seized the British settlements at Hankou and Jiujiang; in the Japanese settlements, Japanese nationals were subjected to violence, and their property was looted.[29] On the morning of 24 March, the opening day of the 52nd Diet in Tokyo, Chiang Kaishek's troops entering Nanjing precipitated the "Nanjing Incident," during which, in their anti-imperialist enthusiasm, they committed "brutal acts of assault and plunder against the Japanese, British, American, and French consulates and those of all other foreigners."[30] To quell the violence and protect the foreigners, British and American naval vessels shelled the foreign settlement and landed marines. The Japanese navy upheld its government's policy of maintaining a neutral posture. On 25 March Japanese naval forces landed, gathered together all Japanese officials and residents, and evacuated them to their ships. The young navy lieutenant responsible for the protection of Japanese nationals ashore during the period of violence, having only a few men at his disposal and following the government policy of noninterference, did not resist. He later committed suicide by disembowelment to atone for his failure. The lieutenant's heroic death further aroused public opinion at home.[31] Nine days later, on 3 April, a mob attacked and entered the Japanese settlement in Hankou, committing acts of violence and pillaging at will. The Japanese landed marines, evacuated the victims to waiting ships, and withdrew to Shanghai.

The passive reaction of Wakatsuki Reijirō's Minseitō government to Chinese violence, even to the point of refusing an earlier British bid for a joint intervention to protect Shanghai, brought the government and Shidehara's diplomacy under heavy fire from the rival Seiyūkai within the Diet and from an aroused public opinion without.[32] The proximate cause of Wakatsuki's downfall was a scandal involving the Bank of Taiwan, but the Nanjing and Hankou incidents were a substantial part of the accumulated pressures that toppled his cabinet and with it Shidehara diplomacy on 17 April.[33] On 20 April Tanaka Giichi assumed the reins of government in a Seiyūkai cabinet in which he held the post of foreign minister concurrently. With this change in government a new phase of Japanese foreign policy ensued. It was during this cabinet shift that Ugaki Kazunari stepped down as army minister, to be replaced by his classmate and ally, Gen. Shirakawa Yoshinori.

The army was, of course, incensed by the Nanjing, Hankou, and related incidents, not only because of the government's feckless handling of the incidents themselves[34] but also because of the long-range danger to Japan's position in Manchuria that revolutionary victory posed.[35] A few days after the Nanjing Incident Maj. Gen. Matsui Iwane called on Foreign Minister Shidehara to present the army opinion that if the revolutionary leadership in China did not seriously reflect on its current course of action, the empire must end its patient attitude and prepare defensive measures in concert with the Powers. With regard to Nanjing, Japan should, he said, support Chiang Kai-shek and other moderate elements in the Guomindang by placing the blame for the incident in Nanjing on communist elements and mediating between Chiang and the British and Americans.[36] The army had good reason to believe that there was serious trouble between left and right within the Guomindang and that this instability was exploitable. Two weeks later, on 12 April, Chiang Kai-shek began his purge of communists in Shanghai.

In the meantime, Ugaki conferred with Wakatsuki, repeating the army view that it was just a matter of time before the Chinese revolutionary movement extended to Manchuria. He recommended, as a policy toward the anti-imperialist movement, that Japan strengthen cooperation with the Powers, adopt a policy of encircling the communist faction in combination with the Powers, and destroy the communists by arms and by military support for moderate elements in both North and South China.[37]

As the Wakatsuki cabinet stepped down and Tanaka Giichi prepared to assume control of the government, the army, divided in so many ways, could agree on one thing—the Shidehara "weak diplomacy" had endangered the empire's position on the continent. A more positive policy was absolutely necessary if Japan was to make secure and permanent its position in Manchuria before the surging Nationalist power in China, backed by meddlesome Americans and revolutionary Russians, could force it to abandon these hard-won and legitimate rights. The army harbored a growing feeling of anxiety about Japan's Manchurian holdings. First, there was the general knowledge that Manchuria promised untold wealth and power to the nation that controlled it. Second, the army felt that both China and Russia were growing in strength and, if Japan did not act immediately, the time to secure its position would pass.[38] Again, visions of total war spurred the army to action.

Tanaka and the First Shandong Expedition

The new prime minister, whose ideas were never far removed from those of the army in which he had served for so many years, agreed with his former colleagues on continental policy. He had, after all, been the principal author. His party had led the fight in the House of Representatives against the Shidehara diplomacy, and he clearly stated to an apprehensive nation that the first business for his government would be to settle outstanding problems with China (the financial crisis that was wracking the nation, notwithstanding). To emphasize his determination, he reserved the foreign minister's portfolio for himself and appointed as his parliamentary vice minister for foreign affairs Mori Kaku (Takashi), who held aggressive views on continental matters.[39] In spite of Tanaka's reputation in the army as the leader of the despised Chōshū clique, his appearance as head of the government was genuinely welcomed in army circles.[40]

Tanaka's positive ideas on how to deal with China in the throes of turmoil and revolution were quickly put to a practical test. Even before his government could formalize its policy, a situation arose in North China that, in the view of the prime minister, the army, and the Seiyūkai, demanded action. On 6 April 1927, Zhang Zuolin raided the Soviet legation in Beijing, seizing documents that revealed the extent of Russian involvement and subversive activity in China.

Zhang's action brought Soviet relations with Beijing to the point of open rupture and acted as a destabilizing factor in Japanese relations with Russia in the *Manmō* region as well. On 12 April Chiang Kai-shek, with-

out the sanction of the national provisional government already established at Wuhan, took action to destroy the Chinese communists' hold on
the Shanghai labor movement and their influence within the Guomindang. Shanghai was in turmoil. On 15 April the British ambassador approached Foreign Minister Shidehara with a new proposal for a joint
intervention in Shanghai and North China to protect the lives and property of foreign residents. A few days later Wakatsuki's cabinet fell. On 22
April, just two days after his government took office, Tanaka announced
in his declaration of administrative policy that Japan continued to be
concerned about the activities of the Communist Party in China, but on 26
April, in reply to the British proposal, he formally denied the need for
an increase in foreign forces.[41] However, the army effectively doubled the
strength of its Manchurian Garrison (Guandong Army) by postponing the
scheduled return of the 10th Infantry Division to Japan even though its
replacement, the 14th Infantry Division, had already arrived. In like manner the army ordered the replacement unit for the North China Garrison
Force to proceed to station ahead of schedule, doubling that force's
strength. The army considered the number of Japanese and other foreign
troops in the Beijing-Tianjin area sufficient for the emergency.

In China, after a delay while Chiang Kai-shek established a second
Nationalist government in Nanjing, the Nationalist army resumed its
northward march with the intention of capturing Beijing. Meanwhile, the
army of the Guomindang left-wing government at Wuhan, which still
maintained its ties with the Chinese Communist Party but had temporarily split with Chiang, also began to advance. With the help of the
warlord Feng Yuxiang, who now joined the Guomindang, the Wuhan
army defeated Marshal Zhang Zuolin's troops in early May in Henan
Province, forcing his army north of the Yellow River. At the same time
Chiang's troops drove the marshal's warlord allies, Sun Chuanfang and
Zhang Zongchang, north to the Shandong-Jiangsu border. By the end
of May it seemed clear that fighting would soon extend to Shandong
Province.

At that time there were approximately 17,000 Japanese residents in
Shandong, in Jinan (Tsinan) and Qingdao and along the railway between
the two cities. Their protection became the pretext, if not the actual reason, for the Japanese army's first Shandong Expedition.[42] On 24 May
Army Minister Shirakawa advised the cabinet that the situation war-
ranted intervention to protect the lives and property of the Japanese in
Shandong. The cabinet responded quickly by approving a policy to protect Japanese nationals. The army chief of staff immediately prepared to

send a full peacetime-strength infantry division to China in accord with the plan of operations division chief Araki Sadao, who wished to provide a "large-scale expedition because Zhang Zuolin could not be depended on to hold even Manchuria." Araki had the support of his chief and the chief of intelligence (G-2) Matsui Iwane, whose younger brother was the senior adviser to Marshal Zhang. The younger Matsui's reports to general staff headquarters did not encourage any dependence on Zhang Zuolin in the face of the determined Nationalist advance.

The prime minister, however, did not conceive of the expedition as a deterrent to Guomindang entry into North China so much as a symbol of Japan's determination to defend her rights. Financial considerations, as well as some fear of Chinese and foreign reaction, tempered Tanaka's view.[43] It was his opinion that only a token force of two battalions should be sent. The army ministry supported Tanaka. In the end the cabinet approved the transport of the 33rd Infantry Brigade of the 14th Infantry Division (four battalions of infantry, reinforced) from the Guandong Leased Territory to Qingdao.[44]

On the following day a government announcement assured the Chinese that the troops were being sent solely to protect Japanese residents and that the Japanese army would in no way interfere with the operations or movement of either contending Chinese army.[45] On 1 June the 33rd Brigade debarked at Qingdao. It was Tanaka's strong desire to hold the expeditionary force in Qingdao, allowing it to advance to Jinan only if circumstances required, but even if an advance became necessary, Japanese troops were not to interfere in what Tanaka accepted as a Chinese internal problem. The situation in the field seemed to improve during June, but in July a part of Sun Chuanfang's army near Qingdao rebelled, declaring for the Guomindang. Sun, who was in Jinan, marched east toward Qingdao to quell the dissidence, uncovering Jinan. On 5 July the cabinet authorized the expeditionary force to advance troops to Jinan for the protection of Japanese residents there. The general staff, wanting no repeat of the Nikolaevsk Incident, recommended the immediate reinforcement of Qingdao with troops (8th Inf. Brigade) from the 10th Division. The cabinet duly authorized this movement on 8 July. Having persuaded both Sun and the rebels to do their fighting in an area removed from Qingdao, the main body of the Japanese expeditionary force proceeded to Jinan, incidentally providing new impetus to the Chinese economic boycott against Japan.[46]

The situation looked bleak for the northern forces, whose repeatedly defeated armies seemed to be disintegrating, but the southern armies, too, were in turmoil. When the Guomindang's Wuhan Army approached the western flank of Chiang Kai-shek's forces by marching east toward Anhui and Jiangsu Provinces on both banks of the Yangzi River, Chiang Kai-shek hastily broke contact with Zhang Zongchang and wheeled to face the Wuhan forces. Sun and Zhang rallied their troops and, attacking from the north, inflicted a serious defeat on Chiang. Placed in an untenable political as well as military situation between the northern warlord armies and Wuhan, Chiang Kai-shek announced his resignation on 14 August in order to facilitate a rapprochement between the Wuhan and Nanjing wings of the Guomindang.[47] In view of this new situation, the Japanese government decided on 24 August to withdraw its forces from Shandong, warning the Chinese that the army would return if further threats to Japanese residents arose.[48] The Japanese forces departed the area of operations on 8 September, ending the first Shandong Expedition without serious incident and setting a precedent for the second.[49]

Tanaka's "Positive Policy" for Manchuria

As a measure of Tanaka's growing confidence in the ability of Chiang Kai-shek to unify China, it is interesting to note that the prime minister asked his old friend, Yamanashi Hanzō, to go to Beijing to persuade Marshal Zhang Zuolin to retreat beyond the Great Wall without further fighting. It was Tanaka's hope that he could then convince Chiang to accept a partition of China, leaving the *Manmō* region in Marshal Zhang's (and Japanese) hands. Yamanashi, accompanied by young Maj. Suzuki Teiichi, proceeded to Beijing in June 1927.[50]

Suzuki tells us that the Old Marshal treated Yamanashi coolly:

He was extremely reluctant to abandon Beijing, largely because it symbolized prestige. He retorted defiantly that it was he who was waging Japan's war against the communist hordes, even to the extent of advancing against them. Therefore he was frankly puzzled as to why Japan should ask him to pull his punches; in his eyes this was tantamount to siding with the Nationalists, who had fallen under communist influence.

Having no good answer, Yamanashi returned to Tokyo.[51] This experience should have been a warning to Tanaka that the Chinese revolutionary struggle could not be so easily manipulated through political bargaining, but he pushed forward boldly with his "positive" program, which was designed to prevent war between China and Japan over Manchuria. The idea of preventing war is a recurrent theme in the prime minister's conversations at this time,[52] but he was convinced, as were his army colleagues, that Japan must secure its position in Manchuria, at the cost of war if necessary. If his last-ditch negotiations failed, war would follow. Manchuria was far too precious to the empire's survival to let slip without a struggle.

The real issue for the Japanese, however, was not the security of Japanese rights in Manchuria, on which there was general agreement, but how far Japan must go to attain security. That Japan must sever Manchuria from China had become the accepted position. It would not be long before the idea that Japan must wrest complete political control of the entire *Manmō* region from China would come to the fore. Meanwhile, as the army tested its wings in the first of a new series of interventions in China, the Tanaka government, with advice from the army, was formulating Japan's new "positive" policy. Beginning 27 June and continuing until 7 July, Tanaka and Vice Foreign Minister Mori Kaku conferred with 21 top foreign, army, navy, and finance ministry officials and field representatives of the foreign ministry and the military services in order to hammer out the new policy. Army representation at this Eastern Area Conference (*Tōhō kaigi*) included Vice Minister Hata Eitarō and general affairs bureau chief Abe Nobuyuki of the army ministry; Vice Chief of Staff Minami Jirō and G-2 Matsui Iwane of the general staff headquarters; and Commanding General Mutō Nobuyoshi from the Guandong Army.[53]

As a result of eleven days' concentrated effort, a policy emerged that reflected closely the long-held ideas of General Tanaka and the army with respect to Manchuria and Mongolia.[54] It was a policy of independence, breaking completely with the Hara-Uchida-Shidehara view that Japan should cooperate as closely as possible with Britain and the United States, and it also rejected the minority position of Gotō Shinpei, who advocated cooperation with China and Russia, a position completely unacceptable to an army that still considered Russia its prime adversary.[55] The Tanaka policy was a Japan First policy; when it was implemented, it was bound to isolate the empire from all the Powers and arouse nothing but opposition and hatred from China.

The conference focused on the solution of the outstanding problems between China and Japan to the almost total neglect of all outside considerations. The geographic emphasis was on Manchuria, where the Japanese bill of complaint was a long one. There was the problem of parallel and competing railway lines to the SMR; China even planned new port facilities at Huludao to eliminate the necessity for using Dairen.[56] The Chinese authorities had made, they said, a dead letter of Japan's right to lease land for commercial purposes by putting heavy official pressure on Chinese individuals willing to rent their land to Japanese. The Chinese attempted to keep out Japanese goods by levying extraordinary taxes on them. They insulted Japanese civil and military officials, oppressed Korean citizens of the empire, and so on. Thus, Chinese reactions to Japanese imperialism became the springboard for Japanese counteraction. Tanaka intended to solve these problems by diplomatic negotiations.[57] For the moment the army was content to let him try.

Foreign Minister Tanaka's eight-point "China Policy Summary," distributed on the final day of the conference, makes it clear that Japan had resolved on a basic policy of recognizing Manchuria (*Manmō*) and China proper as separate entities; the summary also suggested that the "three eastern provinces" were autonomous or independent of China. It viewed the Japanese position in Manchuria as the lifeline of the empire and announced that Japan would resolutely defend its rights and special interests there when menaced from any quarter. In spite of some reassurances concerning the just aspirations of the Chinese people, the document marks the beginning of Japan's official hostility to the Chinese revolution and its determination to secure a commanding position in northeastern China, revolution notwithstanding.[58] The Tanaka government had made a fateful declaration of diplomatic independence, which further alienated China (advancing "anti-imperialist and communist influence" there)[59] and nations friendly to Japan. Moreover, it failed in its diplomatic effort to secure Manchuria, finally losing the confidence and support of the army.[60]

Tanaka Diplomacy in Action

The first step in the implementation of Tanaka's plans was to acquire from Zhang Zuolin a new commercial lease agreement and a promise that the Chinese would construct five new railways in Manchuria. These new treaties, to be extracted from Marshal Zhang before Chiang Kai-shek completed the unification of China proper, would — in the guise of Chinese internal development — secure rights for Japanese business and industry and complete the strategic railway system required by the army. With Japan's rights securely anchored in new agreements with Zhang's Beijing government, Chiang Kai-shek would be forced to recognize and accept them.

As a first step, on or about 14 July 1927, Tanaka conferred with Col. Machino Takema, for much of the time since 1917 a trusted adviser to Zhang Zuolin.[61] Machino held out little hope for success, warning Tanaka that if Zhang acquiesced there would be a rebellion against him. When the prime minister insisted that Japan must undertake the negotiations immediately, Machino reluctantly consented to do what he could to prepare the way. Tanaka then selected Yamamoto Jōtarō, a former director of Mitsui Bussan with close business connections in China and now secretary general of the Seiyūkai, as the chief negotiator; Yamamoto was asked that day to assume the presidency of the South Manchurian Railway.[62] Later he was to proceed to Beijing to negotiate directly and secretly with Zhang Zuolin. Machino, back in Beijing, began the preliminary negotiations to smooth the way for Yamamoto, who did not arrive in the city until October.[63] By keeping the negotiations secret and unofficial, Tanaka hoped to take some of the mounting pressure off Zhang, who found his identification with Japanese interests a political handicap in his contest with the Nationalists. If successful, the results of the negotiations would be announced only after Zhang was safely back in Manchuria.

In order to settle matters that were causing strained relations between Japanese and Chinese in Manchuria, Consul General Yoshida Shigeru opened negotiations with the local authorities in Mukden on 23 July in response to instructions from Foreign Minister Tanaka. The talks began under the cloud of an anti-Japanese reaction to the announced results of the Eastern Area Conference, the troop movement to Jinan, and the arrival of the second wave of Japanese troops of the Shandong Expeditionary Force at Qingdao. Yoshida's approach proved so overbearing that he not only made no progress in spite of threats to cut off military supplies to Zhang Zuolin's armies, but he also aroused anti-Japanese feelings all over China. Japanese civilian entrepreneurs in China, who bore the direct economic effect of the Chinese boycott and most of the abuse that accompanied it, were beside themselves, appealing to their government for relief, but Yoshida forged ahead. In league with Col. Kōmoto Daisaku of the Guandong Army staff and the army's intelligence (*tokumu kikan*) unit in Mukden, the consul general proposed that the Guandong Army and the Chōsen Army send troops to enforce his demands.

As reports of the adverse reaction to Yoshida's bullying poured into the foreign ministry from private and official, even military, sources, an alarmed Tanaka dispatched Parliamentary Vice Minister Mori Kaku to Port Arthur to confer with the diplomats and military officers in the field. Mori met with Minister Yoshizawa Kenkichi, Consul General Yoshida, Lt. Gen. Honjō Shigeru (the army attaché), Maj. Gen. Matsui Shichio (Iwane's brother), Gen. Mutō, and the host, Kodama Hideo (the governor-general of the Guandong Leased Territory), on 15 August to assess the situation. At this meeting, the Dairen or Ryojun Conference, there was a confrontation between Yoshida and the more moderate Yoshizawa, but "because Kodama, Honjō, and Matsui strongly upheld Yoshizawa, even Mori could not speak out openly in support of Yoshida. As a result, it was decided that Yoshizawa would open negotiations in Beijing with Zhang Zuolin on the settlement of outstanding problems and that the Mukden negotiations would be relegated to secondary local problems only."[64]

Changing the site and even the style of the negotiations had little effect. Zhang Zuolin, aspiring to control all of China and rocked by anti-Japanese domestic disturbances in both Manchuria and North China, had no desire to become tainted further with the epithet "tool of the Japanese." Yoshizawa renewed the talks on the unsettled problems connected with Japanese rights in Manchuria while, unknown to him, Machino and later Yamamoto negotiated secretly for an agreement to build the five strategic railways demanded by the army.[65] When Zhang Zuolin saw a map of the five railways, he was reportedly furious with Yamamoto, asking, "Aren't these railroads in preparation for Japan to fight Russia?"[66]

Since the purpose of the proposed agreements with Zhang Zuolin was to secure Japan's position in Manchuria before the Guomindang could unify all of China, speed was absolutely essential to Tanaka's program, and the Old Marshal's adamant refusal to sign government-to-government agreements frustrated the Japanese plans. As a result of Zhang's intransigence, the negotiations dragged on until May 1928, when Yoshizawa, the apostle of the moderate approach, began to lose faith and finally decided that only a return to forceful bargaining would bring results.[67] As foreign ministry officials despaired, the army, which had less faith in the power of peaceful negotiation in the first place, became restive, and voices calling for a military solution to the army's Manchurian dilemma began to rise in chorus. As one might expect, the disturbance centered in the Guandong Army.

Chiang Kai-shek's Unexpected Visit to Japan

In October 1927 a new development in Sino-Japanese relations further complicated the already complex picture, giving hope to Tanaka at the same time that a peaceful solution to the *Manmō* problem was still available. The cause for Tanaka's optimism was a surprise secret visit from Chiang Kai-shek. Chiang had resigned as president of the Guomindang in August, knowing full well that without him the leaderless Nationalists would flounder hopelessly in factional strife. It would be only a matter of time before the party called for him to return.

Taking advantage of his self-imposed exile, Chiang proceeded to Japan, where in October he made discreet contacts through Zhang Qun (a Guomindang officer close to Chiang) to Suzuki Teiichi.[68] Suzuki brought Chiang into talks with army leaders including the G-2, Matsui Iwane,[69] and ultimately Chiang conferred with Mori Kaku and Prime Minister Tanaka.[70] Chiang apparently had come to Japan to confirm what Minister Yoshizawa had implied with respect to the Tanaka government's feelings about the Guomindang.[71] He had reason to believe that through Tanaka he could receive Japanese support for the unification of China.[72]

Tanaka recommended to Chiang that he consolidate his hold on the area south of the Yangzi and complete the destruction of the communists before resuming the Northern Expedition. Chiang countered by saying that Wang Jingwei, leader of the reunified (since 6 September) Guomindang, had requested Chiang to return to his post as commander-in-chief in expectation of a renewed effort northward, but they needed Japanese support. The reason for the anti-Japanese movement in China was that people thought Japan was helping Zhang Zuolin. The people of China, who despised the warlords, mistakenly believed that warlordism depended on Japan. It was necessary, Chiang went on, for Japan to sweep away this erroneous impression by helping those who thought as he did to consummate the revolution quickly. Then the *Manmō* problem, too, could be settled easily and anti-Japanese feeling eradicated.[73] The two men agreed on the evils of communism, but Chiang sought Japanese understanding and noninterference as he completed the unification of China while Tanaka demanded recognition of Japan's special position in Manchuria. The meeting cleared the air somewhat, and Chiang received, in accord with his request, a Japanese army observer. Lt. Col. Sasaki Tōichi joined the Guomindang armies in December 1927. For their part, the Nationalists took measures to restrain the anti-Japanese movement after Chiang's return.[74]

The army and government leaders now held three distinct opinions on how to deal satisfactorily with China on the *Manmō* question. Matsui Iwane, Suzuki Teiichi, and Sasaki Tōichi represented the group of experts who foresaw the ultimate victory of the Nationalist revolution and the eventual unification of China under the Guomindang. With the revolution divorced from communist and Russian connections, they felt that the Guomindang could be brought into friendly relations with Japan. By late 1927, after Chiang Kai-shek's encouraging assurances, this view seemed promising. The prime minister himself was impressed. Rather than hinder its progress, Japan should gain the friendship of the revolutionary forces through open support and negotiate with the victors on mutual problems on the basis of incurred obligation. In good time, the problems of both anti-Japanese feelings in all of China and Japanese rights in Manchuria could be solved amicably. It was an attractive possibility, but it entailed great risk because it depended on the continuing goodwill of the revolutionaries even after they consolidated their control over China.

Matsui Shichio and Machino Takema represented a continuation of the traditional approach to security in Manchuria — support for Zhang Zuolin, the effective army policy since 1915. The Old Marshal's behavior since 1926, however, made this policy less and less attractive. The army was interested in Zhang only insofar as he represented Chinese government in the "three eastern provinces." It had no interest in his pretensions to power in Beijing and to unification of the entire country. By the end of 1927 the Tanaka three-pronged diplomatic offensive to assure Japan's permanent place in Manchuria was meeting obstinate resistance in Beijing and Mukden. Yamanashi's visit in the beginning days of the Tanaka cabinet had been a straw in the wind. The official and unofficial negotiations of Yoshizawa, Yamamoto, and Yoshida had progressed unsatisfactorily. Time was running out for Tanaka if he expected to settle the *Manmō* problem through Zhang Zuolin without resorting to arms.

At the end of 1927 a third army view lurked in the shadows: the military solution. Completely unsympathetic to Chinese claims and having no firm commitment to Chinese revolutionaries or warlords, the military solution found its most ardent spokesmen among staff officers of the Guandong Army — for example, Col. Kōmoto Daisaku, Chief of Staff Maj. Gen. Saitō Hisashi, and, later, Lt. Col. Ishiwara Kanji and Col. Itagaki Seishirō. These men had the general support of their commanding officers, Mutō Nobuyoshi and Muraoka Chōtarō, but perhaps more important, they had the moral support of many staff officers in Tokyo — a support conveyed increasingly after spring 1928 by membership in the Futabakai and, after its formation a year later, the Issekikai.

New developments in China soon dashed the possibility of dealing with Chiang Kai-shek and the Guomindang and ruined any chance of finding a solution through Zhang Zuolin. Under these circumstances the army, after months of hesitation, bared its fangs and claws in September 1931 to seize all of Manchuria — the army's solution to the *Manmō* dilemma.

7

Jinan and Mukden: The Army Sets Its Course in China

> If the gods are in your way, do not be afraid to deny them;
> do not hesitate to forsake them, for *bushidō* is madness, and
> no great deeds will be accomplished without madness.
>
> *Hagakure*

Chiang Kai-shek, restored to his position as commander-in-chief of the Guomindang armies in early January, ordered a general offensive against the northern warlord armies on 7 April 1928. On 16 April the Japanese army attaché in Jinan, Maj. Sakai Takashi, sent a request for troops to Chief of Staff Suzuki Sōroku. Simultaneously, Consul General Fujita, in Qingdao, under pressure from Japanese nationals in the area, sent the foreign ministry a dispatch to the same effect. According to Fujita's report, overseas Japanese feared trouble from the Shandong warlord troops facing attacks from Chiang's army. Because of the difficulty in withdrawing Japanese residents, he recommended a policy of protecting them in situ.

At a cabinet meeting on 17 April Army Minister Shirakawa stated that the time had come to send troops.[1] On 18 April Tanaka conferred once more with Shirakawa and Navy Minister Okada Keisuke. This meeting resulted in a unanimous decision for an expedition. The army ministry then began coordinating talks with the foreign ministry. On 19 April Tanaka held an extraordinary cabinet meeting on the first anniversary of his cabinet's establishment; the group decided to send a force of 5,000 men (6th Infantry Division [Kumamoto]) to Shandong. Tanaka received imperial sanction on the afternoon of the same day. On the following day the Seiyūkai publicly reaffirmed its policy to protect overseas nationals, the army's mobilization order reached the 6th Division, and the government issued the usual statement "disclaiming any intention to interfere with the domestic affairs of the neighbor country, or to favor one faction against another, and declaring the intention of withdrawing the troops as soon as the security of the Japanese residents was assured." Thus began the second Shandong Expedition.[2]

Although the decision to intervene for a second time came quickly, it was apparently not made without serious misgivings.[3] It is now generally acknowledged that the prime minister did not favor sending more than a small force,[4] but his commitment to the principle of protecting Japanese resident nationals in China weighed on him heavily, and he finally decided that the expedition must be sent.[5] There was no consensus within the army either. It seems that the army ministry, which proposed the expedition on 17 April, encouraged and maintained support for the political decision to send troops, but the general staff, perhaps under the influence of the arguments of Matsui Iwane and Suzuki Teiichi, demurred:

On this occasion, too, the army ministry agreed, but the general staff headquarters simply did not. Vice Minister Hata Eitarō tried to convince his good friend, Vice Chief of Staff Minami, and military affairs bureau chief Abe Nobuyuki worked on operations chief Araki and intelligence chief Matsui, but none of them would approve. Araki and Matsui were particularly stubborn according to what Nemoto Hiroshi and Suzuki Teiichi, who were at that time in the general staff headquarters and army ministry, have told us.[6]

When it became clear that dispatching the expedition was a political decision made in spite of the general staff's disapproval, the staff demanded, for safety's sake, a much larger force than that proposed initially.[7]

Within Japan opposition to the expedition was led by Osaka businessmen (who suffered losses as the Chinese boycotted their products), with support from the Minseitō, the leftist parties, and the liberal press.[8] As with the first expedition Tanaka fondly hoped both to protect Japanese nationals in Jinan and to assure the tranquillity of Manchuria by placing the expeditionary forces in Qingdao only, a policy of strength by demonstration. However, on 25 April the 6th Infantry Division commander, Lt. Gen. Fukuda Hikosuke, ordered his troops, who had just that day begun to arrive from Japan, to proceed immediately from Qingdao to Jinan in response to an urgent request from the military attaché, Maj. Sakai Takashi. The general staff headquarters approved his move only after the fact, and on 30 April Tokyo ordered the 460-man temporary guard force from Tianjin, which had entered Jinan on 20 April, to return to station.[9]

The Jinan Incident

The Guomindang Revolutionary Army entered Jinan citadel on 1 May, and the streets overflowed with people enthusiastically greeting Chiang's forces. Guomindang party officials put up posters that read, "Down with Japanese imperialism," and they gave speeches everywhere they could assemble a crowd. On 2 May the Japanese commander of the security guard reported that discipline in the northern expeditionary forces was comparatively rigorous and there was no friction between them and the Japanese army. It was true, he said, that Japanese troops on guard took a markedly contemptuous attitude toward Chinese persons, but not to the extent that an explosive atmosphere had permeated the city. Just as the foreign ministry began to show anxiety over this report, the first notification of a serious incident between the two armies arrived through army channels:

1. The division is placed on an emergency footing.
2. The consul and Sakai, on returning from a meeting with Chiang Kai-shek, learned of a clash between Japanese and Chinese soldiers. [The consulate] immediately sent Lieutenant Colonel Sasaki to [Chinese] general headquarters, and the matter is under negotiation.

Everywhere a warlike situation gradually grows in intensity, and Chiang Kai-shek is unable to control the Chinese troops. It will be necessary for Japan to take drastic steps.

The army ministry excised the final sentence and sent the message to the foreign ministry.[10] Later Japanese and Chinese versions of this first clash differed completely. The Japanese side claimed that revolutionary army soldiers, looting the Japanese-owned Jinan Nippō (daily newspaper) Company, the agent for the *Manshū* (Manchuria) *nippō*, opened fire. On the other hand, the Chinese asserted that one of their soldiers had been shot to death within the Japanese guard perimeter. In any case, fighting continued until the evening of 4 May.[11] Unfortunately, Major Sakai aggravated the situation by continually reporting the course of the fighting in a very exaggerated fashion through telegrams that sought to provoke an aggressive response from the army central authorities. The commanding generals of both the Guandong and Chōsen Armies, receiving copies of Sakai's messages, demanded strong action from Tokyo including the further exercise of military force.

The army center, believing from the intelligence reports that the situation had reached a crisis, not only sanctioned independent action for the troops in the field[12] but also discussed with Prime Minister Tanaka the mobilization and dispatch of more divisions from Japan.[13] Their arguments were couched chiefly in terms of protecting "the honor of the national army." The extraordinary cabinet session on 4 May approved Army Minister Shirakawa's proposal to send reinforcements from the Guandong and Chōsen Armies.[14] However, the army held back its proposal for a one-division increase until the Diet adjourned on 7 May because the Seiyūkai, which held only a one-seat advantage over the Minseitō in the 55th extraordinary Diet session, was at a disadvantage in facing opposition arguments against the expedition.[15]

On 5 May the army released a false statement to the newspapers that more than 300 nationals had been massacred in Jinan, and public opinion began to change. It was true that during the night of 3 May and the morning of 4 May, as armed clashes spread, the Chinese did execute 13 Japanese, presumed to be persons engaged in the opium traffic. Major Sakai's situation reports exaggerated these acts and, on the basis of Sakai's prevarications, the army ministry made an announcement to the press that surpassed the truth by twenty times. On 6 May the *Jiji shinpō* carried the banner headline JINAN in the center of its front page, accompanied by an inflammatory article based on the army's release. At this point civil government and the military services seemed to complete the reversal of roles. The wavering prime minister was suddenly besieged by cries for caution from the foreign ministry and the Seiyūkai. Using information from the commander of Japanese security forces in Jinan that indicated that Sakai's reports were inaccurate,[16] Permanent Vice Minister of Foreign Affairs Debuchi worried that further increases in troop strength would merely make matters worse. However, as a result of the successful combined effect of the army ministry's belligerent attitude and its propaganda, backed now by the general staff headquarters, on the day following the formal end of the 55th Diet (8 May) the cabinet approved a one-division increase.[17] On 9 May the 3rd Infantry Division (Nagoya) received its mobilization order and embarked immediately for Qingdao.[18]

At the height of the 4 May crisis, the chief of staff had hastily decided that three divisions were necessary to reinforce Jinan, and the general staff headquarters pushed its planning forward on that basis. But as the situation in Shandong clarified and the Tanaka government and the Seiyūkai began to have second thoughts about further armed conflict with the Guomindang, the army ministry fell in line with the Tanaka position. Army Minister Shirakawa and Vice Minister Hata convinced Chief of Staff Suzuki and Vice Chief Minami that action in Shandong should accord with the government's foreign policy and that a one-division increase would be sufficient, presumably resolving the difference between the two army organs. However, the egregious Araki, now a lieutenant general and able to speak with more authority, adamantly refused to give ground. He argued that the government had violated the army's right to command and that the army was allowing the government to set a dangerous precedent, which would deprive the army of its constitutional right. The argument between Hata and Araki became heated. The vice minister defended time and again his recent switch to the government's position on the logical basis of its right to final authority concerning Jinan. In response, Araki reportedly bellowed:

What kind of nonsense are you giving me? As a soldier you ought to at least know what a matter of command is. How can you stand there and let the things we decided the other day at the marshals and military councillors meeting, in the presence of a royal prince and with the navy attending, be trampled in the dirt so easily, simply on the basis of government opposition?[19] Aren't you a soldier? If we do that, we're making light of the constitution, and it's going to wind up as an unmitigated disgrace.[20]

Meanwhile, in Jinan General Fukuda came under heavy pressure from his subordinates and the Japanese residents, who, after seeing the bodies of the executed Japanese (discovered on 5 May), agitated for a general accounting of the "accumulated insults" visited upon them by the Chinese. Encouraged by messages of support from the chief of staff and the government in Tokyo for previous actions taken without prior approval, Fukuda decided to maintain the honor of the army by suddenly issuing an ultimatum to Chiang Kai-shek's field commanders on the afternoon of 7 May, which gave them just twelve hours to clear Jinan and the Qingdao-Jinan Railway of Chinese troops.[21] When Fukuda's bombshell burst in Tokyo, the government had little choice but to support him once again, and with approval from Tanaka the decision of 8 May to increase troop strength by one division was reached with reluctance but little internal controversy.[22]

The prime minister received pressure from other army quarters as well. As part of his personal campaign for greater intervention, Araki called shrilly for the punishment of the Chinese. Maj. Gen. Koiso Kuniaki, who then headed the general affairs section of the aviation headquarters in the inspectorate general of military training, a position having no direct connection with the Shandong problem, visited Tanaka to plead for armed interference in China to protect Japanese residents and to prevent the fighting between north and south from affecting the Japanese position in Manchuria.[23]

Receiving from the Chinese what Fukuda deemed an unsatisfactory reply, his forces bombarded Jinan the following day and opened operations to clear the city and the railway of Chinese forces.[24] However, Chiang Kai-shek had already withdrawn the bulk of his forces on the night of 5 May; they had now crossed the Yellow River and were proceeding north.[25] As a result, the Chinese avoided a serious confrontation, although the city of Jinan sustained considerable damage at Japanese hands. By 11 May the Japanese army had attained all its objectives, driving all Chinese units out of the city, and on 12 May the Chinese reopened negotiations with Fukuda. The Jinan Incident was over,[26] but negotiations dragged on until 28 March 1929. At the height of the crisis the Japanese army had 19,000 troops in Shandong Province. Their numbers were gradually reduced, but the last of them left only in May 1929.[27]

The Exploitation of Zhang Zuolin's Defeat

The second Shandong Expedition marked the first of a series of armed clashes between the Japanese and Guomindang China, which continued with increasing frequency and ferocity until the confrontation blended into World War II.[28] The immediate effect of the Jinan Incident was to make Nanjing far more difficult to deal with. The fact that the negotiations to settle it took almost a year attests to the Guomindang's reaction. In the foreign office at Nanjing the pro-American Wang Zhengding (C. T. Wang) replaced Huang Guo, who had been educated in Japan, and Japan replaced Britain as the prime target of Guomindang anti-imperialist propaganda.[29]

The Jinan Incident also marked the parting of the ways between Tanaka Giichi and the army. As soon as the crisis at Jinan had passed, Tanaka attempted to salvage his Guomindang solution by requesting the chief of the general staff to allow Chiang Kai-shek the use of the railway between Jinan and Tianjin so that Chiang could enter Beijing before the warlord Gen. Feng Yuxiang. The general staff headquarters backed Lieutenant General Fukuda as a matter of honor and refused the prime minister's request until Chiang Kai-shek apologized for causing the Jinan affray as the 6th Division commander had demanded.[30]

Tanaka further disturbed the military by his reluctant handling of the plan to reinforce the expedition with the 3rd Infantry Division. The army wanted the situation to be declared a *jihen* (serious incident) and to place a field army headquarters in command of the entire expeditionary force.[31] Tanaka, wishing to make as little of the incident as possible, would not allow this response. Army hotheads led by Araki resented Tanaka's resistance in a matter pertaining to the safety of the command and considered his action unwarranted interference in a command matter within the purview of the chief of staff. Araki's protestations rang loudly in the hallways of Miyakezaka.

The hectic three or four weeks of complicated government and army actions with respect to China between the Jinan Incident and the retreat of Zhang Zuolin further estranged Tanaka from the army. That Tanaka never meant the intervention at Jinan to block the northward advance of the Guomindang Revolutionary Army is clear from the size of the initial force he dispatched as well as from his actions. There were those in the army, however, who wished to use Japanese forces for that purpose, if not at Jinan, perhaps at Tianjin or the Great Wall.[32] The unfortunate Jinan affair delayed the northward sweep of the revolutionary armies for only a few days, though Japanese interdiction, on army insistence, of a main north-south railway at Jinan remained an inconvenience.[33] The northern armies under Zhang Zuolin had no heart for the fight and continued to withdraw before Nationalist forces without making a decisive stand. Japanese army intelligence saw clearly that Marshal Zhang's forces were no match for the revolutionaries,[34] and the imperial army braced for trouble in Manchuria even before Chiang Kai-shek reached Jinan.

Maj. Gen. Saitō Hisashi, the chief of staff of the Guandong Army, proposed as early as 20 April that the army prepare to disarm all Chinese troops entering Manchuria from the south regardless of their affiliation.[35] The new consul general in Mukden, Hayashi Hisajirō, consulted the army authorities in Mukden on arriving at his post and found that there was no longer much support there for the obstinate Zhang.[36] Maj. Gen. Hata Shinji, head of the Mukden *tokumu kikan* unit, urged Hayashi to have the Old Marshal replaced by his son, Zhang Xueliang, presumably because he could be more easily managed, echoing sentiments expressed in Ryojun by men like Saitō and Col. Kōmoto Daisaku, the Guandong Army's senior staff officer. Kōmoto argued that continued government support for Zhang Zuolin was merely a personal alliance between the Chōshū clique leader Tanaka and the Mukden clique leader Zhang.[37] At the same time Zhang's military advisers, Maj. Gen. Matsui Shichio and Maj. Giga Seiya, pinned their hopes on Zhang's chief of staff, Gen. Yang Yuting.

In the meantime, to add to his considerable discomfiture, Minister Yoshizawa and Yamamoto Jōtarō beset the Old Marshal in Beijing. Yoshizawa pressed him for immediate withdrawal beyond the Great Wall while Yamamoto at last gained final approval of almost all of the railway concessions Japan sought for strategic purposes in Manchuria.[38] As Machino pointed out, the railway concessions were not merely the right to build five railways. All the railways had leaseholds attached to them, rendering the Japanese grip complete. The effect "was equivalent to making Manchuria Japan's."[39]

In Tokyo the army minister reported the approach of Guomindang forces and their allies into the Beijing-Tianjin region on 16 May at an extraordinary cabinet session. As a result, the government took firm measures to protect resident nationals in the region in concert with other foreign powers and, more important, considered means to prevent the war from entering Manchuria.[40] Consultations began immediately among army, navy, and foreign ministry officials, and on 18 May the government issued a declaration warning Nationalists and warlords alike that "the imperial government must take appropriate and effective measures to maintain peace and order in Manchuria."[41]

Minister Yoshizawa presented this declaration to the Old Marshal in Beijing late in the evening of 18 May, and he once again urged him to withdraw to Manchuria without fighting, for the good of all concerned. When Zhang refused in spite of Yoshizawa's arguments, possibly hoping against hope that the Japanese would be forced to come to his aid, the Japanese minister requested instructions from Tokyo. He received his answer on 20 May, based on the government policy decisions of the past few days. Yoshizawa was instructed to inform Marshal Zhang that

(1) If the northern and southern armies come into contact and go beyond the [Great] Wall, we shall disarm them without hesitation, regardless of whether they are northern or southern forces.

(2) When the Mukden Army withdraws, if the southern army does not pursue and the Mukden Army enters Manchuria maintaining adequate discipline, and if there is no fear of disturbance to peace and order, depending on the circumstances, it may not be necessary to disarm it.

(3) We will, in short, decide how to handle the withdrawal in keeping with the circumstances.[42]

For a time Zhang continued to resist, but when Maj. Gen. Tatekawa Yoshitsugu, the attaché,[43] informed Zhang Xueliang and Yang Yuting that "in case the Mukden army is routed, the Japanese army will disarm it," the Chinese leaders quickly bowed to the realities of the situation.[44] Since Zhang had little choice, on 23 May he consented to withdraw. According to *Daihon'ei rikugunbu*:

The commanding general of the Guandong Army, Lt. Gen. Muraoka Chōtarō (5th Class), concerned over the situation within the Great Wall and the possibility that the Beijing-Mukden railway might be obstructed, decided on 17 May to send half the 14th Division by rail on 20 May from Mukden to Qinzhou without delay; later, to have the 40th Combined Brigade move to Mukden as a reinforcement, if necessity dictated; and to advance the army headquarters to Mukden as well.[45]

The Guandong Army, spoiling for a showdown, took the attitude that it would not allow "the Mukden Army so much as one step beyond [the border at] Shanhaiguan into Manchuria, no matter what,"[46] indicating its growing impatience with anything but a military solution to the *Manmō* problem.[47]

The Guandong Army and important elements in the army headquarters in Tokyo clashed with the prime minister. The government intended the 18 May declaration to reestablish the possibility for a nonmilitary solution to the *Manmō* problem by offering both the Nationalists and Zhang Zuolin a compromise they could accept while assuring Japan's greatly augmented special rights. The Guandong Army willfully interpreted the declaration to its own advantage, as an acceptance of its two major proposals, the removal of Zhang and the forcible dissolution of his army by disarming it. At about this time, General Shirakawa, probably echoing appeals from military representatives on the continent, especially the Guandong Army headquarters, proposed to Tanaka that he approve steps to retire the Old Marshal from public life.[48] To all such petitions the prime minister turned a deaf ear.

The first check to the Guandong Army's aggressive plans came quickly. The foreign ministry interpreted any movement of the Guandong Army outside the South Manchurian Railway zone as a violation of the Treaty of Portsmouth, and on 19 May the chief of staff had to inform the army in Manchuria to remain within the zone until duly authorized by an imperial order to leave. The Guandong Army leaders protested and asked for a reconsideration, and the following day brought better news. Chief of Staff Suzuki, having talked with Tanaka, told them to prepare for an imperial order to move outside the SMR zone the next day. The fact that the chief of staff had already authorized them to move to Mukden and prepare for action at Qinzhou and Shanhaiguan, steps approved by Tanaka as a show of strength and as a club to force Zhang's submission, only confirmed for the Guandong Army its own interpretation of the 18 May declaration. Muraoka continued to concentrate his forces in Mukden and began preparations for their transportation south on the Beijing-Mukden line. However, that very evening the Guandong Army's high hopes received another blow when Consul General Hayashi showed Chief of Staff Saitō, already in Mukden, the consulate's information copy of a telegram from the foreign minister to Minister Yoshizawa in Beijing, which stated that Zhang Zuolin's troops were to be disarmed only if pursued by the revolutionary army.[49]

On 3 May 1928, the Guandong Army had held a conference of the intelligence officers in its area of jurisdiction. The opinions expressed at that meeting reflected the air of drama and decision that the crisis in North China held for them. Most of the officers advocated detaching the *Manmō* region from China proper. Their plan was to lead the highest responsible Chinese officials of Manchuria to declare the "three eastern provinces" autonomous and, later, independent of China. Then the newly independent state would sign a military alliance with Japan. General Muraoka approved these conclusions in principle but expressed the opinion that the time for the execution of such a plan had not yet arrived.[50]

By 20 May the Guandong Army seethed with excitement and anticipation. The hour to strike appeared to be at hand. Major General Saitō's diary has preserved for us the restless spirit of the moment and the frustration that accompanied the vigil:

Mukden, 21 May.

On the assumption that the imperial order decreed at 9:00 A.M. in Tokyo would become effective at 12:00 noon here, I advised my subordinates to that effect and summoned them at 12:00. But the orders did not come through. I am beginning to think that in all likelihood the plans of the army command have been disrupted by some plot. . . .

Waited all night, but the orders never arrived. The Guandong Army, bursting with spirit, is angered by the government's indecision.

Mukden, 22 May.

At 10:00 A.M. moved command headquarters to the top of the Tōtaku Building. At 3:47 P.M. the commanding general arrived on schedule and immediately occupied the temporary headquarters. . . . I sense a growing warlike mood spreading about us.

Mukden, 23 May.

Colonel Tashiro, chief of the China section of the general staff headquarters, arrived from Tokyo to brief us on the government's position. According to him, Zhang Zuolin is not to be pressed to relinquish his status . . . , although the manifest policy of the government is that both the northern and the southern armies are to be disarmed; in practice, however, the commanding general of the Guandong Army is authorized to use discretion and treat the northern army more leniently.

The Guandong Army in Mukden, expecting mobilization orders at any moment, is in a state of animated suspense. A feeling of antagonism toward the indecisive Tokyo government is mounting daily. Even Beijing is buzzing with rumors of the Guandong Army's pending expedition to Qinzhou and the forcible seizure of the Beijing-Mukden railway.[51]

Back in Tokyo, however, the government was not so united in purpose as the Guandong Army, as it faced serious domestic concerns, including a reconstitution of the Seiyūkai cabinet. Tanaka and the foreign ministry worried over the international repercussions to any bold stroke in Manchuria. On 17 May, the day before the Japanese warning to the participants in China's civil war, Tanaka reassured the British, American, French, and Italian ambassadors that Japan did not intend to change its past policy toward Manchuria. A few days later (22 May), in response to reported expressions of uneasiness in the United States, Ambassador Matsudaira Tsuneo delivered a statement to Secretary of State Kellogg to the effect that Japan accepted Chinese sovereignty in Manchuria.[52] As stated in *Taiheyō sensō e no michi*:

From the beginning Prime Minister Tanaka wanted to have Zhang Zuolin return to Mukden without disarming his Mukden Army, except in the case of an upset to peace and security in Manchuria, and the general staff headquarters knew it, but on the night of 21 May the Guandong Army pressed strong demands on the army center when the expected imperial order was not received. On the one hand, the general staff headquarters put pressure on the foreign ministry for an expedition outside the lands attached [to the SMR] through operations chief Araki, and on the other, it sent China section chief Col. Tashiro Kan'ichirō to the field and had him tell the Guandong Army not to force the retirement of Zhang Zuolin.

On 23 May the government's policy [not to force the marshal from office or disarm his troops] was passed from Tanaka to Zhang's adviser Matsui Shichio (then in Tokyo), who was working out a line of support for Zhang Zuolin, as were SMR President Yamamoto and Machino. In the meantime, the discontent of the Guandong Army toward Prime Minister Tanaka and the government became more violent daily, and on 31 May, when Zhang's withdrawal from Beijing became a matter of time, the Guandong Army again requested instructions from the army central authorities.[53]

General Araki Speaks His Piece

The wrangling among Tokyo bureaucrats over when and whether to deploy the Guandong Army continued until 29 May, when army, navy, and foreign ministry officials met to air their opinions and come to some conclusion. Since this meeting failed to produce any consensus, probably owing to the refractory position of Araki as much as to any other single factor,[54] the bureaucracy was in a highly agitated state. On 31 May, when the telegram arrived from the Guandong Army seeking instructions, the army ministry sent Abe Nobuyuki directly to Arita Hachirō in the foreign ministry to plead for a decision to send the Guandong Army into action. On that evening the pair journeyed to Shūzenji, where Tanaka was spending the weekend. Abe stated his case, and the prime minister answered laconically, "There is still time,"[55] ending for the moment the Guandong Army's chance to separate Manchuria forcibly from China.[56]

It seems obvious that Tanaka made his decision based on his own optimistic estimate of the possibility for a nonmilitary solution to the *Manmō* problem. Certain ominous portents were certainly a factor in his conclusions, but in Tanaka's view Chiang Kai-shek had tacitly accepted Zhang Zuolin's continued governance north of the Great Wall and the position of the Japanese in Manchuria in return for a free hand in China proper. Moreover, the Old Marshal had at last agreed to evacuate North China without fighting (23 May), and he had all but delivered the "three eastern provinces" into Japanese hands when he signed the railway agreements (13 and 15 May). Tanaka would have been a fool to unleash the Guandong Army under the circumstances. He stood at the threshold of success in China without ruffling the feathers of the Great Powers or contravening treaties that Japan had solemnly signed.[57]

Tanaka's views were not kept secret. There were many in the civil bureaucracy and the army who understood his position clearly, and there were more than a few who agreed with him. How could the Guandong Army staff officers persist for so long in their erroneous interpretation of the government's and Tanaka's intentions? First, they lived under the daily pressure of an aggressively vocal anti-Japanese movement aggravated in Mukden by the daily arrival of thousands of hostile Manchurian troops. They felt the enemy all about them.[58] Second, they were psychologically keyed up for the effort to remove Manchuria forcibly from Chinese control, and they held the Japanese soldier's natural suspicion of wishy-washy diplomatic solutions. Many of the officers, Kōmoto Daisaku for example, could no longer rest content with half-solutions to the *Manmō* problem. With or without railway agreements, they wanted Chinese political control extinguished.[59] In his friendly biography of Araki, Kikkawa Manabu writes: "One gathers from Arita [Hachirō] that Abe privately opposed sending troops outside the South Manchurian Railway zone,[60] but Araki, who heard about the postponement from Abe, raged at Tanaka's indecisiveness, saying, "I don't know what's going to happen from now on, but we take no responsibility beyond this, here in operations."[61]

Araki's bitter protests made little visible headway among his establishment peers and colleagues in the army headquarters,[62] but his grandstanding chauvinism, his ardent championing of the army's constitutional rights, and his oblique attacks on the Chōshū-Ugakibatsu power holders in the government and the army found an admiring audience among younger army officers and his nonestablishment friends. His removal from the general staff in August 1928, the next regular periodic rotation date, indicates the disruptive quality of his activities. In August 1929 he was again transferred, this time from the staff college into exile in Kyushu as the commanding general of the 6th Infantry Division, where he spent two years before his forced reemergence in Tokyo as headquarters commandant in the office of the inspector general of military training. Four months after that he became the army minister (December 1931). His banishment from the center did nothing to still his acerbic criticism of the government and army leadership, and his popularity among the younger officers of the army continued to rise.[63]

By mid-1928 Araki had excellent connections with the Futabakai through Obata Toshishirō, who was then his principal (operations) section chief. Several other Futabakai members, including Nagata Tetsuzan, Tōjō Hideki, and Okabe Naosaburō, were stationed in the Tokyo area — Tōjō in the army ministry. Others were close to the situation in China. Kōmoto was, of course, in a key position on the Guandong Army staff; Doihara Kenji had been recently assigned as an adviser to Zhang Zuolin's army in Beijing at Zhang's invitation; Isogai Rensuke and Okamura Yasuji were with the units in Shandong. Ogawa Tsunesaburō, always close to but not a member of the Futabakai, also worked on the general staff in Tokyo.

The men of the embryonic "young officers movement" knew what Araki stood for through their earlier contacts with the Daigakuryō. They, too, found what Araki was saying in Miyakezaka stimulating. When Araki became commandant of the staff college, he came once more into direct contact with numbers of young officers of elite status, and the staff college became an effective forum for his ideas and those of guest speakers, among them civilian ultranationalists such as Ōkawa Shūmei. Araki's radical speech and action found approval among some high-ranking officers outside the mainstream Ugakibatsu as well. Needless to say, the spirited Guandong Army, whose commander, Lieutenant General Muraoka, was of the Sagabatsu, appreciated Araki's efforts on its behalf.

Araki's message to the army was clear even at this early stage. He was calling for a reassertion of the army point of view and the redemption of the army's position of leadership in Japanese society. He wanted the imperial army to guide the way in China in order to regain its self-respect and the respect of the Japanese people, lost almost a decade earlier. He was already asking the army, especially the younger men, to stand behind him in order to sweep away the corrupted Chōshū lineage, which had learned to serve civilian politicians and bureaucrats, and to replace it with soldiers who served only the emperor. He believed in the righteousness of the army's cause, undiluted by political or economic considerations. Araki, an ascetic himself, saw the Japanese military professional as heir to samurai ideals, the noblest expression of sublime purity in the Japanese experience. He brushed aside the pettifogging arguments of foreign ministry bureaucrats who prattled endlessly about the effects of this or that on Japan's relations with foreign powers, and he heaped scorn on politicians who grubbed for votes among the common people, sold their souls to rich capitalists, and played fast and loose with the defense of the empire when it suited their political posture. He had a vision of a united, proud, and fearless people, armed and militant, organized around the person of the divine emperor. For Japan to attain this ideal in the modern world, it must assert itself in China.

Men like Ugaki wanted Manchuria in order to secure Japan's economic lifeline to the vast untapped resources there, so essential for victory in the reality of modern war. To Araki that goal was secondary. He wanted the seizure of Manchuria to be an act of martial spirit—a clarion call to army and people that the *Yamato damashii* (Japanese spirit) had rekindled. Manchuria would be, first and foremost, a symbol of the indomitable *seishin* that had propelled Japan into the modern world, which could make the nation master in Asia and allow it to rise above its present material woes. Therefore, it really was important for the imperial army to secure the *Manmō* region for Japan and thereby advance the spirit of the empire for greater struggles to come.

This kind of talk, young military men could understand. Araki was direct. Here at last was a general who understood the nature of the army's problems and the empire's. He inspired them to a rededication to soldierly ideals and to the assertion of positive leadership for all of Japan. Araki's promotion to lieutenant general gave him a strong voice in high places. The occasion of the China crisis of 1928 gave his views prominence. In spite of the repressive measures of the mainstream officers, Araki's star had begun its meteoric rise.

The Assassination of Marshal Zhang Zuolin

Before the ruckus over the employment of the Guandong Army subsided, the situation in China took a new and unexpected turn. Early in the morning on 4 June, the calm dawn outside Mukden (today's Shenyang), where the Beijing-Mukden railway passed under the SMR, was shattered by an ear-splitting explosion. A bomb had ripped to shreds the railway car carrying Zhang Zuolin back home, and a few hours later the Old Marshal was dead in his Mukden mansion at the age of 55.

Zhang Zuolin's death had terrible repercussions in the years to come. Tanaka's house of cards, the nonmilitary solution to Japan's *Manmō* problem, had appeared near completion, but the bombing of Marshal Zhang collapsed it at a stroke. The "Young Marshal" Zhang Xueliang, Zuolin's son and successor, soon switched Manchuria's allegiance to the Guomindang, sealing the door against any but a military solution for Japan. For the army it was a self-fulfilling prophecy. The Manchurian Incident of 1931 was the direct result. This, in turn, led inevitably to new clashes between the Nanjing government and Japan, ending in the China Incident, which eventually blended into the larger conflagration of World War II.

The effects within Japan were equally disastrous. The chief of the assassins was Col. Kōmoto Daisaku, the senior staff officer on the Guandong Army staff. Though his part was hidden from the Japanese people and the world until the International Military Tribunal, Far East, met after the war, the facts that proved the case against Kōmoto were known to high officials of the army soon after the event. Tanaka's battle with the army to expose the crime and punish the offenders, however, met a stone wall of hostility. In the end Tanaka's position with the emperor and Prince Saionji, both of whom agreed that justice must be meted out in the case, became irreparably compromised, finally forcing the Tanaka cabinet to resign on 2 July 1929. Tanaka Giichi died some weeks later (29 September). There is little doubt that the "great unsolved Manchurian Case" contributed to his demise.[64]

The permanent rupture in the relationship between the army and the government caused by this untoward affair overshadowed Tanaka's death, however. Friction and suspicion between the army and the government never healed, and it was only a matter of time before the emboldened army, led by staff officers of field grade rank, overbore both the political parties and the civil government. The internal effects on army discipline can be imagined. Colonel Kōmoto's only punishment was a belated administrative decision to retire him from the active service (July 1929). That his flagrant breach of discipline and heinous criminal act went unexposed and unpunished amounted to condonation, thereby weakening the established leadership and encouraging new plots. Although the establishment bristled defensively against judging the offenders, some of the army's non-establishment leaders, like Araki and Mazaki, openly applauded the daring of men willing to take matters into their own hands for the sake of right and the empire. These demagogues commanded increasing attention inside and outside the army. A new atmosphere of instability gripped the army, in which it was easy for politically minded groups of officers to wield power far beyond the perquisites of their rank or the numbers of their direct adherents. The Issekikai and Sakurakai, the Kōdōha and Tōseiha, and the wild radicalism of the "young officers movement" in its kaleidoscopic irrationality all now became possibilities. It was the Issekikai, formed during the controversy between Tanaka and the army over the disposition of Kōmoto's case, that led the way, just as the Futabakai had led to the Issekikai. Kōmoto Daisaku could boast of membership in both. Takamiya Tahei, writing in 1951, explained Kōmoto's pivotal role as follows:

After defeating the rebel Guo Songling in a battle at the Liao River, Zhang Zuolin rode into Beijing with the force of a whirlwind, proclaimed himself generalissimo, and acted like the sovereign ruler of China. A petty leader of bandits at the time of the Russo-Japanese War, after he captured the attention of the Japanese army good fortune made him a king in Manchuria and next elevated him near to kingship in China. He had risen to his present position only with Japan's backing. His having recently given Japan the cold shoulder, in spite of this [assistance], was unforgivable. If only he were dead, even though succeeded by his eldest son, Xueliang, there would be little that the son could do. If he [Xueliang] were to fly the flag of rebellion against Japan, [the army] would have to show him what was what. Feelings of this kind permeated leaders and subordinates in the army.

Kōmoto Daisaku was a prominent China expert in the ranks of the army, and his political prowess surpassed that of his colleagues. . . . He was a powerful member of the Issekikai,[65] and with respect to the China problem he was always in a position to lead the members. Okamura Yasuji, Itagaki Seishirō, Doihara Kenji, and Isogai Rensuke were his good friends and figurative younger brothers; Honjō Shigeru, Matsui Iwane, Hata Shinji, and Tatekawa Yoshitsugu were his elder brothers. Moreover, he followed distantly in the tradition of Utsunomiya Tarō. He was always an advocate of a positive policy in China.

One cannot go so far as to say that Zhang Zuolin was anti-Japanese, but it is true that Kōmoto was one of those most disappointed when [he] showed a tendency to be, to say the least, fed up with Japan. Thus, he [Kōmoto] became the leader in laying plans for the assassination of Zhang Zuolin.[66]

By 30 May Zhang Zuolin's northern armies had retreated to a line dangerously close to the capital. On the evening of 2 June Zhang announced publicly his intention to abandon Beijing.[67] The following evening Zhang boarded his special train for the trip to Mukden accompanied by Machino Takema and Giga Seiya, his two Japanese advisers, neither of whom knew of any plot against the marshal's life, although everyone was naturally apprehensive. Zhang's own forces provided a fairly tight security screen along the entire route. Machino detrained at Tianjin to join Zhang Zongchang's army,[68] but Major Giga remained aboard. At Shanhaiguan Gen. Wu Junsheng, a subordinate of Zhang's from Heilongjiang Province who had already moved his forces from the north to Mukden, boarded the train to join Zhang Zuolin for the remainder of the journey.

Zhang, Wu, and Giga were together talking in the marshal's specially appointed car as the train approached the end of its journey. The marshal had risen to don his overcoat just as Kōmoto's henchmen detonated the massive explosive charge. The time was 0523. The force of the explosion turned the car into a maelstrom of flying debris. General Wu was killed instantly, Marshal Zhang received a mortal wound in the chest, which bled profusely, but Major Giga miraculously survived with only minor injuries. At the time of the impact the train was moving very slowly in its approach to the terminal in Mukden. With several cars derailed by the explosion, it quickly came to a full stop. The fatally wounded Zhang Zuolin was carried to his Mukden home, where he died at ten in the morning.[69] People close to Zhang, however, adroitly managed to keep his death secret until 21 June, when his son, Xueliang, was in a position to take over.[70]

Kōmoto's open dislike for the Old Marshal had been apparent for some time. He had called for his removal both privately and publicly,[71] but it is possible that he might never have undertaken the drastic act of assassination had he not known that many of his colleagues and superiors believed that Zhang must be set aside at all costs.[72] Kōmoto began a plot to that end. He first provided himself an intelligence network along the Beijing-Mukden line to inform him in detail of the marshal's progress. This net, manned by younger officers, gave him Zhang's date and time of departure from Beijing and a description of the marshal's train. Others reported up-to-the-minute information from cities along the way.

At the Mukden end Kōmoto selected the site, provided access to it by compromising the regular Japanese railway guard system, engaged an engineer unit from the 20th Engineer Battalion attached to the 40th Combined Brigade from Korea (at one time on guard duty in Mukden) to prepare the explosives, and arranged a rather flimsy cover story for the men at the scene.[73] He even provided an alternate plan for Zhang's murder if the explosive failed to detonate. In that event a device would derail the train a short distance beyond the overpass. Japanese adventurers (China *rōnin*) would then rush aboard to dispatch Zhang in more personal fashion. These precautions proved unnecessary, however; the original arrangement, in spite of its complicated nature, worked splendidly and the unfortunate Marshal Zhang died without a struggle.[74]

Kōmoto hoped that Zhang's assassination would spark local fighting between Chinese soldiers of Zhang's army crowding into Mukden and the Guandong Army troops concentrated there and that these skirmishes would spread into a general conflict. The leaderless Chinese would be no match for the disciplined Japanese troops; they would be defeated, and the administration of Manchuria would fall by default into the hands of Japan and the army. The better to provide a basis for conflict, Kōmoto ordered an infantry brigade to be concentrated before the Yamato Hotel in Mukden, but Chief of Staff Saitō, knowing nothing of Kōmoto's plot, countermanded Kōmoto's order. In any case, no fighting developed between the Chinese and the Japanese except for a brief skirmish between Zhang Zuolin's bodyguard and Capt. Tōmiya Tetsuo's small force at the railway crossing. Aside from the fact that Zhang Zuolin was dead, Kōmoto's plans had come to naught.

The Crisis in Tokyo over Zhang's Assassination

Since there were no plans to take advantage of the situation in Manchuria other than Kōmoto's abortive provisions, neither the Guandong Army nor those sympathetic to its aims in Tokyo were prepared to act in the emergency created by the bombing incident. Representatives of the army, navy, and foreign ministries and the general staff headquarters met once again in Tokyo on 6 June to seek some suitable course of action.[75] The army suggested moving the 3rd Infantry Division in Shandong into a position to interdict the Beijing-Mukden railway to support the still pending Guandong Army operations in the region just outside the Great Wall. The next day Shirakawa brought the proposal before the cabinet to "test the waters." Tanaka completely rejected the idea and received the support of his cabinet, ending once and for all any possibility that the government would approve the use of the army in an offensive role to detach Manchuria from China.[76]

The time, place, and circumstances of the bombing brought immediate suspicion on the Japanese army not only in the Chinese and foreign press but among Japanese newspapers as well. The army ministry, still in the dark about the nature of the crime, accepted reports coming from the field and on 12 June released an official version of the affair that neither offered any convincing explanation for the incident nor implied even the slightest possibility of Japanese army responsibility.[77] It was not long, however, before disturbing reports began to filter in to the government and the army. Retired lieutenant general Kishi Iyajirō, who had Zhang Zuolin's second son in his care, visited the site and found the army's version of the affair very suspicious. He confirmed evidence of a detonating wire and concluded that no agents could have carried to the site surreptitiously the quantity of high-quality explosive necessary to cause such a blast.[78] This news had hardly been imparted to the prime minister when army G-2 Matsui Iwane, fresh from an inspection of the area, announced to the *Mainichi shinbun* in Osaka, "Behind Zhang's recent death by bombing, one can clearly see the hand of the Guandong Army."[79]

Later a China *rōnin* confided that Araki Gorō, the Japanese leader of Zhang Zuolin's bodyguard, had entrusted him to lead the assassination team into the marshal's private railway car if the explosive charge had failed. It seems that officers of the Guandong Army had approached Araki. This news came to Tanaka's attention through his minister of railways Ogawa Heikichi, who had extensive contacts among the China *rōnin*.[80] In August the diplomat Baron Hayashi Gonsuke, returning from Zhang Zuolin's funeral services, added further to Tanaka's mounting suspicions. Finally on 9 September the prime minister had Shirakawa order the provost marshal general, Maj. Gen. Mine Takamatsu, to Manchuria to investigate the case thoroughly.[81]

The army central authorities had similar suspicions and apparently the trail quickly led to Kōmoto, for on 26 June they brought the colonel to Tokyo and began questioning him in detail. In the formal interrogation Kōmoto admitted nothing. This report, forwarded to Tanaka, eased his mind temporarily, but in private Kōmoto was more candid, telling the whole story to Araki Sadao, Koiso Kuniaki, and Obata Toshishirō.[82] By October the prime minister at last had enough evidence from Mine's military police report and from an army ministry, foreign ministry, Guandong governor-generalcy joint special investigating committee to satisfy himself of army complicity in Zhang's death.[83] Meanwhile, the general staff headquarters, already completely though informally apprised of the facts, began work to "bury it in darkness."[84]

By December the Japanese political world was in complete confusion over the "great unsolved Manchurian case." The army wanted the matter to go no further, arguing that exposing the emperor's army to shame would lower imperial prestige in the world. The general staff gradually won over a great proportion of Tanaka's Seiyūkai cabinet to the support of this peculiar proposition. The emperor, whose wishes seemed to matter little to anyone except Prime Minister Tanaka and Prince Saionji, stood firmly for punishing the offenders. The men caught in the middle were Tanaka Giichi and Army Minister Shirakawa, but Shirakawa proved a reluctant warrior on the political battlefield. The corporal's guard who supported Tanaka in this hour of trial included Navy Minister Okada, SMR president Yamamoto Jōtarō, and that battle-scarred veteran of many political campaigns, Itō Miyoji. On 24 December a determined Tanaka reported to the emperor: "In regard to the incident in which Zhang Zuolin was killed by bombing, even though it is regrettable it seems that soldiers of the imperial army were involved, and we are investigating thoroughly at present. If this proves to be true, [they will be] judged rigorously in accord with the law. The details will be reported to you by the army minister when the investigation is completed."[85] The emperor replied, "[It must be done] so as to maintain strictly the military discipline of the national army."[86] With the emperor's reply ringing in his ears, the prime minister peremptorily demanded of Shirakawa that the army punish those responsible by court-martial.

When the angry Shirakawa reported Tanaka's demand to the army, officers of all ranks in the central headquarters reacted violently, as did Marshal Uehara and the military affairs council.[87] According to the navy minister, the stated reason for the reaction was that if a court-martial were held, the truth would be made public. The government would have to acknowledge the fact that Japanese soldiers assassinated the ruler of a foreign nation. The feelings of enmity of Chinese toward Japan would then heighten, and the Chinese would probably call for the withdrawal of all Japanese forces. In addition, Japan would receive the censure of American and world opinion.

The army elders, convening at Uehara's request, wanted to convey to Saionji that the army alone would handle the matter through secret court-martial proceedings, but the line of defense the army finally adopted was the one advocated by Araki and his young staff officer clique, which sought to prevent completely any embarrassing revelation of the truth. If the army was forced to move, it would dispose of the matter administratively by punishing responsible officers for failing to take proper precautions to guard the railway overpass where Zhang was murdered. Once this decision was made, the army central authorities in solid phalanx resisted every attempt to dispose of the case otherwise.[88]

The 56th Diet, reopening on 22 January after a recess for the New Year's holiday, showed the temper of the political world. The Minseitō attacked Tanaka viciously on the failure of his positive China policy and the government's inability to close the Zhang Zuolin assassination incident. However, attacks on the government over the Manchurian affair were not demands for truth or the punishment of possible Japanese army assassins. They were confined to attempts to embarrass the government and topple Tanaka's cabinet in such a way as not to alienate the army.[89] The questions asked revolved around why the Japanese army had abandoned its guard responsibility to the Chinese, thus allowing Zhang to be assassinated.

The Minseitō leaders, who knew in broad outline the true circumstances of Zhang's murder, sensed a chance to resume power soon, and they wanted no trouble with the army when the opportunity came. For this reason they adopted a pusillanimous attitude, abandoning their public trust and tacitly surrendering to the army's demand for administrative disposition of the case. This further proof of the corruption in the political parties emboldened the army leadership to resist more obdurately Tanaka's demands for the trial and punishment of the military men involved in the plot.

Tanaka, largely abandoned by his own party leaders and under attack from the opposition in collusion with the army, found himself more and more isolated. He suffered an attack in the House of Peers by former military men supplied with materials passed to them by the general staff. "It was also said by informed persons of the political world that the activity to bring about the downfall of the cabinet centered on Messrs. Ugaki Kazunari, Adachi Kenzō, and Egi Tasuku."[90] *Taiheiyō sensō e no michi* observes:

The [leaders of the] army, equating the honor of the imperial army with the fate of Japan, was enveloped in the smokescreen of its activities, and it gradually entrenched itself in a policy of no punishment for Kōmoto. The middle grade [staff] officers of the army, who were concentrated among Kōmoto's juniors, laid the plans for a report to the emperor by Army Minister Shirakawa to the effect that since there were "minor irregularities from the standpoint of security," they would "punish those responsible," and they consolidated [army] unity.[91]

Relations between Ugaki and Tanaka probably never were the same after Tanaka replaced Ugaki with Yamanashi as the governor-general of

Chōsen in December 1927. Ugaki's diary reveals an outspokenly critical attitude toward Tanaka's "positive" China policy after mid-1928, reflecting general army disillusionment with Tanaka and the added devastating effect of Zhang Zuolin's murder. Before an unnamed group of officers meeting at the army minister's residence, Ugaki characterized Tanaka's policy as operating on the "three no principle" — no stability, no spirit, and no statesmanship. Later, he outlined four possible objectives for Japanese policy in Manchuria in descending order of harshness: (1) incorporate it into the empire, (2) make it independent — defended by Japan, (3) plan for further economic development and increased rights, (4) guard existing rights. Shidehara, he wrote, concentrated on the fourth possibility. Tanaka talked in the beginning in terms of numbers one and two, but now he was back to number four. He also noted the adverse economic effects of his China policy on Kansai and Nagoya businessmen owing to the rise of anti-Japanese feelings in China, which he characterized as a stinging rebuke toward a China policy that had come full circle back to the Shidehara policy in a year and a half, leaving in its wake only useless disputes and a trade disadvantage. Zhang Xueliang's defection to the Guomindang was the final indignity, an added cost for an ineffectual policy.[92]

All through spring 1929 the pressure mounted on the prime minister. Although his own party members opposed him, they wished to save the cabinet, so they worked diligently to separate Tanaka from Saionji. Tanaka himself let the matter rest undisturbed as long as he could, but he did not change his view of the proper course. When, at last, the emperor again broached the subject and Saionji pressed Tanaka for action against the army, it forced the prime minister's hand.

On 24 May the military affairs council met and decided, in complete contravention of all the evidence, that the army had no connection with the assassination. As a result the army minister sent Vice Minister Abe to Tanaka to request that the matter be settled in accord with the army's wishes.[93] Unmoved, Tanaka continued to maintain that responsibility lay with the army. On 12 June the "big three" met, and both Suzuki and Mutō insisted that the vacillating Shirakawa oppose Tanaka. On 27 June Shirakawa brought the draft of the army's public announcement of the results of the investigation and the proposed arrangements for the punishment of the offenders to the prime minister's official residence for approval. Tanaka did not approve, however, and he called Shirakawa in for personal talks that afternoon, at which he apparently upbraided his army minister, saying that everyone "from Mizumachi [Takezō], the commanding general of the independent [railway] guard unit, and Guandong Army staff officer Kōmoto on down should be tried by court-martial."[94]

The impasse between Tanaka and the army had not yet broken, but Tanaka had held out as long as he was able. Shirakawa left in a rage, meeting later with Abe, Kawashima Yoshiyuki (chief of the personnel bureau), and Sugiyama Hajime (chief of the general affairs bureau), who agreed that they could not give in to Tanaka's demands. Shirakawa, caught between a prime minister who must keep his word to the emperor and an army absolutely determined to lie its way out of an embarrassing predicament rather than lose face, was on the point of resigning. Had he done so, the cabinet would have fallen. Faced with this alternative, the prime minister at last capitulated.[95]

The following day (28 June) the cabinet accepted both Shirakawa's plan for the punishment of the offenders and the official report of the incident. Afterward, Shirakawa immediately reported the details to the emperor, who gave his approval to a simple administrative punishment for the malefactors but warned against allowing such things to happen in the future. At 1:30 P.M. Prime Minister Tanaka proceeded to the palace to face the emperor, whom he found in an unhappy mood. When Tanaka reported that it would be necessary to dispose of the case in the manner recommended by the army minister (which was tantamount to his agreeing that Japanese were not involved in the assassination), the emperor retorted icily, "Is that not different from what the prime minister said last time [December 1928, when Tanaka had promised to bring the perpetrators to justice in accord with the law]?" and left the audience room. In desperation Tanaka attempted to renew contact for further explanation. The newly appointed grand chamberlain, Suzuki Kantarō, put him off, saying, "If you really desire [another] audience, I will try to make arrangements, but if it has to do with the great unsolved [Manchurian] case, [His Majesty] will probably be unreceptive." Thoroughly chastened, Tanaka withdrew.[96]

Having incurred the wrath of his sovereign, the prime minister was left no recourse but to tender his resignation. He had failed the emperor and Saionji, who had faith that, of all people, Tanaka could handle the army. As related in *Taiheiyō sensō e no michi*:

On 1 July the Tanaka cabinet collapsed. In the end, pressure from the army sank the Tanaka cabinet, which had swum along the line that connected Zhang Zuolin to the emperor. Orders dated 1 July suspended Colonel Kōmoto from active duty, placed Lieutenant General Saitō and Major General Mizumachi under arrest in quarters, and relegated Lieutenant General Muraoka to the waiting list, but in the draft ordering the punishments they were explained only as irregularities in the security provisions of the Guandong Army.[97]

For the first time the younger officers of the Japanese army had forced their will not only on their elders but also on the Japanese political world and the government. It is sad to note that only three men — the young emperor, the aging *genrō* Saionji, and Tanaka, who always seemed to adjudge matters clearly when it was too late, opposed the army's initial attack in its final campaign against Japanese civil government. Not only Tanaka's party, but the opposition as well, fell in with the army's scheme.

In the army even the most rational, level-headed men were won over to the cause of Zhang Zuolin's assassin in the name of national honor. Ugaki, the army's leading pragmatist, opportunistically launched a new career mouthing anti-Chōshū and ultranationalist slogans. Later, in 1931, he may have even lent his name to an abortive army officers' coup attempt against the legally constituted civil government. The Japanese army had begun to lead the depressed nation into a new era of militarism and chauvinism.

8

Conclusion

When the Way is that of the Heavenly Sword,
children are the flowers of heartbreak.

Ōkishi Yoriyoshi

In spite of tragic losses, the Japanese nation acclaimed the army as heroes after the Russo-Japanese War without realizing how very narrow the victory was. For the people, the army and the navy had defeated a formidable European enemy, smashing once and for all the myth of Western military invincibility. They could take pride in this race of Japanese, who would no longer be counted as inferior to whites, and they could provide an example to other Asian and nonwhite people suffering under the heel of Western imperialism. Japan was unique — the nonwhite world power and the only one representing an Asian people. Buoyed up by a new self-confidence, the nation turned to a reexamination of the traditional values it had consciously rejected or neglected during the fearful years when Japan modernized in the image of the West to meet the Western challenge. For the army, the Russo-Japanese War confirmed the principles on which army discipline was anchored — nationalism, patriotism, and above all loyalty to the emperor, the living embodiment of the national essence. Like the rest of Japan, the army could, on reflection, attribute its victory in the face of a numerically superior Western enemy as much to the unmatched, traditional qualities of the Japanese fighting man as to the Western weapons and military concepts acquired and applied over the past half century. After all, the Russians had those things, too. There must be something exceptional about Japan and the Japanese people that made their extraordinary victory possible. True nationalism could not, when all was said and done, be built on borrowed values.

The people tended to consider the defeat of Russia as final, while the army and the government elite knew that the country faced a vengeful Russia. They realized that it would be only a matter of time before the tsars would again challenge Japan's foothold on the continent. Fear of a resurgent Russia gnawed at the army even as the adoration of the Japanese people bred in it an attitude of superiority and arrogance. The social-Darwinistic view of nations, common in late nineteenth-century Europe, impressed Japanese military men as it had their counterparts in Europe and America, adding to their perception of their relative importance to the emperor and the nation. The combination evolved into an apocalyptic vision of Japan's future, which the military men, in their view, faced with a realism and awareness more acute than that of the average Japanese.[1] This awareness later gave them license to exhort and lead the nation to "safety" through the formation of a militaristic, almost Spartan, national defense state.

After the Russo-Japanese War, when the victorious nation began to reexamine and reaccept traditional thought and values, this new conservative tendency did not go unchallenged. Japan was now in the mainstream of intellectual communication, and stimulating Western ideas continued to challenge the minds of Japanese. But the army, as a more or less isolated, self-contained subsociety, received perhaps less influence from the Western intellectual world (with the exception of Western military thought, which had to be considered from a professional standpoint), and it placed more emphasis on the reinstitution and reintegration of traditional values. From this time the army and the people began to grow apart.

Within a few years after the Russo-Japanese War, there was a reaction in the civilian community against growing militarism and increasingly frequent interference in civil government by the army and the navy. Even before the end of the Meiji era, the Diet erupted in opposition to military spending, proposed increases in military forces, and the special position of the military ministers in the government. The world war closed ranks in Japan once again, interrupting this confrontation, but in the postwar period the movement against the entrenched military oligarchy gained new momentum, and the battle between the representatives of the people and the military was joined with redoubled vigor. The apparent victory of the world's democracies in the Great War gave the Japanese people and the Diet renewed faith in that amorphous political form. The victory of a kind of socialism in Russia gave many victims of Japan's capitalist system, or those with pangs of social conscience, new gods to worship. The ideas of both democracy and socialism entered the Japanese intellectual atmosphere in all their permutations and perversions, and they attracted an active and articulate proportion of the Japanese community.

Japan emerged from the war a creditor nation, economically well off by previous standards, and an accepted member of the world of nations. It was, in its new international role, receptive to the world of ideas that surrounded it. Like others touched by the horror of the first "total" war, many Japanese felt a revulsion toward war. The postwar flowering of prosperity, plurality, and pacifism, however, contained elements certain to repel the army. Prosperity was, of course, no evil of itself, but the nature of Japan's wartime prosperity was worrisome. Its fruits seemed to accrue largely to the urban middle class and fostered glaring examples of frivolity and selfishness. Besides, the uneven distribution of the nation's profits could cause internal unrest and discontent, a situation antithetical to national solidarity. Intellectual pluralism aggravated these corrupting influences, but, far worse, it permitted the introduction of beliefs inimical to the foundations of the imperial system and the national polity. Pacifism, a pernicious vector of this new pluralism, was the ultimate rejection of the need for military power, the supreme folly in a world of ferociously competing nation-states, especially in the view of men who had dedicated their lives to the defense of the state and whose highest values lay in its glorification.

All three in varying degrees represented a challenge to a central belief of the Japanese army (and the Japanese people in general) that antedated the modern era — the Confucian concept that the goal of society was harmony. The importance of this belief in explaining the army's ability to enlist the support of the people of Japan in the 1920's and 1930's has been forcefully argued by R. P. Dore and Tsutomu Ōuchi as follows:

The collectivist ideology (to which Japan doubtless owed a good deal of her military and economic strength) had a transcendent moral authority in Japan which was not matched in any other contemporary industrial nation. The family, united and transcendent, demanding the subordination of individual interests to the interests of "the house," was a paradigm for all social groups. The state was likened to the family, with the emperor as pater familias; the enterprise was a pseudo-family; family-like unity was the ideal state of the harmonious village; even army officers were spoken of as "mothers" to the other ranks, who were called their "children." . . .

In Japan . . . the emphasis on harmony precluded the view of society as a balancing of conflicting self-interests. The demand for recognition of one's rights was in itself unworthy. All should have the interests of the collectivity at heart, and it was only in terms of Japan's interests that demands for a change in the status quo could properly be framed. Of course, as is usual in such situations, those who held power could claim a monopoly right to interpret what the interests of the nation were.[2]

The unforeseen *après-guerre* reaction against the military in Japan was a shattering experience for the army, neither used to such treatment nor so apt to accept it philosophically as the British or American armies would, which were quite accustomed to an unappreciative public. The estrangement between the army and the people alarmed not just the army leaders but also the younger officers, who felt the barbs of civilian intolerance more directly. Many of the younger men, following a line of reasoning close to that of Satō Kōjirō, believed that at least a portion of the blame for what was happening lay in the oligarchic nature of army (Chōshū) leadership.

Meanwhile, the army, responding to the opportunity presented by Russian political, social, and economic disintegration, attempted to pursue a course of action that aimed to free the empire permanently from the Russian enemy. The plan was probably unworkable and in any case ended in misfortune for the army, but unable to admit its folly, the general staff found ways to blame the result on government vacillation, the divisive tactics of political parties, foreign interference, and weak and indecisive Chōshū clique leadership within the army.[3]

The failure in Siberia again fixed the army's attention on protecting the empire — that is, Japan's continental holdings in Korea and China. But at the time the army had less to fear from Bolshevik infiltration into Manchuria, Mongolia, China, and Korea than from the activities of Japanese statesmen answering the postwar urge for worldwide arms control. The army's lone victory in World War I, at Qingdao, which led to the acquisition of the German concessions in Shandong Province (confirmed at Versailles), was reversed at Washington in 1922, where the Japanese made concessions that trimmed naval expenditures substantially and ended the army presence in Siberia. That year, the army faced a hostile Diet bent on cutting its size and budget. It salvaged a victory in defeat only by persuading the Diet to accept an army retrenchment plan that eschewed internal reform.

It was at about this time that the most significant changes began to take place within the army itself. Unresponsive to outside pressures for reform, the army for the first time in its 50-year history faced an internal challenge to its policies and leadership, from a small group of young field grade officers. Their rebellion, minuscule in its beginnings, had clearly received the influence of European military thought. One of its objectives was to prepare Japan and the army for total war — the lesson of World War I. But just as clearly, the officers involved in the conspiracy were under the influence of the tumultuous postwar European political atmosphere, which introduced mass political movements, mass political awareness, and revolutionary activism to levels of society relatively inert before. In their conspiratorial opposition to Chōshū's monopoly on army power, the movement reflected the impact of European political thought. "The people" were on the move in Europe, acting against traditional or established leadership in their own diverse perceived interests. That these young Japanese officers met in Europe indicates their involvement in this ideological ethos. They had before them the example not only of civilian activism but also of the activism of Russian, German, and Central European soldiery.

The subsequent evolution of this handful of young Japanese officers reflects the method, though not the ideology, of Europe's activism. Their value system had been set by their upbringing and their military schooling; it was bolstered by the inculcation of nationalism and the habits of collectivism that permeated all of Japan. They had no complaint against the value system of which they were a part; they merely sought reform to restore harmony and justice to it. Neither democracy nor socialism nor any other of Europe's "isms" attracted their notice except as a threat to Japan's emperor-centered national polity, but in using subversion and conspiracy to attack Chōshū, they displayed a current mode of European revolutionary political activism that was by no means new to Europe or Japan but had only recently come into common use.

This slowly expanding movement among the elite young staff officers was the single most important agency internal to the army leading to the unfortunate political-military situation of the 1930's and 1940's. Their organization, the Futabakai, was the focal point of the anti-Chōshū movement. The Futabakai and its offspring, the Issekikai, helped spawn the anti-government revolt against Tanaka Giichi in 1929, which succeeded in covering up one member's responsibility for an infamous international political assassination. Later, in 1931, Issekikai members planned and executed the seizure of Manchuria, and their support helped bring the ultranationalist General Araki to power in the army ministry. Ensuing political differences within the army split its elite members into two primary factions, the Kōdōha and the Tōseiha.[4] Former Issekikai members were active in each. This situation resulted in an ugly internal conflict solved only after the February 26th Incident of 1936 with the victory of the Tōseiha. Many of these former Issekikai men were in the forefront of army leadership during the China Incident and the Pacific War.

This is not to say that the Futabakai/Issekikai led the army, but the organization was at the core of a critical mass of an explosive political movement within it. Their discussions formed and reinforced the thoughts and fears of members and outsiders alike and gave the members the resolution to act individually and collectively in a general reflection of the less well articulated concerns and fears of the entire army. Although the group effectively disbanded in 1934, the army had already gained the great political momentum with which it swept everything before it until 1945, and former members of the Issekikai continued to perform duties at the political center.

The less rational and less sophisticated "young officers movement" reflected the indirect effect of European ideologies and mass movements on Japan in that the inspiration for these men came from Japanese revolutionary sources. Unlike the senior group, they had no direct contact with Europe, but, more amenable to changes in the social structure, many of them espoused homegrown (national) forms of socialism or agricultural communism without ever abandoning the emperor as the central figure of the *kokutai*. The "young officers movement" influenced the trend of army and civil politics for about five years, but neither it nor its individual members ever wielded great power and authority as did the men who rose from the Issekikai.

There seems little doubt that the psychological atmosphere in the decade after the war contributed to the rise of the army in the 1930's. The economic high of 1918 was followed by inflation and the rice riots in 1918 and a depression in 1920. The country had not recovered when the great earthquake struck a crippling blow to the capital in 1923. This was followed by another, more serious depression in 1927 and the world depression in 1929. The army was, of course, no less affected by those events than the civilian populace. As an institution it endured two sizable (and to it ominously threatening) retrenchments, one by popular demand and one by economic necessity. Army personnel suffered economic privations and the loss of livelihood, and young officers responded sympathetically to the depressed economic lot of the army's constituency, especially the hard-pressed peasantry.

The postwar period aggravated old intra-army tensions and added new ones. Yamagata Aritomo's ties to the imperial person had made the position of Chōshū in the army unassailable while he lived, but the changing structure of the army officer corps began to place heavy pressure on Chōshū hegemony even before he died in 1922. The *hanbatsu* system was the first casualty of the still lingering Meiji army structure. But favoritism for Chōshū (and Satsuma) in matters of promotion, assignment, positions after retirement from the army, and elevation to court rank was only a part of the army's postwar problems. Pay and living standards for young active army officer personnel were not subjects for legitimate open discussion, but the economic pressures on the young officers were a certain, perhaps underestimated, factor in army discontent.[5]

External pressures added to the army's problems. Changes in world military thought fanned controversy in an army whose traditions and standards were set in the Russo-Japanese War and which had virtually no experience in World War I. Standards for organization, equipment, strategy, and tactics were debated endlessly. The importance of psychological and economic factors in total war was discussed.

Though the army engaged in no foreign war in the 1920's, its soldiers fought several crucial battles in Japan. Among themselves they battled for a truly national army, which would do away with the privileges long held by cliques built on feudal clan loyalties. By a strange twist of fate the outcome was a new pernicious elite system with its foundation in the graduates of the staff college. A reaction against staff officer domination became a problem of the 1930's. Although the mass of line officers remained politically inert, the "young officers movement" articulated the unspoken grievance of the line by criticizing "staff fascism" and refusing to compete for places in the staff college. Permutations of various loyalties and beliefs factionalized this new elite into warring interest groups by the 1930's. Thus, the sub-rosa movement for army unity ended in further disunity, and the preoccupation with basically nonmilitary problems weakened the army and its leadership significantly.

This internal political struggle was complicated by the impact of postwar European military thought, which emphasized thorough preparation for war on a gigantic national scale to include political, economic, and psychological as well as purely military considerations. It also stressed military organization based on the massive use of firepower. All officers generally agreed on the national collective aspects of total war, but not on the absolute necessity for the provision of new weapons and ammunition in prodigious quantities. As a result, modernization became a political football dividing the army roughly into two camps, one of modernizing pragmatists and the other of those who scorned the unattainable goal of modernization in favor of a "native" spiritual approach to military problems. A reformer like Ugaki Kazunari found himself at a disadvantage because the economic constraints of the decade hamstrung his program for change. The advantage fell to men like Araki Sadao, who stressed inexpensive irrational solutions such as dependence on the human spirit instead of expensive materiel that Japan could not afford. The irrationalists received the support of the young officers, whose philosophy was similarly irrational, and the unit officers, whose outlook and training were rooted in the traditions and perceptions of a war fought in 1904–5.

Ugaki temporarily solved the vexing internal problem of dual leadership in the army by bringing the chief of staff's office under the control of his Ugakibatsu, but when Shirakawa became army minister, Araki was able to use the general staff headquarters as a springboard to launch his own rise to power and to form the ranks of the spiritually oriented Kō-dōha. In 1931, when the momentarily triumphant Araki emerged as the minister of the army, he was unable to duplicate Ugaki's feat. Less radical elements blocked the elevation of Araki's ally Mazaki Jinzaburō to the post of chief of the general staff, and Prince Kan'in filled the office as a compromise candidate. This solution proved durable, for the imperial prince remained chief of staff until fall 1940.

The wave of antimilitarism that struck the army in the years 1920–23 and the growth of ideologies destructive to the established view of the national polity, which stressed collectivism and denied plurality in society, gave the army reason to suspect the loyalty and good sense of the common people. These phenomena led them into a debate with the people that cast army men in the role of teachers to the nation in order to rectify wayward thought by reestablishing the collective ethic and love of country. They thereby reflected their own social-Darwinist fears for the safety of the Japanese state and race in a world struggle for survival. The changed international atmosphere of the middle and late 1920's, which seemed to put increasing economic and political restraints on Japan, swung the debate in the army's favor. The concessions at the Washington Conference in 1922, America's alien exclusion laws, rising tariff walls, increasing opposition throughout the world to Japan's continental policies, and finally, the London Naval Conference, all enhanced the credibility of the army's argument.

In the beginning years of the decade when antimilitarism was rife, the army first defied and then submitted to the demands of the civil government to reduce the size of the army, but international pressures on Japan and the devastating earthquake of 1923 conspired to present the army an opportunity to neutralize its critics and later, under Ugaki, to take the offensive. Popular opinion was as changeable as the economic situation in Japan, but the army clung steadfastly to the righteousness of its position, spurred on by the vision of a future total war. The tide turned when the army placed its officers in the nation's secondary and higher schools and enlisted the Reservists Association to train the youths who did not go on to secondary education. Ugaki laid the basis for the assault on the minds of young people. Araki later greatly expanded the scope of army activity in these psychological operations to the adult population. Both sought an alliance with civilian ultranationalists, and, as the relationship between the army and the political right wing grew, it affected army leaders, the staff officers, and the "young officers movement" in the army and the credibility of the political parties without.

Another major external challenge to the army in the postwar "democratic era" was the rise of political parties and the emergence of party governments. The army faced the situation soberly. Like Yamagata, it had no taste for party governments, but the truth is that the army as an institution handled the parties with relatively little difficulty, at times playing one off against another, but more often effecting advantageous compromises with the "democratic" forces. In the end, economic and psychological conditions weakened popular confidence in the parties, and the parties lost confidence in themselves.[6] Beginning with Tanaka Giichi, the only party prime minister of military background, the army applied divide-and-conquer tactics to force its will on the ruling party's leader and his civil government.

Hara Kei, the first of the party prime ministers, had to establish his bona fides with the bureaucracy, with the army and navy, and above all with the *genrō* Yamagata. He trod lightly with regard to military reform, establishing his own and his party's loyalty to the system as he nudged the army toward change. He held out the hope (since he had no other recourse) that the army could police and reform itself. In this he was mistaken. Army Minister Tanaka, who appeared to favor certain reforms, failed to avail himself of his opportunities. Yamanashi Hanzō, his successor, obdurately refused to countenance reform, given the chance. Uehara Yūsaku, as chief of staff, did not lead the army in those days; he anchored it. When it came Ugaki's turn he accepted the challenge to effect a partial internal reform in which all the initiative lay with him and his followers. By this time, however, the process of change was no longer governed by a tiny group of men at the pinnacle of the army pyramid. A ground swell of rebelliousness within the army itself rose to aid in the defeat of the reformists. In Ugaki's relationship with the parties, however, things went quite smoothly. During his tenure the government under Katō Kōmei had its attention fixed on reform, but its primary focus was not on the army. What Ugaki proposed, the civil government approved, even to the subversion of the public school system. Meanwhile, a new problem had arisen to plague army-government relations.

In Tanaka, Hara had an ally on matters of continental policy through whom army opposition could be partially controlled, but Katō Kōmei, Wakatsuki Reijirō, and Shidehara Kijūrō found no champion in Ugaki. The changing world situation had estranged Japan from the United States and Britain. The reemergence of Russia as a power and the threatened unification of China caused nightmares in the army, whose lifeblood seemed to flow in Japan's continental holdings. Even Prime Minister Tanaka's "positive" policy in China, which stopped short of using force to settle the *Manmō* problem, proved insufficient to mollify the army, whose attitudes toward China grew increasingly aggressive as fear for its position in Manchuria mounted. The army destroyed Tanaka's government, as it had helped to topple Wakatsuki's, in reaction to failures in continental policy. It is ironic that army impetuosity contributed substantially to the failure of the policy.

Added to this amalgam of intra-army and extra-army strife, the individual rivalries between classmate and classmate, the conflicts between officer and officer for the satisfaction of personal ambition within the army bureaucracy, and the individual officer's struggle for economic survival complete a picture of subtle but nonetheless intense competition at all levels of army life. The nature of the military service, based on a spirit of willing lifelong sacrifice, forbade the outward display of ambition. Autobiographies and friendly biographies of army officers may attribute the curse of ambition to the less scrupulous fellows who were in rivalry with the biographic subject, but never to the subject himself. Ambition tended to be sublimated into the support of principle, thus justifying acts that incidentally advanced the subject's own interests. This may have resulted in intensifying belief and sharpening the difference in positions not really far apart. The perpetuation of cliques was at least in part a device to assure personal success through collective action.

It is probably unnecessary to remind ourselves of the bitter personal rivalries that darken the pages of this work — Uehara and Tanaka, Tanaka and Fukuda Masatarō, Ugaki and Uehara, Ugaki and Mutō Nobuyoshi, to mention just a few. Tanaka was a man of towering ambition. The egotistical Ugaki sanctimoniously deplored this flaw in Tanaka's character (as did many others) while he carefully constructed a clique to ensure his own success. These personal rivalries, present in all the army but affecting its performance most seriously among the elite, added in some incalculable measure to the stresses of life within the rigid military bureaucracy.

The Japanese army of the 1920's presents a strange and contradictory picture — a mixture of pride, arrogance, and hubris on the one hand, and the haunting fear of impending calamity on the other. Under assault by advancing technology and aggressive ideologies, the army, fighting a rear-guard action against both, sought refuge in the established traditions of Meiji. The Confucian view of the state as a harmonious family under an imperial pater familias fit nicely into the concept of national solidarity for the successful prosecution of a total war. The idea of the transcendent value of morale and spirit in combat provided a satisfying, if erroneous, answer to a technologically advanced war machine too expensive for Japan to afford. The army's problem was to re-create the lost consensus of the Russo-Japanese War, and it was compounded by the lack of harmony within its own ranks, which, paradoxically, began as a reaction to the injustices of the Meiji system. The warring factions all recognized the need for internal agreement, but each blamed the other for the discord. Even so, by maintaining secrecy on internal disharmony, the army managed a fa-çade of unity toward the civilian population and successfully represented itself as the one institution on which the nation could depend in a time of adversity. The army stood as a shield for the emperor, his people, and the sacred soil of his empire; it was a sword to hew the nation's destiny in the face of world revolutions and international hostility.

It is little wonder that when the army bullied its way to power over the debilitated and ineffectual political parties, it provided no better leadership for Japan than the discredited parties had. The army had failed to reach a viable internal consensus, and soon the disarray within it moved to the stage of national politics.

Reference Matter

Notes

Preface

1. A general officer of the Ground Self-Defense Force who had graduated from the Japanese Naval Academy and served as a naval officer in the Pacific War once told me there were three reasons for the army's domination over the navy in political affairs. First, the army controlled the military police; second, it ran the Reservists Association; and third, it directed the education of the imperial family.

1. The Background to Army Politics

1. *Asahi shinbun*, 1 May 1906.

2. The term *han*, usually translated as clan in English, does not signify an extended family grouping as the term clan does in the West. The Japanese *han* was a hierarchical fraternal military organization, formed only in part of blood relations, based on principles of feudal loyalty passed down from generation to generation, holding in its power a specific geographic area whose people it ruled and from which it gained economic sustenance. In the Tokugawa era (1600–1868) it came to mean the land, the administration, and the people of a feudal lord's jurisdiction.

3. See Hackett, *Yamagata Aritomo in the Rise of Modern Japan*, 54–57.

4. Matsushita, *Chōheirei seiteishi*, 221–27.

5. Imai and Takahashi, *Kokkashugi undō* 1: 31.

6. Matsushita, *Meiji gunsei shironshū*, 78–79.

7. The steps that led to the removal of all civilian controls from the army (and navy), the breakdown of unified command within each of the services, and the establishment of the principles of *tōsuiken no dokuritsu* (independence of command) and *iaku no jōsō* (the right of direct access to the emperor) under Yamagata's influence are most clearly outlined in Itō, *Meiji kokka ni okeru seigun kankei* 1: 3–20, 36–46.

8. For a more thorough discussion of the qualifications for the selection of the two service ministers, see Itō, *Meiji kokka ni okeru seigun kankei* 2: 73–76. The military took the last formal step to complete its independence of civil government on 2 September 1907, with the institution of a system of *gunsei*, or military orders, a special class of imperial edict that did not require the countersignature of the prime minister. The signature of the army or navy minister sufficed to bring *gunsei* into force. Itō, *Meiji kokka ni okeru seigun kankei* 2: 61–73, and Izu and Matsushita, *Nihon gunji hattatsushi*, 165–67.

9. Matsushita, *Nihon gunbatsu no kōbō* 1: 340–50.

10. Ibid. 2: 32–33.

11. Ibid. 2: 9–10.

12. See, for example, Matsushita, *Meiji no guntai*, 164–69.

13. Six generals or retired generals served as ministers of education before 1945.

14. Rikugunshō, *Gunrei, riku, daijūshichigō, guntai naimusho*, 1. See also Rikugunshō, *Guntai naimusho kaisei riyūsho*, esp. 1–14; and Fujiwara, *Gunjishi*, 116. For Tanaka Giichi's role in rewriting the *Guntai naimusho*, see Tazaki, *Hyōden Tanaka Giichi* 1: 249–60.

15. Katogawa, *Sanjūhachi shiki hoheijū*, 136.

16. Smethurst, *A Social Basis for Prewar Japanese Militarism*, 2–3, 20. For more on Tanaka's role, see Tazaki, *Hyōden Tanaka Giichi* 1: 261–67.

17. Katogawa, *Sanjūhachi shiki hoheijū*, 129, quoting the book *Teikoku rikugun* (1913), compiled by the infantry section of the army ministry for the use of the Reservists Association.

18. Bōeichō, *Senshi sōsho*, chap. 2.

19. Uehara Yūsaku Kankei Monjo Kenkyūkai, *Uehara Yūsaku kankei monjo*, 50–55 (Utsunomiya Tarō to Uehara), 140–41 (Ōsako Naomichi to Uehara), 173–74 (Kōno Michinari to Uehara), 463–72 (Machida Keiu to Uehara), 578–90 (Yuhi Mitsue to Uehara).

20. Ibid., 469.

21. Matsushita, *Nihon gunbatsu no kōbō* 2: 112–13; Uehara Yūsaku Kankei Monjo Kenkyūkai, *Uehara Yūsaku kankei monjo*, 150–54 (Oka Ichinosuke to Uehara).

22. In the course of research for a story about whom the army would choose to follow Hasegawa, one newspaper learned that the army's marshals, a Chōshū majority, considered Uehara too inflexible and too prone to involve himself in detail to make a good chief of staff. Uehara Yūsaku Kankei Monjo Kenkyūkai, *Uehara Yūsaku kankei monjo*, 480 (Machida Keiu to Uehara).

23. Imai, "Taishōki" 402: 109–10.

24. General Tanaka's plan for Japanese economic cooperation with and penetration into China is contained in a lengthy report that he prepared shortly after his return to Japan. The text appears in Takakura, *Tanaka Giichi denki* 1: 676–712. See also Tazaki, *Hyōden Tanaka Giichi* 1: 552–81.

25. Imai, "Taishōki" 402: 106–7; Rikugunshō, *Meiji Sanjūshichinenshi*, 326;

and Nihon Kindai Shiryō Kenkyūkai, *Nihon rikukaigun no seido*, 200, 208–9, 214, 217.

26. The U.S. army attaché reported:

The activities of this section [intelligence, general staff headquarters] indicate that large funds are at its disposal. Military attaches abroad entertain lavishly; while the maintenance of Intelligence parties in Siberia, Manchuria, and China to the extent that those countries are fairly honeycombed with military agents, cannot fail to require large sums of money, which are apparently always forthcoming.

It is believed that there is no "common hopper" as far as the General Staff and Foreign Office are concerned, these two organs are non-cooperative, to say the least, and there is no question that the General Staff maintains the more extensive and more efficient service of the two.

Letter from the Military Attache, Tokyo, Japan, to the A.C. of S., G-2, Washington; dated 4 Mar. 1922; subject: "Military Intelligence in the Japanese Army"; signed C. Burnett, Lt. Col., Cavalry; National Archives of the United States, Modern Military Records Division, Records of the War Department General Staff, Record Group 165, MID 2023-386.

27. Takakura, *Tanaka Giichi denki* 2: 140–42.

28. Humphreys, "Imperial Japanese Army," 37–39.

29. Ibid., 56–57. The entire subject of the Siberian intervention and Tanaka's and Uehara's involvement is covered in detail in Tazaki, *Hyōden Tanaka Giichi* 2: 931–1110.

30. Hara, *Hara Kei nikki* 8: 573.

31. Humphreys, "Imperial Japanese Army," 63–65.

2. *The Army Faces Change*

1. Nihon Kindai Shiryō Kenkyūkai, *Nihon rikukaigun no seido*, chap. 1. Takahashi Masae observes that the number of a man's graduating class from the military academy in the early Meiji period corresponds almost exactly to the year of Meiji in which he was born. Thus, Ugaki, born in the 1st year of Meiji, graduated in the first class of the *shikan gakkō* (*Shōwa no gunbatsu*, 14).

2. Saionji Kinmochi, the junior member of the *genrō*, lived on till 1940, but his status was always different from that of the older members. Although relatively inactive, Matsukata Masayoshi, the last of the original *genrō*, survived Yamagata by only two years.

3. Matsushita, *Nihon gunbatsu no kōbō* 2: 204–7.

4. Ibid. 1: 18. The term *gunbatsu* in Japanese military writing is confusing. It can designate the army leaders as a clique or a clique of officers within the army. I use it exclusively in the second, more restricted sense.

5. By 1887 the army had for all practical purposes completed the establishment of its officer training school system. There were many changes over the years, but it basically comprised three tiers. At the lowest level there were the several *yōnen gakkō*, or youth schools, preparatory high schools for the military academy. The second level was the *shikan gakkō*, or military academy, which accepted

graduates of the youth schools plus qualified applicants from the civilian middle school system. The third level was for the commissioned officers of the army. These were branch and specialty schools; by far the most important was the *rikugun daigakkō*, or staff college, whose graduates are the main actors in this chapter and the ones that follow.

6. Fujiwara, *Gunjishi*, 149–50. Fujiwara states that in early Meiji 70–80 percent of all officers were of *shizoku* background, in late Meiji 50–60 percent, and in Taishō only 10–20 percent.

7. Imai and Takahashi, *Kokkashugi undō* 1: 31. The Chōbatsu consisted of not only Yamaguchi Prefecture but also certain clients, often determined by earlier feudal relationships. These included Oita, Okayama, half of Kumamoto, and Ishikawa Prefectures. The Satsubatsu is often described as having as its allies "Kyushu minus Oita." Itō, *Gunbatsu kōbōshi* 2: 212.

8. Takakura, *Tanaka Giichi denki*, chap. 10, and Tazaki, *Hyōden Tanaka Giichi* 1: 440–44, provide the details of his activities in the youth movement.

9. Matsushita, *Nihon gunbatsu no kōbō* 2: 191.

10. Takakura, *Tanaka Giichi denki* 2: 336.

11. Ōtani, *Shōwa kenpeishi*, 13–15.

12. Inaba, *Okamura Yasuji taishō shiryō* 1: 367; Funaki, *Shina hakengun sōshireikan*, 27–34.

13. By far the most important position in the army ministry below the minister and vice minister, who were generals or lieutenant generals, was the *gunmu kyokuchō*, or chief of the military affairs bureau. This post, the only one at this level normally held by a major general, was considered the stepping stone for advancement to the highest positions in the army and was highly coveted by the army's best and brightest. In addition to the signal honor bestowed on its recipient, it was a most powerful office. The bureau dealt with the fundamentals of national defense, armament, and military administration; the peacetime organization and equipment of the army; mobilization of military forces, etc. Because it also dealt with the army budget, this bureau was the contact point between the army, the other departments of government, and the Diet. The *gunmu kyokuchō* was, in short, the only officer besides the army minister and his vice minister authorized to deal with Japan's civilian political world. As a measure of the office's importance, of the first ten incumbents (from 1890) six were Chōshū men and the other four were chosen from their friends and allies. They included Katsura Tarō (the first to hold the office), Kodama Gentarō, Kigoshi Yasutsuna, and Tanaka Giichi. Of the five men who held the post between 1922 and 1935, two later became prime ministers of Japan (Abe Nobuyuki and Koiso Kuniaki).

14. Johnson, *Peasant Nationalism and Communist Power*, 55–58. Okamura authorized the notorious "kill all, burn all, destroy all" policy in North China after July 1941.

15. Takahashi, *Shōwa no gunbatsu*, 54.

16. Nakamura, *Shōwa rikugun hishi*, 28. Also see Nagata Tetsuzan Kankōkai, *Hiroku Nagata Tetsuzan*, 400, 434–35; and Bōeichō, *Senshi sōsho*, 303, quoting Okamura's "Sensō taiken kiroku."

17. The most complete analysis of the Baden-Baden meeting appears in Takahashi, *Shōwa no gunbatsu*, 78–82, a somewhat expanded version of the analysis in his *Niniroku jiken*, 142–44. In both, Takahashi emphasizes the importance of these officers' European experience in recognizing the rise of technology, its complexity, its academic quality, and the close connection of military technology to the people of the nation. He suggests that they felt deeply the necessity for a national total war system because of Germany's experience in the war and the success of the Russian revolution, which revealed the fragility of an imperial system hundreds of years old before an onslaught of soldiers, peasants, and workers. These events also revealed to them that the army must take into account not merely military but also ideological enemies. See also Nagata Tetsuzan Kankōkai, *Hiroku Nagata Tetsuzan*, 433–50.

18. Nakamura, *Shōwa rikugun hishi*, 139, and with more detail, Imanishi, *Shōwa rikugun habatsu kōsōshi*, 36–37. Tōjō Hidenori graduated number one in the first class of the staff college (1885). Terauchi retired the senior Tōjō in 1907 so that he would not have to give high office to a brilliant outsider. According to Imanishi, 37 years later the younger Tōjō avenged his father by vehemently opposing Terauchi's son Marshal Terauchi Hisaichi's appointment as prime minister of Japan. Terauchi languished in Saigon and died there in 1946.

19. Nakamura, *Shōwa rikugun hishi*, 29. Okamura lists six classmates contacted afterward: Ogasawara Kazuo, Isogai Rensuke, Itagaki Seishirō, Doihara Kenji, Kuroki Shinkei, and Ono Hirokata. The group also began enlisting support in other classes. Recruitment took place over several years. Nagata did not return from Switzerland until spring 1923.

20. Uehara's eligibility for consideration for the staff college ran out while he was studying in France (1881–85); Imanishi, *Shōwa rikugun habatsu kōsōshi*, 30.

21. Matsushita, *Nihon gunsei to seiji*, 90–91.

22. Imamura, *Kōzoku to kashikan*, 52. There were stories in the late Taishō period that Chōshū officers taking written entrance exams, where numbers rather than names were used to identify the answer sheets, wrote their names on the backs of their examination papers in tiny characters so that Chōshū instructors could give them special consideration. Whether true or not, it indicates growing resentment at the unfairness of Chōshū predominance in the army at that time.

23. Actually, status within the staff college elite had more than a *Satchō*/non-*Satchō* basis. Top graduates, usually six each year, received the imperial gift, a sword. These men, the *guntō gumi*, or sword group, were almost assured eventual general officer rank. The recipients of the sword and those who graduated only slightly behind them were usually given the choice assignments for study abroad or for service as military attachés. Lower-ranking staff college graduates could expect less exotic staff assignments, although most graduates eventually attained general officer status. Nihon Kindai Shiryō Kenkyūkai, *Nihon rikukaigun no seido*, 271–328. Others identify a special elite among language study groups, the students of the German language having preferred status, students of English, not taught at the *yōnen gakkō*, the lowest.

24. The best description of the *rikudai* selection process appears in Kawabe, *Ichigayadai kara Ichigayadai e*, 14–16.

25. Majima, *Gunbatsu antō hishi*, 15.

26. Nakamura, *Shōwa rikugun hishi*, 139. Horike entered the staff college on 14 December 1922. He testifies that there were no Yamaguchi Prefecture officers selected for his class, although in the class preceding his there were several who made excellent records. He describes his own adventure when he was mistakenly identified as a possible Chōshū clansman during the oral examination; ibid., 137–38. Inada Masazumi, a classmate of Horike, confirms the exclusion of the Chōshū officers but does not agree that the method used resulted from a conspiracy. He feels that the anti-Chōshū officers acted independently. Kido Nikki Kenkyūkai, "Inada Masazumi-shi danwa sokkiroku," 22–25. See also Imamura, *Kōzoku to kashikan*, 52–54.

27. Majima, *Gunbatsu antō hishi*, 15. Gen. Horike Kazumaro tells the story of an officer accused of changing his place of origin by having himself adopted into another family in northern Japan in order to enter the staff college. Nakamura, *Shōwa rikugun hishi*, 138. Tanaka Giichi's gifted adopted son, Nishimura Toshio, was also the target of this type of anti-Chōshū abuse. It may have been a factor in severing the adoption ties between him and Tanaka. Takakura, *Tanaka Giichi denki* 2: 336–37n. Tanaka's biography quotes Lt. Gen. Banzai Ichirō, whom it characterizes as very anti-Chōshū, as saying when a young officer, "There is one SOB we've just got to get, that Chōshū SOB Nishimura. He's smart, by far their best." Nishimura did enter the staff college in 1926. His career was distinguished though not outstanding. He was a major general when the imperial army disbanded in 1945. Nihon Kindai Shiryō Kenkyūkai, *Nihon rikukaigun no seido*, 56.

28. Takamiya, *Gunkoku taiheiki*, 21; Maeda, *Shōwa hanranshi*, 80. Utsunomiya was promoted to the rank of major in October 1898 and became a lieutenant colonel less than five years later, in January 1903 (Nihon Kindai Shiryō Kenkyūkai, *Nihon rikukaigun no seido*, 13). If Takamiya's information (repeated in Maeda) is correct, the Sagabatsu was a venerable institution by the end of Taishō.

29. Takamiya, *Gunkoku taiheiki*, 20–21.

30. Ibid., 21–22. On the occasion of Utsunomiya's death the story was told that, as he lay in extremis, several younger officers of kindred spirit gathered at his bedside, among them Col. Araki Sadao. On the wall of his bedroom was a huge map of the world. Calling to Araki in a weak voice Utsunomiya bade him draw two lines on the map in pencil, one at 60° east longitude, the other at 170° east longitude. "Make just that much Japan's," he said. "All right, do all of you understand?" When they replied affirmatively, he said, "My last will and testament is that alone. I'm finished." He never spoke again. The area encompassed by the two lines included everything in Asia east of the Urals and the present Pakistan-Iran border, Australia, and a part of New Zealand.

31. Itoya and Inaoka, *Nihon no sōran hyakunen*, 106–13.

32. Just one day after the government published in the *Offical Gazette* the declaration of Japan's intention to join the Siberian Expedition.

33. Description based on data in Itoya and Inaoka, *Nihon no sōran hyakunen*, chap. 8.

34. Matsushita, *Rikukaigun sōdōshi*, 186–204. Statistics vary according to sources. Fujiwara, *Gunjishi*, 140, quoting Matsuo Son'in, *Kome sōdō to guntai*, states, "More than 58,000 troops were sent to 34 cities, 50 towns, and 22 villages, a total of 106 places. The dead from the army's bayonets and bullets climbed to 30."

35. Terauchi, as head of the Zaigō Gunjinkai, was shocked to learn that former soldiers actually participated in the riots and were among those arrested. In October he admonished those who performed acts "very regrettable for this association." At the coal mining town of Ube, where a dozen men died in clashes with army troops, former soldiers among the miners organized and led them, using their military skills shrewdly. Fujiwara, *Gunjishi*, 140.

36. Fukuchi, *Gunkoku Nihon no keisei*, 188. A fresh and innovative look at the turbulent social and political scene of the 1920's appears in Gordon, *Labor and Imperial Democracy in Prewar Japan*, chaps. 5–8.

37. Rikugunshō, *Meiji sanjūshichinenshi*, appendix: tables 2-1, 2-2.

38. Fujiwara, *Gunjishi*, 137.

39. Itō, *Gunbatsu kōbōshi* 2: 90.

40. Hara, *Hara Kei nikki* 8: 503 (entry for 5 Mar. 1920). Inukai had not opposed the intervention in 1918.

41. Japan's uneven economic performance in the decade of the 1920's has long been recognized as a factor contributing to political discontent in Japan (including that of the army) and to rising support for the military and popular acquiescence to military leadership. This book makes no attempt to correlate economic performance with military history except in a general way. For excellent, tentative confirmation of the part economics played in the formative stages of the Japanese national defense state, see Patrick, "Economic Muddle of the 1920's."

42. Fukuchi, *Gunkoku Nihon no keisei*, 187.

43. Matsushita, *Nihon gunsei to seiji*, 62.

44. Fujiwara, *Gunjishi*, 138; Ikei, "Kindai Nihon ni okeru gunbu no seijiteki chii," 106–7.

45. Ikei, "Kindai Nihon ni okeru gunbu no seijiteki chii," 106.

46. Utsunomiya Naokata, interview with the author, 6 July 1969. This is in marked contrast to the treatment accorded a regiment (34th, 3rd Division) on its march to Mount Fuji from Shizuoka in June 1919, as reported by Malcolm Kennedy. Captain Kennedy, a British army language officer attached to the regiment, reported, "At every place at which we halted we were given tea and, generally, fruits and cakes as well by the local inhabitants." Kennedy, *Military Side of Japanese Life*, 88–90.

47. Many sources touch on these kinds of incidents. I have used Kido Nikki Kenkyūkai, "Inada Masazumi-shi danwa sokkiroku," 13 and 17; Fukuchi, *Gunkoku Nihon no keisei*, 188–91; Kido Nikki Kenkyūkai, "Nishiura Susumu-shi danwa sokkiroku" 1: 5–7; Kikkawa, *Hiroku rikugun rimenshi*, 354–56; Fujiwara, *Gunjishi*, 138; and Utsunomiya, interview, 6 July 1969.

48. Kido Nikki Kenkyūkai, "Inada Masazumi-shi danwa sokkiroku," 13. For economic reasons young officers usually deferred marriage until they attained the rank of captain. Since *rikudai* students were, or became, captains during their

three years at the school, many of them married during those years. When the author interviewed Major General Utsunomiya (6 July 1969) at his home in Tokyo, the general told stories of the adverse public attitudes toward soldiers while he was in *rikudai*. When I asked him what years those were, he called to his wife in the kitchen to ask what year they were married.

The attitudes toward the imperial army in 1921–23 are similar to those faced by Japan's Self-Defense Forces in the early postwar era. Both Utsunomiya and Nishiura (Kido Nikki Kenkyūkai, "Nishiura Susumu-shi danwa sokkiroku," 8) have noted the similarity. Suematsu, *Watakushi no Shōwashi*, 22–23, also draws this analogy.

49. Fukuchi, *Gunkoku Nihon no keisei*, 189.

50. Matsumura, *Miyakezaka*, 23.

51. Fukuchi, *Gunkoku Nihon no keisei*, 189.

52. Bōeichō, *Senshi sōsho*, table 2. The number of graduates for the fifteen years between 1918 and 1932 are as follows:

Year:	1918	1919	1920	1921	1922	1923	1924	1925	1926
Graduates:	632	489	427	437	344	315	330	302	340
Year:	1927	1928	1929	1930	1931	1932			
Graduates:	294	225	239	218	227	315			

53. Rikugunshō, *Meiji sanjūshichinenshi*, appendix: table 5, shows a sharp decline in the number of second lieutenants after about 1919. Although the Rikugunshō source does not confirm it, Satō, *Guntai to shakai mondai*, 232, testifies that the army was having a very difficult time persuading young soldiers to volunteer to become noncommissioned officers in this period for economic as well as psychological reasons.

54. Matsumura, *Miyakezaka*, 23.

55. Ibid., and Kido Nikki Kenkyūkai, "Nishiura Susumu-shi danwa sokkiroku," 7–8. Nishiura feels that the problem of insufficient pay, combined with popular reaction against the army, later had a strong influence on the actions of young officers.

56. Kikkawa, *Hiroku rikugun rimenshi*, 355–58.

57. Ibid., 358–61.

58. Kennedy, *Military Side of Japanese Life*, 48.

59. Kikkawa, *Hiroku rikugun rimenshi*, 354; Fukuchi, *Gunkoku Nihon no keisei*, 189.

60. Utsunomiya, interview, 6 July 1969.

61. The March revolution prompted Tanaka Giichi, then vice chief of the general staff, to write an article for the army's official magazine in which he attributed the enlisted men's participation in the revolution to the coldness and cruelty of the relationship between officers and men in the Russian army and the distance between the army and the people. He enjoined the Japanese army to let Russia's fate stand as a lesson, emphasizing once more one of his favorite themes — the army as a family; Tanaka, "Rokoku kakumei shokan," 1–3.

62. Matsushita, *Nihon rikukaigun sōdōshi*, 204–9.

63. Fukuchi, *Gunkoku Nihon no keisei*, 190.

64. Kido Nikki Kenkyūkai, "Nishiura Susumu-shi danwa sokkiroku," 8.

65. Fujiwara, *Gunjishi*, 141–42.

66. Kawabe, *Ichigayadai kara Ichigayadai e*, 37. Utsunomiya (interview, 6 July 1969), who served with the Guards Division throughout this period, emphatically corroborates Kawabe's observation of the sudden conversion. Inada Masazumi, attached to the Guards Division, noted, as did Kawabe, that after the earthquake a soldier walking on the street would be quickly picked up by any passing vehicle and sped toward his destination; Kido Nikki Kenkyūkai, "Inada Masazumi-shi danwa sokkiroku," 8.

67. Nakamura, *Shōwa rikugun hishi*, 122–23. This phenomenon has been recorded by civilians as well. See Imai, "Taishōki" 402: 117.

68. The most complete source for data on the army's part in the relief operations in the Kantō area is Rikugunshō, *Meiji sanjūshichinenshi*, appendix: addendum 7, pp. 167–68.

69. Kawabe (*Ichigayadai kara Ichigayadai e*, 36) recalls that he was confronted with unbelievable eyewitness reports of the violent acts of the Koreans when he reached Tabata Station in Saitama Prefecture, north of Tokyo, on his return trip from Hokkaido. Imamura Hitoshi, then Marshal Uehara's aide-de-camp, returning with the marshal by ship from a trip through Japan's South Sea island territories, writes that they received word of the disaster while sailing north past the Ogasawara Islands. "[News of] the violence of resident Koreans was repeatedly received. A message that read, 'Three hundred outlaw Koreans attacking Funabashi Naval Wireless Station. Urgently request aid.' was received from the commanding officer of that station, arousing great confusion in the minds of the men on this lone ship floating in the middle of the ocean." Imamura, *Kōzoku to kashikan*, 20–21.

70. Kido Nikki Kenkyūkai, "Inada Masazumi-shi danwa sokkiroku," 10, reports a colonel in the army finance corps murdered in the Sugamo district because his poor pronunciation of Japanese identified him as Korean to the local vigilantes. Utsunomiya (interview, 6 July 1969) tells of one of his army platoons on patrol rescuing a warrant officer whom vigilantes had trussed up and would have put to death. The man was in uniform, but because he spoke with a Tōhoku (northeast Honshu) accent, in their misdirected zeal they thought he was a Korean masquerading as an army man.

71. *Gendaishi shiryō* 6 (Tokyo, 1963), Kaisetsu, xiv–xv, 91–137.

72. Kido Nikki Kenkyūkai, "Inada Masazumi-shi danwa sokkiroku," 7–10. See also Murakami, *Konoe rentaiki*, 195–200.

73. Itoya and Inaoka, *Nihon no sōran hyakunen*, 237–40.

74. Kantō Daishinsai 50 Shūnen Chōsenjin Giseisha Tsuitō Gyōji Jikkō Iinkai Chōsa Iinkai, *Rekishi no shinjitsu*, 16–38, devotes a chapter to the broadcasting activities of the Funabashi Wireless Station.

75. The imperial edicts and the military government's orders appear in Rikugunshō, *Meiji sanjūshichinenshi*, appendix: addendum 7, pp. 264–70.

76. The details of these incidents are not central to this study, and with one

exception are not treated here. For further information see Itoya and Inaoka, *Nihon no sōran hyakunen*, 230–36; Matsushita, *Nihon rikukaigun sōdōshi*, 238–68; and in English, Stanley, *Ōsugi Sakae*, chap. 11. Itoya and Inaoka claim the government's emergency edicts giving powers to a military government caused the incidents involving the killing of radicals and the Koreans; *Nihon no sōran hyakunen*, 231. There is no evidence to substantiate their contention in the case of the Koreans and little to support it in the incidents where radicals were involved. Neither the government's edicts nor the martial law regulations authorized anyone to kill anyone. The deaths of Koreans and radicals came from two primary causes; first and foremost, panic among the people; and second, individual or group excesses by men in official positions acting contrary to their instructions. The number of recorded incidents in the second category with respect to leftists is relatively small. Matsushita counts fourteen deaths attributable to the military. Ten of these murders, it seems, were of radical workers by troops led by 2nd Lt. of Cavalry Uchimura Haruyoshi (in the incident known as the Kameido affair; in English, see Gordon, *Labor and Imperial Democracy in Prewar Japan*, 177–81 and appendix B), but the number of radicals killed by officials in the abuse of their positions might well be higher than those recorded. Maj. Gen. Utsunomiya Naokata recalls having citizens report to his unit that "socialists" had barricaded themselves in a building in his unit's area of responsibility. Investigating the report, they rounded up twenty socialists whom the unit planned to execute. They thought they could dispose of the bodies in a downtown factory area where many had died in the earthquake and fire. The intervention of the Guards Division chief of staff, Terauchi Hisaichi, prevented the massacre, and the group was turned over to the police. Utsunomiya, interview, 6 July 1969.

77. The most detailed and probably the most reliable account of the "Amakasu affair" appears in Matsushita, *Nihon rikukaigun sōdōshi*, chap. 14. For the argument that the Ōsugi and Kameido affairs tended to reverse the army's popular image once again, see Imai, "Taishōki" 402: 117n.

78. Takakura, *Tanaka Giichi denki* 2: 344; Tazaki, *Hyōden Tanaka Giichi* 2: 48–51.

79. Takakura, *Tanaka Giichi denki* 2: 327 and 334n; Tazaki, *Hyōden Tanaka Giichi* 2: 48–51.

80. Fukuchi, *Gunkoku Nihon no keisei*, 197.

81. Ugaki, *Ugaki Kazunari nikki* 1: 448–49 (entry for 19 Sept. 1923). Within four months Ugaki would be the army minister. History views Ugaki as a liberal and progressive in comparison with most of his contemporaries.

82. Matsushita, *Nihon rikukaigun sōdōshi*, 258.

83. Ikei, "Kindai Nihon ni okeru gunbu no seijiteki chii," 112.

84. This sort of criminal justice in Japan in the 1930's drew withering criticism from European and American observers. Byas, *Government by Assassination*; Young, *Imperial Japan*; and Storry, *Double Patriots*, are well-known works that deal with these trials in varying detail.

85. Matsushita, *Nihon rikukaigun sōdōshi*, 266.

86. Ibid., 267. Amakasu appeared as a character in the motion picture *The*

Last Emperor as the éminence grise behind Pu Yi, the puppet emperor of Manchukuo.

3. The Changing of the Guard

1. Araki, *Gensui Uehara Yūsaku den* 2: 134.
2. Imai, "Taishōki" 402: 114. In 1921 the plans of the general staff still prescribed an enlarged force of 38 divisions. Itō, *Gunbatsu kōbōshi* 2: 102.
3. Imai, "Taishōki" 402: 114.
4. Some people contend that support for military expansion was the pound of flesh Yamagata cut from Hara in payment for his appointment as prime minister. Itō, *Gunbatsu kōbōshi* 2: 74, for example.
5. Fukuchi, *Gunkoku Nihon no keisei*, 191.
6. The triangular division was the basic organizational structure of most modern armies in World War II.
7. Fujiwara, *Gunjishi*, 141.
8. Imai, "Taishōki" 402: 116.
9. Ibid.
10. Araki, *Gensui Uehara Yūsaku den* 2: 134–36.
11. Fukuchi, *Gunkoku Nihon no keisei*, 191–92; Itō, *Gunbatsu kōbōshi* 2: 107; Matsushita, *Nihon gunsei to seiji*, 283; Bōeichō, *Senshi sōsho*, 265. Yamanashi's original "Seiri-an oboegaki" (Reduction plan memorandum) appears in Araki, *Gensui Uehara Yūsaku den* 2: 133–34. Rudimentary work on the development of army air units had begun in 1919 when Army Minister Tanaka, at the urging of Capt. Sakai Kōji, who had recently returned from France, arranged to have a Colonel Faure of the French air force come to Japan for one year with a 61-man air advisory group. This, it seems, was the single exception to the utter poverty of the army in the field of mechanization before 1922. Itō, *Gunbatsu kōbōshi* 2: 103; Kennedy, *Military Side of Japanese Life*, 326–31.
12. Itō, *Gunbatsu kōbōshi* 2: 108.
13. Nihon Kindai Shiryō Kenkyūkai, *Nihon rikukaigun no seido*, 133, 145; Ugaki, *Ugaki Kazunari nikki* 1: 624. Ugaki's statement is open to question, however. At that time Tanaka and Fukuda were supposedly still friends; in fact, Tanaka recommended Fukuda as his replacement. See Takakura, *Tanaka Giichi denki* 2: 336.
14. Takakura, *Tanaka Giichi denki* 2: 336–37.
15. Matsushita, *Nihon gunbatsu no kōbō* 2: 188–89.
16. For the six-year period between 1918 and 1923, only two Chōshū clansmen, Tanaka and Oba Jirō, served in the army's five key jobs. There were others in these positions, however, who can be identified as from clans more or less allied to Chōshū.
17. Matsushita, *Nihon gunbatsu no kōbō*, 13–14.
18. Fukuchi, *Gunkoku Nihon no keisei*, 82. Actually Uehara ranked second behind Marshal Oku Yasukata, who was then 76 years of age and politically inactive.

19. Matsushita identifies the growth and flourishing of a "Uehara clique" during Uehara's long tenure as chief of staff. Primarily a Satsuma or Kyushu clique, it had the strong scent of the staff college about it. This is in keeping with Matsushita's view of a "Tanaka clique" — a mixture of Chōshū and staff college adherents. "Even Uehara, who might have rested content as the army's senior officer, could not forever avoid the winds of autumn as the specter of a revived Chōbatsu, long in eclipse, loomed its great bulk before him." Matsushita, *Nihon gunbatsu no kōbō* 2: 168–69.

20. Matsushita, *Meiji gunsei shironshū*, 125.

21. There are several differing accounts of the entire sequence of events leading to Ugaki's appointment as army minister. Among the earliest and most often quoted is the one in Takamiya, *Gunkoku taiheiki*, 11–14. Major discrepancies between Takamiya's and other versions appear in the works' footnotes and text. Kōno, *Kokushi no saikokuten*, 21–23, carries a version of the affair in general agreement with my own.

22. Araki, *Gensui Uehara Yūsaku den* 2: 202. According to this account, which is probably correct, Uehara provided Kiyoura with a choice of two names, Gen. Fukuda Masatarō and Gen. Ono Minobu.

23. Takamiya describes the two most important individuals so engaged as *machiai seijika*, which might be translated loosely as cathouse politicians, i.e., behind-the-scenes political operatives. Takamiya, *Gunkoku taiheiki*, 11.

24. Takakura, *Tanaka Giichi denki* 2: 330. Tazaki, *Hyōden Tanaka Giichi* 2: 59–76, contains a detailed discussion of Tanaka's problems with Uehara over the appointment of Tanaka's successor that agrees in essentials with my own.

25. Araki, *Gensui Uehara Yūsaku den* 2: 202–3; Takakura, *Tanaka Giichi denki* 2: 329.

26. Takakura, *Tanaka Giichi denki* 2: 330–31, professes some inside information on the discussion of Fukuda's candidacy within the Kiyoura headquarters. Fukuda had become the target of vengeful "socialists" after Amakasu murdered Ōsugi. If appointed army minister, the biography alleges, he would appear in public with the emperor at, for example, the annual grand maneuver, and his presence would greatly endanger the life of His Imperial Majesty. In any case, Tanaka did use Fukuda's relief as his major argument to advance the candidacy of Ugaki. See also Tazaki, *Hyōden Tanaka Giichi* 2: 67.

27. Araki, *Gensui Uehara Yūsaku den* 2: 203.

28. Ibid. 2: 203–5.

29. Takamiya, *Gunkoku taiheiki*, 14.

30. Tanaka, *Nihon gunbatsu antōshi*, 7; Fukuchi, *Gunkoku Nihon no keisei*, 83.

31. Imamura, *Kōzoku to kashikan*, 50–51.

32. Araki, *Gensui Uehara Yūsaku den* 2: 205–6. Ugaki, then 55, was three years younger than Ono, two younger than Fukuda.

33. Takakura, *Tanaka Giichi denki* 2: 331. No text is really clear on this point. Imamura, *Kōzoku to kashikan*, 51–52, whose veracity I question, asserts that Tanaka saw Uehara and received Uehara's reply. All other texts indicate the

contrary. Tanaka's interpretation of his rights in this matter obviated any obligation to await Uehara's reply, since it in no way bound Tanaka.

34. Takakura, *Tanaka Giichi denki* 2: 331.

35. Imamura, *Kōzoku to kashikan*, 52.

36. Araki, *Gensui Uehara Yūsaku den* 2: 206.

37. Takamiya, *Gunkoku taiheiki*, 14.

38. Tanaka, *Nihon gunbatsu antōshi*, 6.

39. Takakura, *Tanaka Giichi denki* 2: 331; Tazaki, *Hyōden Tanaka Giichi* 2: 67–68.

40. Takakura, *Tanaka Giichi denki* 2: 331; Ugaki, *Ugaki Kazunari nikki* 1: 454.

41. Araki, *Gensui Uehara Yūsaku den* 2: 206–12, as summarized in Imai, "Taishōki" 402: 121. A strange argument for Uehara to make considering his record, but in this case he was quite correct. According to Suzuki Teiichi, Uehara wanted to follow precedent and choose the senior man for army minister. To do otherwise would break down the discipline of the seniority system. On the other hand, Tanaka felt that the times called for the ablest man available to fill the position. The episode left the impression that Chōshū still held its monopoly on the personnel system and aroused anti-Chōshū sentiment, which tended to coalesce around support for Uehara. Kido Nikki Kenkyūkai, "Suzuki Teiichi-shi danwa sokkiroku" 1: 262–63.

42. According to Takakura, *Tanaka Giichi denki* 2: 329, on 28 December the day after the Yamamoto cabinet resigned, Uehara, Tanaka, and other high-ranking generals met at a graduation ceremony at the artillery-engineer school. In social conversation Uehara was heard to suggest that the army should agree not to nominate any particular person for the next army minister since the prime minister would probably be Kiyoura and his cabinet would doubtless be short-lived. It was only three days later that Uehara got Kiyoura's ear.

43. Ibid., 331–33. At one point Uehara was supposed to have raged, "This is the dirty work of that SOB Tanaka! He only had his secretary bring me the result of the big three meeting and didn't come himself. That Tanaka's really a bastard!" Other sources contradict the Tanaka biography. *Gensui Uehara Yūsaku den* (2: 212), which would not sully the army officer corps with the charge of lasting internal disagreement, claims that Uehara allowed the disagreement to stand by itself and resumed normal relations with Tanaka. Knowing something of Uehara's character, I find this assertion doubtful.

44. Ugaki, *Ugaki Kazunari nikki* 1: 448–49.

45. Takakura, *Tanaka Giichi denki* 2: 333. The editor makes the claim that Tanaka and Fukuda had been very close friends from their youth. Fukuda's mother was supposed to have said, hyperbolically, that she loved the youthful Tanaka more than her own son.

46. Imamura, *Kōzoku to kashikan*, 52–53. See also Kido Nikki Kenkyūkai, "Suzuki Teiichi-shi danwa sokkiroku" 1: 261–64. Suzuki sees the Ugakibatsu as a spinoff from, if not a continuation of, the Chōbatsu. For him Chōshū power was finally eliminated when Araki Sadao assumed control of the army ministry in 1931; Kido Nikki Kenkyūkai, "Suzuki Teiichi-shi danwa sokkiroku" 1: 271.

47. Imamura, *Kōzoku to kashikan*, 53, attributed to Lieutenant Colonel T. (Tōjō?) and Major K.

48. Tanaka, *Nihon gunbatsu antōshi*, 7.

49. Fukuchi, *Gunkoku Nihon no keisei*, 82.

50. Ugaki, *Ugaki Kazunari nikki* 1: 624. In fairness to Ugaki the circumstances of this diary entry should be made clear. It was written on 1 December 1927, at a moment of great disappointment after Prime Minister Tanaka Giichi had relieved Ugaki as acting governor of Korea in favor of his old crony Yamanashi Hanzō.

51. Ibid. 1: 624.   52. Ibid., 454–55.

53. Ibid., 409.   54. Ibid. 2: 924.

55. Ibid. 1: 455.   56. Ibid., 454.

57. Maeda, *Shōwa hanranshi*, 79.

58. Ugaki, *Ugaki Kazunari nikki* 1: 456.

59. Ugaki, *Shōrai seidan*, 98.

60. Matsushita, *Nihon gunbatsu no kōbō* 3: 28.

61. Ugaki, *Ugaki Kazunari nikki* 1: 455.

62. Takamiya, *Gunkoku taiheiki*, 16–17; Matsushita, *Nihon gunbatsu no kōbō* 3: 32; and Maeda, *Shōwa hanranshi*, 79–80. Of the seventeen men who formed the basis of the Ugakibatsu, thirteen became (full) generals; among these were six army ministers, three chiefs of staff, and two inspectors general of military training. Two, Hata Shunroku and Sugiyama, were promoted to marshal; three became cabinet ministers; and two, Abe and Koiso, were prime ministers. Of the remaining four, all of whom became lieutenant generals, Tsuno died at 54, Tatekawa became ambassador to Russia (1940–42), and Ninomiya became minister of education in Koiso's cabinet. These talented men were all graduates of the staff college. Compiled from data in Matsushita, *Nihon gunbatsu no kōbō* 3: 297–305, and Nihon Kindai Shiryō Kenkyūkai, *Nihon rikukaigun no seido*.

63. Matsushita, *Nihon gunbatsu no kōbō* 3: 32, and Takamiya, *Gunkoku taiheiki*, 18. Itō, *Gunbatsu kōbōshi* 2: 119–20, also points out that the Ugaki (Taishō) *gunbatsu* marked a transition from the Meiji *gunbatsu* of the *hanbatsu* variety to the Shōwa *gunbatsu* of the *gakubatsu*, or school clique, variety. Itō counts Tanaka, Ugaki, and — for the navy — Katō Tomosaburō as founders of new-style "rational cliques," which eschewed militarism and denied the routine use of special privilege for the benefit of the military. In this sense the Taishō *gunbatsu* were different from their predecessors and successors.

64. Imai, "Taishōki" 402: 121.

65. Matsushita, *Nihon gunbatsu no kōbō* 3: 32.

66. Takamiya, *Gunkoku taiheiki*, 18–19.

67. Takakura, *Tanaka Giichi denki* 2: 379.

68. Ibid., 381–82.

69. Matsushita, *Nihon gunbatsu no kōbō* 3: 32; Takamiya, *Gunkoku taiheiki*, 16. Takamiya assures us that forcing the retirement of his seniors caused Ugaki unendurable pangs of compassion. This probably was not the case. Ugaki would have been more likely to relish the prospect. Yamanashi Hanzō probably

saw no disadvantage to leaving the army when he did because he stepped into a position of leadership in the Seiyūkai beside his old friend and benefactor Tanaka Giichi.

70. Matsushita, *Nihon gunbatsu no kōbō* 3: 32. There has been a great deal stated and repeated in books commenting on army politics concerning Tanaka's motives toward the army and Ugaki in his voluntary retirement into the reserves. Several volumes—e.g., Takamiya, *Gunkoku taiheiki*, 16; Matsushita, *Nihon gunbatsu no kōbō* 3: 31; Itō, *Gunbatsu kōbōshi* 2: 126—indicate that one important, if not the sole, reason for Tanaka's retirement was to give Ugaki a free hand for his reform plans and to help him get rid of dead wood at the top of the army hierarchy. I find no evidence to support this contention in Takakura, *Tanaka Giichi denki* (2: 378–81), which states that, quite to the contrary, Tanaka had lost interest in army affairs and was thinking almost completely about his own career in politics. That he did not sever his army ties until his presidency of the Seiyūkai was assured, indicates that he was principally interested in protecting Tanaka Giichi. The coincidence of Tanaka's retirement and Ugaki's opportunity to trim the army upper ranks was probably fortuitous.

4. Reduction and Modernization

1. Tanaka, *Nihon gunbatsu antōshi*, 13.
2. Ugaki, *Shōrai seidan*, 98.
3. The army sent attachés to the legations and embassies in many European states; officers of various ranks went on European trips. Leading graduates of the *rikudai* were regularly sent for further study in Europe. Statistics show that, among the first 25 classes of the staff college from 1885 to 1913, fully half of the graduates went to the Central Powers: Germany 79, Austria 2, France 28, Russia 26, Great Britain 21, others 5. Compiled from data in Nihon Kindai Shiryō Kenkyūkai, *Nihon rikukaigun no seido*.
4. Ludendorff, *My War Memories*, 2–12, 360–78, and 765–71, carries the essence of Ludendorff's argument on the demoralization of the German government and populace and the effectiveness of Allied psychological warfare.
5. Fukuchi, *Gunkoku Nihon no keisei*, 191.
6. Hayashi, *Taiheiyō sensō rikugun gaishi*. See also Fujiwara, *Gunjishi*, 148–49. For the most complete discussion of Japanese army strategy and defense planning in this period, see Bōeichō, *Senshi sōsho*, 229–311.
7. Nakamura, *Shōwa rikugun hishi*, 125 (Horike interview).
8. Matsumura, *Miyakezaka*, 33–34. At that time the Japanese army clung to the doctrine of "artillery and infantry on the same line." To place the artillery far behind and shoot at the enemy from concealed positions was thought cowardly and debilitating to the morale of one's forces. In some measure the army's persistence in this reasoning right up to the end of the Pacific War was one of the reasons for its weakness in combat against Western armies. Kobayashi was such a controversial figure that he retired in 1924 as a colonel. He published his well-known *Rikugun no konpon kaizō* (Basic reform of the army) in that year.

9. Nihon Kindai Shiryō Kenkyūkai, *Nihon rikukaigun no seido*, 34.

10. Ibid., 9.

11. Yokoyama, *Hiroku Ishiwara Kanji*, 128–39; Peattie, *Ishiwara Kanji and Japan's Confrontation with the West*, 49–50.

12. Itō, *Gunbatsu kōbōshi* 2: 101–2.

13. Kennedy, *Military Side of Japanese Life*, 331–32.

14. Itō, *Gunbatsu kōbōshi* 2: 104.

15. Tanaka, *Nihon gunbatsu antōshi*, 11.

16. Nakamura, *Shōwa rikugun hishi*, 127 (Horike interview).

17. Itō, *Gunbatsu kōbōshi* 2: 104.

18. Tanaka, *Nihon gunbatsu antōshi*, 12.

19. Fujiwara, *Gunjishi*, 139.

20. Itō (*Gunbatsu kōbōshi* 2: 102) likens the army's action to that of "a country samurai lording it over the peasants of the area with sword and spear." He also recollects that "every one of the army officers that this writer knew in England and France at that time, without exception, deplored the fact that the Japanese army would fall into a weak third- or fourth-rate status if it did not terminate the Siberian Expedition and use its military appropriations to modernize immediately."

21. Bōeichō, *Senshi sōsho*, 268.

22. Fujiwara, *Gunjishi*, 140.

23. For one explanation of this process in Japan, see Gordon, *Labor and Imperial Democracy in Prewar Japan*, 13–63.

24. Ugaki, *Ugaki Kazunari nikki* 1: 448. Ugaki became Tanaka's vice minister in October.

25. Rikugunshō, *Meiji sanjūshichinenshi*, appendix: 381; Imai, "Taishōki" 402: 118. Proposed for the army budget of 1924 under Tanaka; passed by the Diet after Ugaki became army minister.

26. "A strange sequel to the Conference was a book published in the United States, *The Black Chamber*, by Herbert O. Yardley, formerly of the Telegraph Section of the State Department. According to this book, the United States decoded secret instructions sent to the Japanese delegates. Knowing that they were being instructed to accept as the last alternative the 5-5-3 ratio, the other Powers demanded of the Japanese the utmost in concessions. Yardley's book was a sensational best-seller in Japan. It was used by the Army to discredit the Foreign Office and to colour the picture of the 'world against Japan'." Lory, *Japan's Military Masters*, 164.

27. Ōtani, *Shōwa kenpeishi*, 59–62, carries a detailed account of this incident.

28. Rikugunshō, *Meiji sanjūshichinenshi*, appendix: 381.

29. Imai, "Taishōki" 402: 117–18; and Ikei, "Kindai Nihon ni okeru gunbu no seijiteki chii," 108–9.

30. Itō, *Gunbatsu kōbōshi* 2: 102. "To change the minds of the army leaders would have been as difficult as changing an old scholar of the Chinese classics into an English professor. There was no way to treat these stoneheads other than to

replace them. Though it was 1920, they pursued the ideas of 1900 and gainsaid the new knowledge. Even though they mouthed agreement with the new weapons and scientific change, they did the opposite in action."

31. Ugaki, *Shōrai seidan*, 98.

32. Bōeichō, *Senshi sōsho*, 265.

33. Ugaki, *Ugaki Kazunari nikki* 1: 464.

34. Ibid. Having had their own way for so long, Ugaki and the army were apparently disturbed by the pressures the political parties could now bring to bear on them. See also Ikei, "Kindai Nihon ni okeru gunbu no seijiteki chii," 107–8.

35. Imai, "Taishōki" 402: 122.

36. Takamiya, *Gunkoku taiheiki*, 16.

37. Bōeichō, *Senshi sōsho*, 265–66.

38. Ibid.

39. Ugaki, *Ugaki Kazunari nikki* 1: 459. Ugaki, elated, wrote of its passage as "my military operations in both houses."

40. Itō, *Gunbatsu kōbōshi* 2: 114.

41. Fukuchi, *Gunkoku Nihon no keisei*, 193.

42. Imai and Takahashi, *Kokkashugi undō* 1: 33.

43. Bōeichō, *Senshi sōsho*, 266; Matsushita, *Nihon gunsei to seiji*, 285. The army provided officers for all public secondary schools and colleges and to private schools and colleges on request.

44. Fukuchi, *Gunkoku Nihon no keisei*, 245.

45. Fujiwara, *Gunjishi*, 150–51. Fujiwara is a bit extreme when he deduces from Ugaki's comments on military training in the schools that the army did not seek it for its military value, but in order to gain control over the people and lead them to militarism.

46. Pyle, "Technology of Japanese Nationalism," 52–53, notes "the significance of political initiative in the making of Japanese nationalism and the role of decision-making in the maintenance of political integration. The Local Improvement Movement and similar campaigns which followed in the 1920's and 1930's are evidence of bureaucratic concern with what I would call 'the technology of nationalism.' In these efforts bureaucrats were devising techniques to mobilize the material and spiritual resources of the population in order to cope with social problems and to provide support for Japanese imperialism. Leadership faced a continuing challenge to find ways of absorbing newly awakening groups into the political community so as to prevent alienation and disruption. These campaigns, carried out largely under the auspices of the home ministry, played a decisive role in shaping the political community of the 1930's." The cooperation of the army ministry and the education ministry in these instances seems to support Pyle's thesis that the bureaucracy consciously manipulated segments of the population for the purpose of developing a spirit of nationalism.

47. Fukuchi, *Gunkoku Nihon no keisei*, 246–48.

48. Fujiwara, *Gunjishi*, 146, 151. That Ugaki was most concerned with this problem is quite evident. His career had close connections with the army personnel administration system for years, and entries in his diary express this anxiety. For

example, in *Ugaki Kazunari nikki* 1: 409 (spring 1923), he notes, "Hand in hand with the drop in volunteers for student officers, there has been a decline in their educational attainments and a lowering of their social status. In other words the number [of volunteers from] aristocratic and wealthy families has decreased." A discussion of the makeup of the army officer corps for the late Taishō and early Shōwa periods appears in Fujiwara, *Gunjishi*, 156–61.

49. Itō, *Gunbatsu kōbōshi* 2: 108–9. Itō (*Gunbatsu kōbōshi* 2: 114) states that the army patterned the school training program after the U.S. R.O.T.C. program provided for in the National Defense Act of 1919.

50. Fukuchi, *Gunkoku Nihon no keisei*, 194.

51. Ugaki, *Ugaki Kazunari nikki* 1: 467–68.

52. Fujiwara, *Gunjishi*, 152.

53. Itō, *Gunbatsu kōbōshi* 2: 230.

54. Crowley, "Japanese Army Factionalism," 313.

55. Matsushita, *Nihon gunsei to seiji*, 260, 268, 285–86.

56. Fukuchi, *Gunkoku Nihon no keisei*, 194.

57. Itō, *Gunbatsu kōbōshi* 2: 111.

58. Tazaki, *Hyōden Mazaki Jinzaburō*, 32–33. Original in "Arashi no ato-saki: Niniroku jiken no okiru made," *Jiron*, August 1949.

59. Koiso, *Katsuzan kōsō*, 453–64.

60. Humphreys, "The Imperial Japanese Army, 1918–1929," 207.

61. Tanaka, *Nihon gunbatsu antōshi*, 14. That these officers were not accepted, created a serious and lasting problem, but not one unexpected among Japanese. Tanaka attributes the inability to absorb these transferred officers to the "exclusive and feudal Japanese character."

62. Matsushita, *Nihon gunbatsu no kōbō* 3: 31.

63. Nakamura, *Tennōsei fuashizumu ron*, 88.

64. Nakamura, *Shōwa rikugun hishi*, 125 (Horike interview).

65. Bōeichō, *Senshi sōsho*, 266.

66. Itō, *Gunbatsu kōbōshi* 2: 112.

67. Ugaki, *Ugaki Kazunari nikki* 1: 468–69.

68. Tanaka, *Nihon gunbatsu antōshi*, 14.

69. Ikei, "Kindai Nihon ni okeru gunbu no seijiteki chii," 107.

70. Takahashi, *Shōwa no gunbatsu*, 42.

71. Tanaka, *Nihon gunbatsu antōshi*, 15–16.

72. Fukuchi, *Gunkoku Nihon no keisei*, 194–95.

73. Kennedy, *Military Side of Japanese Life*, 120–22.

74. Itō, *Gunbatsu kōbōshi* 2: 231.

75. Bōeichō, *Senshi sōsho*, 268.

76. Fujiwara, *Gunjishi*, 147–48.

77. Matsumura, *Miyakezaka*, 32–33.

78. Nakamura, *Shōwa rikugun hishi*, 130 (Horike interview). Horike's reference to a third and fourth arms reduction means that he counts the two Yamanashi reductions as one and the Ugaki reduction as the second. This is often done because the second Yamanashi reduction (1923) was really not significant.

79. Ibid. Horike returned from Russia in 1932, where he had been overwhelmed by the concepts of armored warfare being developed in cooperation with officers of the German army. Horike's phrase "human bullets" (literally, "meat bullets," but not usually so translated) refers to Japanese tactics of the Russo-Japanese War when army troops stormed position after position in the face of withering Russian fire, at terrible human cost but with victorious result. The famous book *Nikudan* (Human bullets; Tokyo, 1906) by Sakurai Tadayoshi, translated into every major European language and widely read throughout the world, glorified the Japanese army, its soldiers, and their *seishin*. This spirit of sacrifice became the ideal of the army thereafter.

80. Matsumura, *Miyakezaka*, 33.

81. Itō, *Gunbatsu kōbōshi* 2: 105.

82. Nakamura, *Shōwa rikugun hishi*, 126 (Horike interview).

83. Ugaki, *Ugaki Kazunari nikki* 1: 632–33.

84. Tanaka, *Nihon gunbatsu antōshi*, 7–8.

85. Nihon Kindai Shiryō Kenkyūkai, *Nihon rikukaigun no seido*, 146, 150; Kikkawa, *Arashi to tatakau tesshō Araki*, 67–68. (Kikkawa is in error concerning the time of Kawai's retirement.)

86. Imamura, *Kōzoku to kashikan*, 54–55.

87. Koiso, *Katsuzan kōsō*, 474.

88. Ibid., 478, 482.

89. Kikkawa, *Arashi to takakau tesshō Araki*, 68.

90. Ibid., 51, 61; Takahaski, *Kokkashugi undō* 2: 685.

91. Bōeichō, *Senshi sōsho*, 267. Araki is generally credited with bringing the term *kōgun*, literally "army of the emperor," into general use. The quote is a passage from *Tōsui kōryō*.

92. Kikkawa, *Arashi to tatakau tesshō Araki*, 70–73.

93. Tsuchikata, " 'Gunjin seishin' no ronri," 32.

94. Maeda, *Shōwa hanranshi*, 79.

5. The Growth of Dissidence

1. Matsushita, *Nihon gunbatsu no kōbō* 2: 181–82.

2. Ibid., 185.

3. Ibid., 184.

4. Tanaka, *Nihon gunbatsu antōshi*, 14.

5. Maeda, *Shōwa hanranshi*, 83.

6. Matsushita, *Nihon gunsei to seiji*, 79–80.

7. Takahashi, *Shōwa no gunbatsu*, 55–60; Funaki, *Shina hakengun sōshireikan*, 184–89; and Itō, *Shōwa shoki seijishi kenkyū*, 284–89. Almost all detail on meetings of the Futabakai comes from Okamura Yasuji's diary. The Futabakai was an informal organization and is sometimes referred to as the Dōjinkai (Friends Club). Okamura identifies the eighteen members of the association, in his diary entry for 1 January 1929, as Kōmoto Daisaku, Yamaoka Shigeatsu, 15th class; Doihara Kenji, Isogai Rensuke, Itagaki Seishirō, Kuroki Shinkei, Nagata Tetsuzan,

Obata Toshishirō, Ogasawara Kazuo, Okamura Yasuji, Ono Hirokata, 16th class; Kudō Yoshio, Matsumura Masakazu, Tōjō Hideki, Watari Hisao, 17th class; Okabe Naosaburō, Nakano Chokuzō, and Yamashita Tomoyuki, 18th class. Kuroki had left the service in 1920 but was active in the group because of a continuing friendship with his classmate Obata. A nineteenth member, Iida Sadakata, 17th class, joined in April 1929.

8. "Issekikai to Futabakai yurai," in *Daitōa (taiheiyō) sensō senshi sōsho*, appendix 8: 1; and Kido Nikki Kenkyūkai, "Suzuki Teiichi-shi danwa sokkiroku" 1: 10, 215–16, 258–59.

9. Kido Nikki Kenkyūkai, "Suzuki Teiichi-shi danwa sokkiroku" 1: 10; and Takahashi, *Shōwa no gunbatsu*, 55–60. The names of these associations remain something of an anomaly. Okamura, who apparently likes names for things, freely uses the terms Futabakai, Mokuyōkai, and Issekikai (Takahashi, *Shōwa no gunbatsu*, 55–63). Only the last of these seems to have an agreed basis. Suzuki Teiichi insists that his group (Mokuyōkai) never had any name at all, and he also states that he knew of the Futabakai, but never by that specific name or any other (Kido Nikki Kenkyūkai, "Suzuki Teiichi-shi danwa sokkiruku" 1: 10, 2: 323). The Issekikai was apparently named on the eve of its foundation by Tsuchihashi Yūichi (Takahashi, *Shōwa no gunbatsu*, 61). To muddy the waters, Tanaka Kiyoshi (29th class), an active member of the Sakurakai in the early 1930's, tells us in his memoir that soon after he joined the army ministry in August 1928 he was approached by Major Suzuki and asked to participate in a study group. Tanaka writes that the group's aims were not clear, but they seemed to be the reform of the state. He also tells us that there were widely divergent views within the group and that it broke up when Suzuki went to Europe (Feb. 1929); subsequently, he (Tanaka) and three other officers of the 29th and 30th classes continued their own researches, later joining the Sakurakai when it was founded. OO Shōsa, "Iwayuru jūgatsu jiken ni kansuru shuki," in Imai and Takahashi, *Kokkashugi undō* 1: 651. Itō (*Shōwa shoki seijishi kenkyū*, 289 n3) comments that no member of the 29th or 30th classes ever entered the Issekikai, and he surmises that Tanaka Kiyoshi's group, carrying on their research separately, gravitated to the Sakurakai, which was formed largely of men from their own classes. Suzuki Teiichi mentions recruiting Takashima Tatsuhiko (30th class) into the Mokuyōkai. Kido Nikki Kenkyūkai, "Suzuki Teiichi-shi danwa sokkiroku" 1: 259. He mentions no other juniors specifically, but the implication is that there could have been others. Itō, *Shōwa shoki seijishi kenkyū*, 287, provides an annotated list of Mokuyōkai members. See also Funaki, *Shina hakengun sōshireikan*, 194–204.

10. Kido Nikki Kenkyūkai, "Suzuki Teiichi-shi danwa sokkiroku" 1: 3–4, 10–11, 58–61, 258–59.

11. Ibid., 257–58.

12. Only two sources give us the scant firsthand detail that is available on the merger, and some of that is mistaken or contradictory. They are Okamura Yasuji's diary and Tsuchihashi Yūichi's "Issekikai to Sakurakai," pertinent parts of which appear in *Daitōa (taiheiyō) sensō senshi sōsho*, appendix 8. Other attempts to explain what happened appear in Takahashi, *Shōwa no gunbatsu*, 57–63; Funaki,

Shina hakengun sōshireikan, 205–9; and Itō, *Shōwa shoki seijishi kenkyū*, 284–89. Suzuki Teiichi is of no help in describing the merger because he was posted to Great Britain in February 1929.

13. The Issekikai continued to meet until 1934, although a rift had long since developed between Obata and Nagata. Several neutral members attempted to mediate between them but to no avail, and meetings apparently ceased completely in April of that year. See Inaba, *Okamura Yasuji taishō shiryō*, 368–69; Funaki, *Shina hakengun sōshireikan*, 244–51.

14. Data complete except for Matsumura Masakazu, Nakano Chokuzō, and Ono Hirokata, for whom I have no information. Data largely from Nihon Kindai Shiryō Kenkyūkai, *Nihon rikukaigun no seido*; and Takahashi, *Shōwa no gunbatsu*, chap. 2.

15. Matsushita, *Nihon gunbatsu no kōbō* 3: 99. (As one example of this prejudice, Okamura Yasuji once admitted that, beginning in August 1929, when he took over, he allowed no high school graduates in his officer personnel section. Takahashi, *Shōwa no gunbatsu*, 71.) Matsushita considers the *yōnen gakkō* clique and the *rikudai* clique to be the two great cliques in the army from the late Meiji period on. Matsushita, *Nihon gunbatsu no kōbō* 2: 186. Virtually all the smaller cliques (subcliques?), whether based on geographic background, language study, personal following, or political belief, traced their roots to officers whose background classified them as members of one or both of these two "generic" cliques. The *yōnen gakkō* clique (or cliques) is the more complicated of the two because it was differentiated not only vertically by year and class standing but also geographically. There were six of these youth schools. The Hiroshima *yōnen gakkō* was dominated by Chōshū students. The Kumamoto *yōnen gakkō* was identified with Kyushu generally; in addition, strong clan rivalries persisted among the students from Kagoshima (Satsuma) and Saga (Hizen), etc. The clan-based cliques (*hanbatsu*), which continued into the Shōwa era — e.g., the Sagabatsu — probably depended on common experiences in *yōnen gakkō*, in this case in Kumamoto, for the continuation of clan identification among Saga officers.

16. All statistics compiled from material in Nihon Kindai Shiryō Kenkyūkai, *Nihon rikukaigun no seido*. Takahashi, *Shōwa no gunbatsu*, 70, identifies three exceptions: Watari Hisao, Suzuki Teiichi, and Okada Tasuku.

17. Matsushita, *Nihon gunbatsu no kōbō* 3: 101.

18. Takahashi, *Shōwa no gunbatsu*, 68; Takahashi, *Niniroku jiken*, 145.

19. Takahashi, *Shōwa no gunbatsu*, 59 and 61–63; Nagata Tetsuzan Kankōkai, *Hiroku Nagata Tetsuzan*, 449–50; Kido Nikki Kenkyūkai, "Suzuki Teiichishi danwa sokkiroku" 2: 367–87.

20. Among them, Kōmoto, Okamura, Isogai, Itagaki, Doihara, Suzuki Teiichi, and Nemoto Hiroshi. As Okamura Yasuji said, "From the time I was young, I had the dream of working on the continent in China and made an agreement with kindred souls and classmates Doihara, Itagaki, and Isogai, who shared the same dream." Inaba, *Okamura Yasuji taishō shiryō* 2: 367. It was this man who devastated North China in the early 1940's.

21. All three officers had broad contacts with younger officers, Hayashi and

Araki at the staff college and Mazaki at the military academy. Mazaki was in charge of the regular course (*honka*), August 1923–February 1924. He became assistant commandant in May 1922 and commandant from March 1926 until August 1927. Young officers who graduated during his tenure were the central figures in the "young officers movement" and the February 26th Incident of 1936. Mazaki invited the civilian nationalist Ōkawa Shūmei to speak as a guest lecturer at the military academy. Tanaka, *Nihon gunbatsu antōshi*, 18–19. Araki extended the same privilege to Ōkawa at the staff college.

22. Takahashi, *Shōwa no gunbatsu*, 68; Takahashi, *Niniroku jiken*, 145; Itō, *Shōwa shoki seijishi kenkyū*, 284–85.

23. Imai and Takahashi, *Kokkashugi undō* 1: 27. The most important of these was Dr. Ōkawa Shūmei, an employee of the South Manchurian Railway Corporation, who had worked for the army as a translator from his college days. He was able to come and go freely at Miyakezaka (the site of the army ministry and the general staff headquarters in Tokyo), and after 1919 Ōkawa began, over a period of years, to make lasting contacts with young staff officers including, it is said, Koiso Kuniaki, Shigeto Chiaki, and Futabakai members Okamura Yasuji, Itagaki Seishirō, Doihara Kenji, and Kōmoto Daisaku. From these personal friendships, and perhaps emboldened by the example of older officers like Araki and Mazaki, the Futabakai-Issekikai group began to invite exchanges of ideas with civilian nationalists, a circumstance that Ōkawa exploited.

24. Maeda, *Shōwa hanranshi*, 81. In a sense the Tōseiha was not really a faction; it had no designated leaders. Although Nagata Tetsuzan was always clearly identified as its central figure, it really consisted only of officers who opposed the Kōdōha. Nagata himself explicitly denied the existence of the Tōseiha in his often quoted statement, "There is but one faction [in the army]; there are no others." Nagata Tetsuzan Kankōkai, *Hiroku Nagata Tetsuzan*, 113–14. "Both terms *Kōdōha* and *Tōseiha* were coined by pro-*Kōdōha* pamphleteers. Therefore, *Kōdōha* was from the beginning a laudatory term, whereas *Tōseiha* remained a pejorative appelation. Thus, no group or individual ever referred to themselves as *Tōseiha*." Shillony, *Revolt in Japan*, 37–38; see also Itō, *Gunbatsu kōbōshi* 2: 226–27. See also Crowley, "Japanese Army Factionalism," 317; and Kido Nikki Kenkyūkai, "Suzuki Teiichi-shi danwa sokkiroku" 1: 268–70, 2: 323–24. Suzuki vehemently denies the existence of either faction. Okamura Yasuji sheds some light on the quarrel between Nagata and Obata in Inaba, *Okamura Yasuji taishō shiryō* 1: 366–69. He agrees that the Kōdōha and Tōseiha names were arbitrarily designated by the media.

25. Kikkawa, *Arashi to tatakau tesshō Araki*, 70, 74–75.

26. Kojima, *Shisetsu Yamashita Tomoyuki*, 11.

27. Apparently more a reflection of choice than ability. The leading figures of the "young officers movement," unlike the bulk of the *taizuki* (unit) officers, were men of tremendous potential. Shillony, *Revolt in Japan*, 24–25.

28. Imai and Takahashi, *Kokkashugi undō* 1: 33. As far as I can determine, the unit officers prominently involved in the "young officers movement" were, with one exception, graduates of the *yōnen gakkō*. The exception, 1st Lt. Kurihara

Yasuhide, was the son of an army colonel. Most of them seem to have come from military families. For example, of the fifteen young officers condemned to death as a result of their part in the February 26th Incident, eleven were the sons of military men (seven sons of generals, two sons of admirals, one son of a colonel, and one son of a sergeant). Fujiwara, *Gunjishi*, 161. For further analysis of the background of the young officers, see Shillony, *Revolt in Japan*, 21–25. Shillony also observes that almost half of the men involved in the February 26th Incident were from Kyushu.

29. At the military academy Nishida assiduously cultivated an association with his classmate Prince Chichibu, second son of the Taishō emperor and brother of the Shōwa emperor Hirohito. The connection between them proved useful at times to Nishida, but an embarrassment to the dynasty in later years. Suematsu, *Watakushi no Shōwashi*, 21; Nishida, "Sen'un o sashimaneku," 238–44.

30. Nishida, "Sen'un o sashimaneku," 236–38; Imai and Takahashi, *Kokkashugi undō* 1: 24. Nishida met Michikawa in February 1922 and Kita in April.

31. The 1926 edition of *Nihon kaizō hōan taikō*, edited by Nishida, appears in Takahashi, *Kokkashugi undō* 2: 3–40.

32. It was here that Nishida first established a direct liaison with Ōkawa Shūmei and Yasuoka Seitoku (from June 1924). Nishida, "Sen'un o sashimaneku," 254.

33. Nishida's brother told Shillony that Nishida used this illness as an excuse to resign so that he could "resume political activities" in Tokyo. Shillony, *Revolt in Japan*, 16n6.

34. Imai and Takahaski, *Kokkashugi undō* 1: 25–26; Wilson, *Radical Nationalist in Japan*, 105–6.

35. The Daigakuryō was the successor to the Social Education Institute (Shakai Kyōiku Kenkyūjo) of Yūzonsha days. The felicitous location was possible because of Ōkawa's friendship with Makino Nobuaki, the imperial household minister. It was to these institutions that officers of higher rank—Araki, Hata Shinji, and Watanabe Jōtarō—came to encourage the students and perhaps to engage in discussions with leaders of the civilian nationalist movement. Imai and Takahashi, *Kokkashugi undō* 1: 25, 34; see also Ōkawa's testimony at the International Military Tribunal, Far East, in Takahashi, *Kokkashugi undō* 2: 685–86. The term "military science" used to describe Nishida's teaching duties is apparently a euphemism for "ideas for the reorganization of the state." Ōtani, *Shōwa kenpeishi*, 89.

36. Kita's *Nihon kaizō hōan taikō* does not name the military as the executor of reform, but the Reservists Association. Nishida is generally credited with introducing the argument that only undefiled young officers could purify the nation and bring about the reorganization of the state, although this would have been a logical conclusion for young officers to reach without Nishida.

37. Suematsu, *Watakushi no Shōwashi*, 18–22. Suematsu maintains that the most brilliant cadet in his class, Shibukawa Zensuke, recipient of a gold watch from the emperor on his graduation from the preparatory course, became so involved with Nishida that he lost some 30 places in class standing and eventually withdrew from the regular course without graduating. Suematsu, *Watakushi no*

Shōwashi, 24. Shibukawa was later executed for his part in the February 26th Incident.

38. Imai and Takahashi, *Kokkashugi undō* 1: 34.

39. Ibid., 26.

40. Ibid., 35–39, contains most of the *Tenkentō* covenant.

41. Suematsu, *Watakushi no Shōwashi*, 17–18, 26. Mazaki Jinzaburō was the commanding general of the 5th Infantry Division at the time. Since the affair was triggered by patriotic motives, Mazaki did not censure his officers, but the final disposition came from Tokyo.

42. Ibid., 36. He attributes the *Tenkentō* to Nishida's loneliness after Suematsu's 39th class graduated and his disciples within it were posted to units all over Japan.

43. Takahashi, *Shōwa no gunbatsu*, 103.

44. Ibid., 26. See also Ōtani, *Shōwa kenpeishi*, 91.

45. Takahashi, *Kokkashugi undō* 2: 733; Wilson, *Radical Nationalist in Japan*, 110. An interesting interpretation of the relationship among Kita, Nishida, the young officers, and Mitsui appears in Tiedemann, "Big Business and Politics in Prewar Japan," 300–301.

46. Imai and Takahashi, *Kokkashugi undō* 1: 42–43; Ōtani, *Shōwa kenpeishi*, 91–92; Suematsu, *Watakushi no Shōwashi*, 26–30. The *Heika* episode falls within the genre of *kaibunsho* (scurrilous pamphlets or pamphleteering), a time-worn device for dissident expression in Japan and particularly prevalent from this period on. Army officers had used the *kaibunsho* as a means of communicating discontent for some time. (Suematsu classifies the *Tenkentō kiyaku* as a *kaibunsho*.) Ironically, one of the most celebrated earlier cases directly involved Ugaki Kazunari, who, as a colonel in the army ministry, received Diet criticism, an army reprimand, and transfer to a troop unit for writing and circulating one such tract entitled *Rikukaigun daijin mondai ni tsuite* (On the problem of the army and navy ministers) in 1913. Ugaki's chef d'oeuvre attacked those who advocated the changes necessary to make the army and navy ministers civilians. Ugaki later admitted that writing the *kaibunsho* could have ruined his career.

If his *kaibunsho* did not ruin it, however, the system it defended did, for in 1937 the army refused Prime Minister–Designate Ugaki an army minister, thwarting his chance to form a cabinet. Ugaki never donned his uniform again. Ugaki, *Shōrai seidan*, 65–75; also Takahashi, *Shōwa no gunbatsu*, 40, and Matsushita, *Nihon gunbatsu no kōbō* 3: 27.

47. Takahashi, *Shōwa no gunbatsu*, 98–99. See also Crowley, "Japanese Army Factionalism," 312. Other distinctive designations separated the two groups. The *bakuryōha* meant the staff faction. The *rikudaiha* (staff college faction) or *Tenpō(sen) gumi* distinguished the staff from the *mugakuha* (nonschool faction) or *muten gumi*, the line. These terms all had differences in nuance, but all compared the staff to the line.

48. Takahashi, *Shōwa no gunbatsu*, 101.

49. Imai and Takahashi, *Kokkashugi undō* 1: 58. For example, Nemoto Hiroshi was one of the leaders of the Sakurakai. Tsuchihashi Yūichi attended the first

meeting, but he liked neither the coup d'état formula nor the inclusion of *taizuki shōkō* and young officers in the membership so he withdrew. Takahashi, *Shōwa no gunbatsu*, 76.

50. Nihon Kokusai Seiji Gakkai, *Taiheiyō sensō e no michi* 1: 376.

51. Inoue Nisshō was the civilian ultranationalist founder of the Ketsumeidan (Blood Brotherhood), which had followers and supporters among young army and navy officers, including several who were intimates of Nishida (Ōkishi Yoriyoshi, Suematsu Tahei, Ōkura Eichi, Suganami Saburō, and Tsushima Katsuo). Takahashi, *Shōwa no gunbatsu*, 144–46; Imai and Takahashi, *Kokkashugi undō* 1: 71–90.

52. Takahashi, *Shōwa no gunbatsu*, 140.

53. For coverage of the Sakurakai and its activities in the March and October incidents, see Hata, *Gun fuashizumu undōshi*, chap. 2; and in English, Storry, *Double Patriots*, chap. 4.

54. Maeda, *Shōwa hanranshi*, 84.

55. Ikei, "Kindai Nihon ni okeru gunbu no seijiteki chii," 114; Fujiwara, *Gunjishi*, 156.

56. Matsushita, *Nihon gunbatsu no kōbō* 3: 140–41.

57. Maeda, *Shōwa hanranshi*, 81.

58. When Oba retired in March 1926, he was replaced by Gen. Kikuchi Shinnosuke, who died the following August. The clique wished to replace Kikuchi with Sugano Hisaichi, but Shirakawa gave in to Uehara, and Mutō became *kyōiku sōkan*. Uehara also succeeded in placing another Sagabatsu man, Muraoka Chōtarō, in Mutō's old assignment as commanding general of the Guandong Army. Takamiya, *Gunkoku taiheiki*, 23.

59. Ibid., 60–64; Ugaki, *Ugaki Kazunari nikki* 1: 754–56. See also Kōnō, *Kokushi no saikokuten*, 26–28.

6. The Manmō *Problem*

1. Itō, *Katō Takaaki*, 215–21.

2. Nihon Kokusai Seiji Gakkai, *Taiheiyō sensō e no michi* 1: 35–38; Bōeichō, *Senshi sōsho*, 242–43; and Young, *International Relations of Manchuria*, 129–46, 197–209.

3. McCormack, *Chang Tso-lin in Northeast China*, 27–28.

4. Bōeichō, *Senshi sōsho*, 199–201, 214–17.

5. Hayashi, *Waga shichijūnen o kataru*, 333.

6. Imai, "Taishōki" 402: 110.

7. Bōeichō, *Senshi sōsho*, 261. In English, see Young, "Hara Cabinet and Chang Tso-lin," 125–26.

8. Humphreys, "Imperial Japanese Army," 36–62.

9. Ugaki, *Ugaki Kazunari nikki* 1: 375 (undated, 1922).

10. Ikei, "Kindai Nihon ni okeru gunbu no seijiteki chii," 109.

11. Imai, "Taishōki" 402: 112.

12. Araki, *Gensui Uehara Yūsaku den* 2: 278–80.

13. Ibid. 2: 278–80; Ikei, "Kindai Nihon ni okeru gunbu no seijiteki chii,"

109; Ugaki, *Ugaki Kazunari nikki* 1: 560–61. Ugaki's diary makes it clear that he disapproved of the foreign policy toward China maintained by the government in which he served as army minister. The entry for 14 January 1927 (Ugaki, *Ugaki Kazunari nikki* 1: 560–61), for example, summarizes his (and the army's) condemnation of Japanese official neutrality in the second Mukden-Zhili War, Guo Songling's rebellion against Zhang Zuolin in 1925, the battle for control of Beijing between Zhang Zuolin and Feng Yuxiang in 1926, and the Guomindang's Northern Expedition. In every case he favored aid to Zhang Zuolin (and in every case army aid was to some extent forthcoming). For coverage of this war in greater detail in English, see McCormack, *Chang Tso-lin in Northeast China*, 119–43. McCormack maintains that the differences between government policy and army actions were more apparent than real.

14. Takamiya, *Gunkoku taiheiki*, 40–41; Ikei, "Kindai Nihon ni okeru gunbu no seijiteki chii," 110; Bōeichō, *Senshi sōsho*, 264. The Guandong Army judged Guo to be pro-Guomindang, and, since that organization was under Russian influence, his victory "would invite Red Russian influence into Manchuria. . . . It was clear that Guo Songling's army met defeat because his way was blocked owing to Japan's interference. The policy of noninterference in [China's] internal politics had to give way to our first priority policy, the protection of our rights." Bōeichō, *Senshi sōsho*, 264. Also see McCormack, *Chang Tso-lin in Northeast China*, especially 149–51, 163–87. As in the case of the second Mukden-Zhili War, McCormack avers, "the positions of the army and foreign ministers have generally been distinguished, but the difference, we would suggest, relates not so much to principle as to the degree of reluctance with which the decision to support certain measures was agreed upon, or to the insistence on maintaining the rhetoric of nonintervention while authorizing the intervention." Just as the Japanese threw their weight behind Zhang, the Russians apparently did their bit for Guo by denying Zhang's troops passage on the CER without prepayment of railway fares. Infuriated, Zhang Zuolin arrested the Soviet Russian manager and directors of the CER, precipitating a crisis in Sino-Russian affairs. Young, *International Relations of Manchuria*, 229–34.

15. Takamiya, *Gunkoku taiheiki*, 40.

16. Imai, "Taishōki" 402: 112–13. Count Uchida Yasuya was foreign minister from September 1918 to September 1923.

17. Ibid., 113. Baron Shidehara Kijūrō was foreign minister from June 1924 until April 1927 and from July 1929 until December 1931.

18. Young, *International Relations of Manchuria*, 223–27, 283–94.

19. Nihon Kokusai Seiji Gakkai, *Taiheiyō sensō e no michi* 1: 261–63; Bōeichō, *Senshi sōsho*, 287.

20. Young, *International Relations of Manchuria*, 228–29, 295–300.

21. Zhang Zuolin cordially disliked the Soviet Union and all its works. He had refused to recognize the Koo-Karakhan agreement, which restored Russian rights in the CER, but he was forced to sign the agreement in September 1924 when the Russians threatened him by massing troops on the Manchurian border just as Zhang faced a showdown with Wu Peifu in the second Mukden-Zhili War.

Yoshihashi, *Conspiracy at Mukden*, 32; McCormack, *Chang Tso-lin in Northeast China*, 113–14.

22. Nihon Kokusai Seiji Gakkai, *Taiheiyō sensō e no michi* 1: 262; also see Bōeichō, *Senshi sōsho*, 262.

23. Nihon Kokusai Seiji Gakkai, *Taiheiyō sensō e no michi* 1: 263–64; Bōeichō, *Senshi sōsho*, 258. (It was in this year that the United States officially superseded Russia as the most likely enemy in Japanese joint military planning.)

24. Nihon Kokusai Seiji Gakkai, *Taiheiyō sensō e no michi* 1: 264.

25. Ibid., 283.

26. Ibid., 265.

27. Bōeichō, *Senshi sōsho*, 288.

28. Sources for the developing army opposition to government foreign policy in the late Taishō period are fairly extensive. I have relied largely on "Jo'an zuisōroku," in Ugaki, *Ugaki Kazunari nikki* 1: 353–559, for the recorded views of an articulate and powerful army officer presenting personal opinions probably well within the army consensus; and Nihon Kokusai Seiji Gakkai, *Taiheiyō sensō e no michi*, vol. 1, part 2, chap. 4.

29. Bōeichō, *Senshi sōsho*, 272. As the Wakatsuki cabinet fretted over the spread of communism in China under the auspices of the Guomindang, Army Minister Ugaki called Suzuki Teiichi from his troop assignment as a battalion commander in December 1926 to send him on a mission to China. Major Suzuki, already well versed in Chinese affairs, had orders to contact Chiang Kai-shek through Suzuki's friend Huang Guo. Suzuki attempted to persuade the Guomindang to carry out a national revolution under Chiang Kai-shek based solely on Sun Yat-sen's three principles of the people. Huang argued that Japan should encourage the Nationalist revolution by not presenting obstacles to its advance; i.e., it should persuade Zhang Zuolin through his Japanese military advisers to withdraw into Manchuria. Nakamura, *Shōwa rikugun hishi*, 103–4 (Suzuki interview). See also Usui, "Chō Sakurin bakushi no shinsō," 23–24. Eventually Suzuki met Chiang in Jiujiang, where, according to Suzuki, Chiang told him that "if Japan helps us, we will break relations with Russia and carry on in accord with the three principles of the people." Kido Nikki Kenkyūkai, "Suzuki Teiichi-shi danwa sokkiroku" 1: 4. Suzuki returned to Tokyo in May 1927 to make his report to the new army minister and prime minister. In it he advocated support for Chiang as the best way to stop the spread of communism. He felt that when Chiang completed the Northern Expedition, an agreement on *Manmō* problems could easily be reached, and he even went so far as to advocate an alliance between Nationalist China and Japan. The G-2, Matsui Iwane, made an inspection trip to China and reached similar conclusions. Mitarai, *Minami Jirō*, 155.

30. Bōeichō, *Senshi sōsho*, 272.

31. Ibid., 273, and Takakura, *Tanaka Giichi denki* 2: 530–31.

32. Bōeichō, *Senshi sōsho*, 272. Actually, on 2 February Shidehara requested of the British ambassador that Britain consider not landing the three brigades of infantry brought to Shanghai for that purpose, but to withdraw them to Hong Kong for the time being. Shidehara's decision not to entertain the British request

was contrary to the army general staff's advice. Nihon Kokusai Seiji· Gakkai, *Taiheiyō sensō e no michi* 1: 277, 287.

33. Itō Miyoji launched a blistering attack against the government at a privy council meeting in the presence of the emperor on 17 April 1927. He said, among other things, that the insults to the nation received at Nanjing came as the result of diplomatic effeminacy and that the foreign ministry did not know what diplomacy was. Nihon Kokusai Seiji Gakkai, *Taiheiyō sensō e no michi* 1: 280. Wakatsuki's response to Itō's intemperance appears in Takamiya, *Gunkoku taiheiki*, 37–38. See also Takakura, *Tanaka Giichi denki* 2: 548–59.

34. Araki, *Gensui Uehara Yūsaku den* 2: 286–87. On 3, 4, and 5 April Uehara reported to his diary the views of several officers, all China experts, who felt that the situation in China called for intervention. Those mentioned who expressed, or agreed to, this opinion included the chief of staff of the Guandong Army, Maj. Gen. Saitō Hisashi; the army attaché in Beijing, Lt. Gen. Honjō Shigeru; Col. Tashiro Kan'ichirō, China section, general staff headquarters; Col. Tatekawa Yoshitsugu; Lt. Col. Okamura Yasuji; Lt. Col. Iwamatsu Yoshio; and Maj. Suzuki Teiichi. Lt. Gen. Sasaki Tōichi, in 1927 a lieutenant colonel and the assistant army attaché in Beijing, recalls that the Nanjing Incident "truly closed the books on our Shidehara diplomacy." Bōeichō, *Senshi sōsho*, 273. Finally, Araki Sadao, then chief of operations in the general staff headquarters, tells us that "the problem of whether, at the risk of people's lives, to be cautious or to interfere and suppress it [the Nanjing Incident] before it began was the great decision before the military then on the spot. As an example of how to invite disaster through caution this [incident], along with the havoc of the Nikolaevsk Incident in the Siberian affair, served as a warning to those responsible for security in foreign territories." Quoted in Bōeichō, *Senshi sōsho*, 273–74, after which the editors point out, "This became the bitter resolution of the army at that time, which led to the origins of the Manchurian Incident."

35. Ugaki, *Ugaki Kazunari nikki* 1: 568. The army ministry pointed out to the government that it was just a matter of time before the communist movement reached the *Manmō* region if the Powers did not intervene.

36. Bōeichō, *Senshi sōsho*, 272.

37. Ugaki, *Ugaki Kazunari nikki* 1: 568–70. On this occasion (7 Apr. 1927) Ugaki made an oral presentation of material from an army position paper entitled "Research on the Protection of the Empire's Position in China," which noted the failures of present policies and offered suggestions for more positive action. On 12 April Army Vice Minister Hata Eitarō presented the document to the foreign ministry. See also Bōeichō, *Senshi sōsho*, 273.

38. Ugaki, for example, directed very strong criticism at the sanctimonious American policy aimed at destroying the position of Japan and other nations in China. Ugaki, *Ugaki Kazunari nikki* 1: 468, 566, 570.

39. An extensive account of the baleful influence of Mori Kaku on the Tanaka cabinet's positive policy in China can be found in Yamaura, *Mori Kaku*, 565–648; and Yamaura, "Bōshō Mori Kaku." For coverage of Mori's influence on Tanaka's China policy in English, see Morton, *Tanaka Giichi*, 64–65, 91–92. The usual role

of a parliamentary vice minister was one of legislative liaison. The permanent vice minister of foreign affairs, a bureaucrat and career diplomat, was at that time Debuchi Katsuji, later the highly respected ambassador to Washington during that embarrassing period for Japanese diplomats, the Manchurian Incident. Stimson, *Far Eastern Crisis*, 4–10. When Mori made his determination known in the foreign ministry to take an active part in foreign policy matters with regard to China, he caused considerable consternation. Tanaka apparently placated Debuchi and the professionals, but in spite of Tanaka's reassurances, much of the content of official China policy stemmed from the parliamentary vice minister, who consciously aligned his views with those of army militants. Nakamura, *Shōwa rikugun hishi*, 108–9 (Suzuki interview).

40. Ugaki expressed his approval to his diary. Ugaki, *Ugaki Kazunari nikki* 1: 570.

41. Nihon Kokusai Seiji Gakkai, *Taiheiyō sensō e no michi* 1: 287–88. In this decision, Tanaka apparently saw the wisdom of placating Chiang Kai-shek, whose leadership he considered preferable to the left-leaning Wuhan government.

42. It is difficult, if not impossible, to assign relative weight to government considerations in this case. The protection of Manchuria by intervening to retrieve Zhang Zuolin and his allies from defeat was certainly a factor in determining whether to dispatch troops, but other factors, including the Seiyūkai promise to protect Japanese residents, weighed heavily in the decision. The Tokyo *Asahi shinbun* flatly accused Tanaka of intervening in the name of protecting Japanese residents in order to prevent Chiang Kai-shek from marching north, and according to Nihon Kokusai Seiji Gakkai, *Taiheiyō sensō e no michi* 1: 288, this may well have been the intention of Mori Kaku and a hawkish faction of the Seiyūkai. See also Banba, *Manshū jihen e no michi*, 185–92.

43. "Araki's opinion was that it would be better to send no expedition than one that was inadequate, but Tanaka, whom Araki criticized as weak-kneed in the same way for the Siberian Expedition plan when he [Tanaka] was vice chief of staff, had now become the person of highest responsibility in the government with the confidence of Saionji [Kinmochi, the remaining *genrō*]. He adopted a policy that would see him through the turmoil caused by the retreat of the Northern Army by protecting resident nationals there and keeping the public promise he made before the establishment of his cabinet when the Seiyūkai attacked Shidehara's diplomacy as weak." Nihon Kokusai Seiji Gakkai, *Taiheiyō sensō e no michi* 1: 288–89, 456nn 6–10.

44. The disagreement between Tanaka and the army general staff over the first Shandong Expedition presaged the split between Tanaka and the army that followed. Araki remained in the van of opposition to Tanaka's suddenly cautious approach.

45. Gaimushō, *Nihon gaikō nenpyō* 2: 96.

46. Nihon Kokusai Seiji Gakkai, *Taiheiyō sensō e no michi* 1: 289.

47. The Wuhan force approaching Chiang from the west was General Zhang Fakui's 4th Army. On 1 August 1927, communist elements within this army revolted at Nanchang. The incident is considered by the Chinese communists to

mark the founding of their armed forces, known today as the Chinese People's Liberation Army. The Wuhan government broke with the communists in July, but the final reconciliation with Chiang Kai-shek did not take place until December.

48. Yamaura, *Mori Kaku*, 610–11.

49. This account, except as noted, follows closely the one in Bōeichō, *Senshi sōsho*, 274–76. A longer, more politically oriented account appears in Takakura, *Tanaka Giichi denki* 2: 620–39. See also Tazaki, *Hyōden Tanaka Giichi* 2: 401–29.

50. Nakamura, *Shōwa rikugun hishi*, 10 (Suzuki interview).

51. Yoshihashi, *Conspiracy at Mukden*, 21. See also Kido Nikki Kenkyūkai, "Suzuki Teiichi-shi danwa sokkiroku" 1: 13–15.

52. For example, see Machino, "Chō Sakurin bakushi no zengo," 77. For much more detailed accounts of the Tanaka government's diplomatic and political activities with respect to China in this era, see Iriye, *After Imperialism*, especially chaps. 3–6, and Morton, *Tanaka Giichi*. See also Banba, *Manshū jihen e no michi*, 193–200.

53. Takakura, *Tanaka Giichi denki* 1: 645.

54. Nihon Kokusai Seiji Gakkai, *Taiheiyō sensō e no michi* 1: 282 and 287. "Tanaka Giichi was the mastermind behind the plans to cut Manchuria from China proper, and he interfered time and again in the war between north and south in China during his tenure as vice chief of staff" (287).

55. Ibid., 282.

56. Many Japanese thought these new, "competing" railways used British or American capital for their construction (see, for example, Itō, *Gunbatsu kōbōshi* 2: 132), but they apparently did not. Although two of them were in effect sections of the old Qinzhou-Aihui (Chinchow-Aigun) line, proposed by the United States in 1909 and 1910, the capital for all three of the lines in question came solely from Chinese sources, an interesting commentary on the growing strength of modern Chinese capitalism. Young, *International Relations of Manchuria*, 278–82.

57. Itō, *Gunbatsu kōbōshi* 2: 132.

58. Maeda, *Shōwa hanranshi*, 74.

59. Nihon Kokusai Seiji Gakkai, *Taiheiyō sensō e no michi* 1: 281–82.

60. The most complete accounts of the *Tōhō kaigi* I have found appear in Takakura, *Tanaka Giichi denki* 2: 640–74 (which refers to it as the *Renraku kaigi*, or Liaison Conference); and Yamaura, *Mori Kaku*, 575–601. Other sources include Nihon Kokusai Seiji Gakkai, *Taiheiyō sensō e no michi* 1: 289–91; and Yamamoto, *Nihon o horoboshita mono*, 24–30. The China Policy Summary can be found in Gaimushō, *Nihon gaikō nenpyō* 2: 101–2, as well as Yamamoto, *Nihon o horoboshita mono*, 24–30; and Bōeichō, *Senshi sōsho*, 276–77. Takakura, *Tanaka Giichi denki* 2: 652–58, provides not only the summary but also Vice Minister Mori's "Explanation of the Important Points in Foreign Minister Tanaka's Instructions," which amplifies it.

61. Machino began his career as adviser to Zhang Zuolin while on active duty. He entered reserve status in 1923, served a term in the lower house of the Diet, and returned to advisory duties with Zhang in 1925 as a reserve officer. Nihon Kindai Shiryō Kenkyūkai, *Nihon rikukaigun no seido*, 68; and Machino,

"Chō Sakurin bakushi no zengo," 72–80. The date given in Takakura, *Tanaka Giichi denki* 1: 677, for Machino's meeting with Tanaka is the most logical. Without being specific, other accounts suggest that the meeting could have taken place as early as the end of April 1927.

62. Nihon Kokusai Seiji Gakkai, *Taiheiyō sensō e no michi* 1: 294. Several different and somewhat contradictory versions of this conversation between Tanaka and Machino exist, one in Machino, "Chō Sakurin bakushi no zengo," 77, repeated in abbreviated form in Shinmyō, "Shōwa seiji hishi." In another version, Machino avers that Tanaka feared an army occupation of Manchuria by military force if the government did not act; Nihon Kokusai Seiji Gakkai, *Taiheiyō sensō e no michi*, vol. 1, appendix: 2. All emanate from Machino himself, but long after the fact. Takakura, *Tanaka Giichi denki* 2: 677–78, presents yet another version, directly quoting Yamamoto Jōtarō, but it provides no source. That Yamamoto took up his duties as president of the SMR on 19 July 1927, is a matter of record.

63. Machino, "Chō Sakurin bakushi no zengo." Yamamoto's private diplomacy soon ran afoul of the official foreign ministry negotiations of Minister Yoshizawa concurrently under way in Beijing. Details of Yamamoto's negotiations can be found in Takakura, *Tanaka Giichi denki* 2: 678–88. See also Banba, *Manshū jihen e no michi*, 201–7; and Morton, *Tanaka Giichi*, 103–6. The negotiations later ran into snags that prolonged them until May 1928, when Zhang finally signed agreements giving the Japanese the right to build four of the five railways and the promise to complete negotiations on the fifth. The marshal's assassination less than one month later added monumental complications. See also Iriye, *After Imperialism*, 179–80; and a still different interpretation in McCormack, *Chang Tso-lin in Northeast China*, 241–44.

64. Nihon Kokusai Seiji Gakkai, *Taiheiyō sensō e no michi* 1: 292. Within the month Mutō had returned to Tokyo to take up his new post as inspector general of military training. His replacement was Lt. Gen. Muraoka Chōtarō.

65. Tanaka and the army still thought in terms of railways for strategic mobility, a novel concept in the Austro-Prussian War and a central theme in the strategic planning and fighting of World War I, but declining in importance in the strategic thinking of Europe and America at this time. Ugaki seems to be among the few who sensed the misplaced emphasis in Japan's Manchurian planning when he wrote in his diary that the completion of the railway network was important but not the paramount issue. The real urgency lay in the provision of natural resources, the commercial leasing of land, the development of mining and forestry enterprises, and commerce and industry. He accused army authorities of thinking in terms of ten years before. Ugaki, *Ugaki Kazunari nikki* 1: 621 (entry for 4 Nov. 1927); Bōeichō, *Senshi sōsho*, 278.

66. Bōeichō, *Senshi sōsho*, 280; Banba, *Manshū jihen e no michi*, 205.

67. Nihon Kokusai Seiji Gakkai, *Taiheiyō sensō e no michi* 1: 298–99.

68. Suzuki's special relationship to Tanaka gave him more importance than his rank would normally warrant. An explanation of that relationship appears in Nakamura, *Shōwa rikugun hishi*, 106–7; and in English in Humphreys, "Imperial Japanese Army," 305n2.

69. After Matsui talked to Chiang, he changed his mind about continuing

support for Zhang Zuolin in spite of his brother's relationship with the marshal. From this time on, the elder Matsui was considered, along with the very junior Suzuki, to be the most ardent supporter of the Guomindang within the army. Mitarai, *Minami Jirō*, 155. Matsui retired in 1935, but by an ironic twist of fate his enthusiasm for the Guomindang cost him his life. He was recalled to active duty in 1937 to lead the Japanese invasion of Shanghai during the China Incident. (Army leaders believed that he would be most able to reach a compromise solution with Chiang Kai-shek in the field.) In October 1937 troops under his command committed the infamous "rape of Nanjing." Matsui, sick in bed at the time, was not present. He was so crushed by that incident that he left the military service completely in March 1938. Tried as an A-class war criminal by the Tokyo International Military Tribunal, Matsui was held responsible for the murders at Nanjing and sentenced to death. He was executed in December 1948.

70. Gaimushō, *Nihon gaikō nenpyō* 2: 102–6; Tazaki, *Hyōden Tanaka Giichi* 2: 568–76; Takakura, *Tanaka Giichi denki* 2: 741, 828–29n.

71. Takakura, *Tanaka Giichi denki* 2: 737–38.

72. Mitarai, *Minami Jirō*, 155–56, contains a statement Chiang made to Matsui Iwane on 27 October 1927, preserved in the records of the general staff headquarters. In it Chiang plays on Japan's fear of Russia and opposition to communism in order to solicit a helping hand from the Japanese, ending rather wistfully, "If Japan helps me, I will return to work hard for the revolution. Otherwise I have no alternative but to watch in silence for the time being."

73. Bōeichō, *Senshi sōsho*, 280.

74. Nihon Kokusai Seiji Gakkai, *Taiheiyō sensō e no michi* 1: 297.

7. Jinan and Mukden

1. Shirakawa and Chief of Staff Suzuki had been in conference since at least 9 April with foreign ministry officials, officers of the SMR, and representatives from Guandong, discussing the China situation and Japanese government policy toward it. Takeuchi, *War and Diplomacy*, 249; Tazaki, *Hyōden Tanaka Giichi* 2: 580. The army presented contingency plans for a second intervention to the cabinet in December 1927, which approved them at that time. Takakura, *Tanaka Giichi denki* 2: 862; Tazaki, *Hyōden Tanaka Giichi* 2: 580.

2. Takeuchi, *War and Diplomacy*, 250–51; full text, Takakura, *Tanaka Giichi denki* 2: 825–26. Also see U.S. Department of State, *Papers Relating to Foreign Relations* 2: 136–37. Another excellent account of the Jinan (Tsinan) Incident, using somewhat different sources, appears in Iriye, *After Imperialism*, 193–205. Iriye quite rightly emphasizes the insubordination of the Japanese army in this affair and states that its consequence was to frustrate "all attempts at further Sino-Japanese *rapprochement*." See also Morton, *Tanaka Giichi*, 111–22; Tazaki, *Hyōden Tanaka Giichi* 2: 580–82.

3. Tanaka's thinking in view of his private understanding with Chiang Kai-shek in November can be found in Takakura, *Tanaka Giichi denki* 2: 827–28.

4. Suzuki Teiichi is emphatic about Tanaka's reluctance. In fact, he claims that

the army did not support either the first or the second expedition, but he admits that he participated only in the decision for the second one. (He was on his trip to China during the first.) "I had no connection with the first expedition, although at the time of the second I was directly involved, but I was completely against it. I met and talked with both the army minister and the prime minister. That was because I had a special relationship with the prime minister . . . , but the prime minister didn't want the expedition either. This is what he said: 'I don't want to send them, but when I pulled out the first expeditionary force, I said in the Seiyūkai declaration, "If this happens again, I'll send troops any time." So at a time like this we have to do something as a party. Over at the general staff headquarters you want to send two companies from Tianjin. Wouldn't that be just an evasion of the party declaration?'

"I replied, 'That's not impossible, but if worst came to worst and something like the Nikolaevsk Incident occurred, it would be terrible. If we send anybody, we'll have to send the proper number.' " Nakamura, *Shōwa rikugun hishi*, 101–2 (Suzuki interview). See also Kido Nikki Kenkyūkai, "Suzuki Teiichi-shi danwa sokkiroku" 1: 11–12. By "the army" Suzuki really meant his colleagues on the general staff, because there is ample evidence that the other decision-making body, the army ministry, supported intervention.

5. Yamaura, *Mori Kaku*, 617, argues that Tanaka was pressured by Mori and the Seiyūkai hawks, but Takakura, *Tanaka Giichi denki* 2: 828 and 866, discounts Mori's importance in this matter. The editor states that the decision for intervention was Tanaka's alone and that he based it on dispatches received on 16 April from Consul General Fujita and his consular representative Nishida in Jinan, both of whom saw the situation as very dangerous. Neither believed that there was any way that resident nationals could be evacuated because the Chinese would quickly cut the railway. Both felt strongly that all Japanese would be roughly handled by the Chinese army, whose slogans were filled with anti-Japanese propaganda. If Tanaka had been successful in persuading Zhang Zuolin to withdraw beyond the Great Wall, things might have been different, but because that effort had failed so far, Japan had to prepare for the worst.

6. Mitarai, *Minami Jirō*, 160. Major Nemoto, wounded in the Nanjing Incident of March 1927, was next assigned to the China section of the military affairs bureau in the army ministry. With respect to the historical interpretation that places blame for the second Shandong Expedition (and the Jinan Incident) squarely on the army (and on Prime Minister Tanaka), Suzuki tells us, "That is a very great mistake. It was the army's opinion that there should be no expedition. I can say this unequivocally because I myself participated directly. Because we were soldiers, people believed that we always advocated war, so they thought that there must be those within the army who called for the expedition, but really, we thought that the Shandong Expedition should not be sent under any circumstances." Nakamura, *Shōwa rikugun hishi*, 101 (Suzuki interview). If we substitute "army general staff" for "army" in Suzuki's statement, we probably come close to the truth. See also Kido Nikki Kenkyūkai, "Suzuki Teiichi-shi danwa sokkiroku" 1: 11–12.

7. Kikkawa, *Arashi to tatakau tesshō Araki*, 77, confirms this. "But in the following year (April 1928), with signs of worsening conditions in Shandong for the second time, the general [Araki] requested of the government that *if they were to protect resident nationals* [my emphasis], they should, this time also, take preventive measures against the outbreak of incidents in connection with the arrival of the northern expeditionary forces by sending troops without neglecting the requirement for safety [in numbers]."

8. Yoshino, *Gendai kensei no un'yō*, 444–50.

9. According to Iriye (*After Imperialism*, 197–98), the troops from Tianjin were under orders from the general staff to "avoid all interference with the Chinese civil war. . . . Also, you should take care that the action of the contending armies be not interfered with by our troops, unless to do so is necessary in order to protect our residents around Tsinan."

10. Nihon Kokusai Seiji Gakkai, *Taiheiyō sensō e no michi* 1: 300–301.

11. Takakura, *Tanaka Giichi denki* 2: 829–30; Tazaki, *Hyōden Tanaka Giichi* 2: 590–92. A somewhat divergent account from different sources appears in Iriye, *After Imperialism*, 199–200. A reliable, but limited, eyewitness account of the situation in Jinan appears in Sasaki, *Aru gunjin no jiden* 1: 226–38. The observer, then lieutenant colonel Sasaki Tōichi, was the army liaison officer to Chiang Kai-shek's forces. He shuttled between the two headquarters during the fighting.

12. One message from the chief of staff to the commanding general, 6th Infantry Division, read as follows: "With the worsening of the situation, it will now be necessary for drastic action based on all-out reinforcement from Japan." Bōeichō, *Senshi sōsho*, 281.

13. The exaggerated reports from Sakai in Jinan were the only communications being received by the general staff headquarters. Greatly agitated by them, the staff officers contacted their chief, Suzuki Sōroku, then in Shikoku on a trip. In view of the supposed emergency, Suzuki told the staff to prepare three divisions for immediate transport to China, and he himself returned to the capital posthaste. Kikkawa, *Arashi to tatakau tesshō Araki*, 78–79.

14. The 28th Combined Brigade from the Guandong Army, and a provisional aircraft expeditionary unit from Korea. At the same time, the 40th Combined Brigade from the Chōsen Army replaced the 28th in Manchuria, but the 28th was returned to the Guandong Army on 17 May. Bōeichō, *Senshi sōsho*, 281–84.

15. The government was under fierce attack in both houses of the Diet. Representative Nagai Ryūtarō accused the army ministry of using the expedition for political purposes. Shirakawa denied the charge. Takeuchi, *War and Diplomacy*, 251–53.

16. Major Sakai was never called to account for his actions at Jinan. He rose steadily in rank, becoming a lieutenant general in August 1939. He entered reserve status in March 1943. Sakai was executed by the Chinese in Nanjing in September 1946. Nihon Kindai Shiryō Kenkyūkai, *Nihon rikukaigun no seido*, 34.

17. A year later (21 Mar. 1929) a member of the House of Peers asked Shirakawa in a Diet interpellation if the decision to send the extra division to Shandong

had not been delayed till the end of the Diet session to prevent embarrassment to the government. The army minister "flatly denied" that it had. Takeuchi, *War and Diplomacy*, 253.

18. Actually, by the time the 3rd Infantry Division was ready to move, the crisis in Shandong was over, and a new one was brewing in the Beijing-Tianjin area as Chiang Kai-shek and the warlord general Feng Yuxiang converged there. As a result, two battalions of the 3rd Division were diverted to reinforce the China Garrison Army. Bōeichō, *Senshi sōsho*, 283. In English, see U.S. Department of State, *Papers Relating to Foreign Relations* 2: 138–39, 144–45.

19. Ugaki reports a meeting of the military affairs council at 0830 on 8 August 1928 in the army minister's official residence. He gives us no details except to say that in their first briefing the authorities concerned wished "to take this opportunity to increase troop strength further and sweep away the contemptuous attitude of the Chinese people toward us by a show of authority and power, thus opening the way for the expansion of the nation's destiny." At this point Ugaki posed a series of searching questions on the national and international implications of such a dangerous step. The "authorities" retreated, saying that "this troop increase did not mean a fundamental solution to [problems] of the nation's China policy, just a settlement of the Jinan Incident and aid to the troops already there, who were in danger." Ugaki replied that he trusted the present army leaders and posed no objection to what they were doing, but he wondered why there was any necessity in this situation to call the military affairs council into session. Ugaki, *Ugaki Kazunari nikki* 1: 659–60.

20. Kikkawa, *Arashi to tatakau tesshō Araki*, 79–81. Apparently, Araki continued to raise such a storm of protest over the Jinan decision that the army authorities transferred him to the staff college as commandant the following August to be rid of him. Mitarai, *Minami Jirō*, 162–63.

21. Bōeichō, *Senshi sōsho*, 282. The text of Fukuda's five-point ultimatum appears in Takakura, *Tanaka Giichi denki* 2: 859.

22. "A storm of criticism and denunciation was showered upon this extravagantly militaristic and irresponsible measure adopted by the government. The criticism was so instantaneous and so widespread that the government had to issue a public statement approving the Japanese commander. Thus, on 13 May both the war minister and the chief of the general staff sent messages to General Fukuda at Tsinan commending his measures." Takeuchi, *War and Diplomacy*, 254. A detailed public report of the incident from the army ministry dated 13 May and a discussion of the incident by Consul General Fujita of the same date appear in Takakura, *Tanaka Giichi denki* 2: 831–37. The army ministry report lists 13 Japanese residents dead, 28 missing, 2 presumed dead, 2 women raped, and 9 persons wounded. Fujita's figures differ somewhat.

23. Koiso, *Katsuzan kōsō*, 487.

24. Although it was never proved conclusively, there is reason to believe that renewed fighting early on 8 May came as a result of a plot on the part of Major Sakai, who may have ordered a man from the Jinan *tokumu kikan* (intelligence) unit to open fire in an area where Japanese and Chinese troops faced each other in close

proximity. This touched off a firefight that spread quickly throughout the city. See, for example, Nihon Kokusai Seiji Gakkai, *Taiheiyō sensō e no michi* 1: 302–3.

25. Bōeichō, *Senshi sōsho*, 282.

26. This account of the Jinan Incident follows closely the outlines contained in Nihon Kokusai Seiji Gakkai, *Taiheiyō sensō e no michi* 1: 299–303, except where noted otherwise. An official view of U.S. observers near the scene is contained in U.S. Department of State, *Papers Relating to Foreign Relations* 2: 148–50.

27. Takeuchi, *War and Diplomacy*, 255–61.

28. For consideration of this period with respect to Sino-Japanese relations, see Iriye, *After Imperialism*, 205–23. See also Morton, *Tanaka Giichi*, 122–30.

29. Yamaura, *Mori Kaku*, 624–27.

30. Nihon Kokusai Seiji Gakkai, *Taiheiyō sensō e no michi* 1: 303, 305, 460 n38; Takakura, *Tanaka Giichi denki* 2: 951. Araki, supporting Fukuda, strongly advocated punishment for Chiang Kai-shek and the Guomindang army for the Jinan Incident, which he assumed on the basis of Japanese reports and investigation to have been caused by the Chinese. He also apparently favored supporting Zhang Zuolin to hold Beijing. The outspoken Araki carried his argument beyond his dispute with Hata Eitarō to Minami, Abe, Shirakawa, Mori Kaku, and others in the foreign ministry and in the cabinet.

31. Takakura, *Tanaka Giichi denki* 1: 951–52.

32. One scheme brought before the cabinet by the army apparently went so far as to suggest that the navy land an army infantry division at Shanhaiguan to block Zhang Zuolin's retreat into Manchuria completely. The theory was that, stripped of all Chinese forces and military leadership, Manchuria would then fall like a ripe plum into Japanese hands. According to Navy Minister Okada, the navy opposed the plan resolutely, and he convinced the prime minister with his arguments. Okada, *Okada Keisuke kaikoroku*, 33–35. Okada supplies no dates, but the incident may have taken place between 30 May and 7 June 1928. It is possible that it is the same incident as the one referred to in Takakura, *Tanaka Giichi denki* 2: 956–57.

33. See Jordan, *Northern Expedition*, 163.

34. Takakura, *Tanaka Giichi denki* 1: 940–41. For details of the campaign, see Jordan, *Northern Expedition*, chap. 17.

35. Nihon Kokusai Seiji Gakkai, *Taiheiyō sensō e no michi* 1: 303–4; Bōeichō, *Senshi sōsho*, 282.

36. There is no question that the Guandong Army headquarters burned with resentment toward Zhang. The Japanese military had raised Zhang to his high status and had supported him for years. Now they felt betrayed. Since Zhang had left Manchuria for Beijing, he had gradually come to spurn Japanese advice, and in his bid for national unification he had even jumped on the anti-Japanese bandwagon. Manchuria seethed with ill-feeling toward the Japanese in 1927 and 1928. This the Guandong Army laid to Zhang's policies. Usui, "Chō Sakurin bakushi no shinsō," 30, 35; also Kawamoto [Kōmoto], "Watakushi ga Chō Sakurin o koroshita." The latter article contains some interesting and perhaps authentic material,

but it is very doubtful that it was written by Kōmoto, for he had been languishing in jail since 1945 in Taiyuan, China, where he died in 1956.

37. Nihon Kokusai Seiji Gakkai, *Taiheiyō sensō e no michi* 1: 304.

38. Ibid. Marshal Zhang, inwardly pleased over the turn of events in Jinan, thought that Japan had finally agreed on a policy to block the northward march of the revolutionary army, which, in his view, was turning China red. He now anticipated Japanese aid in his fight against the southerners. As a result, on 7 May he secretly consented to sign the railway agreements already approved in principle earlier. He signed two agreements on 13 May and two more on 15 May. He agreed to sign the remaining one later. When Yamamoto secured Zhang's agreement in principle the previous November, he is said to have exulted, "It's just as if we've bought all Manchuria!" Banba, *Manshū jihen e no michi*, 206.

39. Machino, "Chō Sakurin bakushi no zengo," 79.

40. The text of the cabinet's "action plan" appears in Bōeichō, *Senshi sōsho*, 283.

41. Ibid.; and Takakura, *Tanaki Giichi denki* 2: 942. The 18 May declaration acted as a signal to Chiang Kai-shek that Japan, in spite of the Jinan affair, would not oppose Nationalist conquest of all of China south of the wall. Although the Nanjing government protested against the declaration officially, it acknowledged Japan's position in private communications with Japanese Consul General Yada Shichirō in Shanghai by intimating that it did not intend to pursue Marshal Zhang into Manchuria. For Zhang Zuolin the signals were equally clear. He could survive only if he withdrew behind the protective shield of the Japanese army, which would not under any circumstances extend beyond the borders of the "three eastern provinces." Nihon Kokusai Seiji Gakkai, *Taiheiyō sensō e no michi* 1: 305; and Usui, "Chō Sakurin bakushi no shinsō," 29.

42. Takakura, *Tanaka Giichi denki* 2: 944–45; Tazaki, *Hyōden Tanaka Giichi* 2: 606.

43. Tatekawa replaced Honjō Shigeru in March 1928. Nihon Kindai Shiryō Kenkyūkai, *Nihon rikukaigun no seido*, 46.

44. Usui, "Chō Sakurin bakushi no shinsō," 29; Takakura, *Tanaka Giichi denki* 2: 945. Also see McCormack, *Chang Tso-lin in Northeast China*, 246–47.

45. Bōeichō, *Senshi sōsho*, 284.

46. Takakura, *Tanaka Giichi denki* 2: 945.

47. At this same time Matsui Shichio and Machino Takema were still working frantically for a Zhang Zuolin solution to the *Manmō* problem by attempting to convince Zhang to withdraw to Manchuria with his forces intact. Takakura, *Tanaka Giichi denki* 2: 945. In their view Yamamoto had won Manchuria for Japan. All that remained was to assure the proper implementation of the railway agreements that Zhang had agreed to make public in July. There is evidence that Guandong Army officers like Senior Staff Officer Kōmoto had nothing but contempt for the ideas of men like Machino and Matsui.

48. Shidehara Heiwa Zaidan, *Shidehara Kijūrō*, 361; and Usui, "Chō Sakurin bakushi no shinsō," 30. In the foreign ministry Mori Kaku and Asia bureau chief

Arita also agreed that Zhang had outlived his usefulness. Usui, "Chō Sakurin bakushi no shinsō"; and Takakura, *Tanaka Giichi denki* 2: 952.

49. Nihon Kokusai Seiji Gakkai, *Taiheiyō sensō e no michi* 1: 305–6; also Bōeichō, *Senshi sōsho*, 284; and Usui, "Chō Sakurin bakushi no shinsō," 31.

50. Takakura, *Tanaka Giichi denki* 2: 956.

51. Usui, "Chō Sakurin bakushi no shinsō," 32; Yoshihashi, *Conspiracy at Mukden*, 38–39. Yoshihashi's translation (modified slightly).

52. U.S. Department of State, *Papers Relating to Foreign Relations* 2: 224–25, 227–28, 229–30. Also mentioned in Usui, "Chō Sakurin bakushi no shinsō," 32–33.

53. Nihon Kokusai Seiji Gakkai, *Taiheiyō sensō e no michi* 1: 306–7.

54. Deduced from the opinions attributed to Araki by his adulatory biographer. Kikkawa, *Arashi to tatakau tesshō Araki*, 86. Those present included Yoshida Shigeru, the new permanent vice minister of foreign affairs; Mori Kaku and Arita from the foreign ministry; Generals Abe, Araki, and Matsui Iwane from the army; and Rear Adm. Yonai Mitsumasa of the navy.

55. Nihon Kokusai Seiji Gakkai, *Taiheiyō sensō e no michi* 1: 308; Tazaki, *Hyōden Tanaka Giichi* 2: 618–19.

56. Another, older version of these events appears in Yamaura, *Mori Kaku*, 633–36, and it is often repeated in later secondary sources (in English, see Yoshihashi, *Conspiracy at Mukden*, 38–40). Yamaura calls the meeting another Eastern Area Conference (which it clearly was not, since there were no representatives from the field) and gives the dates as 20–25 May. This version places the "five-day" meeting under the chairmanship of Mori, who, after endless and fruitless debate, declared unilaterally in conclusion that Japan must "go with the already established policy." Yamaura interpreted this vague phrase as support for Guandong Army intervention. Arita and Abe then carried the conference's nondecision to Tanaka, resting at his country villa near Kamakura, and during a moonlight stroll on the beach with the pair Tanaka declared his opposition to Guandong Army intervention. On the following day (26 May) Arita and Abe reported to Tokyo that it was "the prime minister's decision to stop all action." Tanaka based his decision, according to Yamaura, on a warning from the United States that said in substance, "Is not Japan embarking on some kind of positive action in Manchuria? If this is true, we wish you to reveal its content to America beforehand." The Yamaura interpretation, written before the Pacific War, is easily refuted by primary materials written or revealed later and simply by the fact that the United States never issued such a warning, but it has persisted because it confirms the Guandong Army's fervent belief that Tanaka acted in a cowardly fashion, backing down in the face of foreign pressure, thus depriving the Guandong Army of the glory of seizing Manchuria for the empire. Takakura, *Tanaka Giichi denki* 2: 952–56, refutes the Yamaura text; Usui, "Chō Sakurin bakushi no shinsō," and Nihon Kokusai Seiji Gakkai, *Taiheiyō sensō e no michi*, vol. 1, damn it by omission. U.S. Department of State, *Papers Relating to Foreign Relations* 2: 226, 227–28, 231, makes it quite clear that the U.S. secretary of state was more concerned about (1)

U.S. involvement in joint ventures with other powers in North China and (2) denying Japanese press reports that falsely expressed his concern over Japanese intentions in Manchuria than he was about what the Japanese were actually doing there.

As to allegations of the prime minister's cowardice, Takakura, *Tanaka Giichi denki* 2: 952–56, attributes it to Mori Kaku "blowing his bugle," but I feel that one should not overlook the influence of chauvinists in the general staff headquarters. If the information about Tashiro's conversations in Guandong Army headquarters is correctly rendered in Kikkawa, *Arashi to tatakau tesshō Araki,* 86, it is likely that Colonel Tashiro, as a visitor from the general staff, left or reinforced that impression among the Guandong Army staff in Mukden by reflecting the inflamed feelings held by many in the general staff headquarters.

57. Usui, "Chō Sakurin bakushi no shinsō," 33.

58. Kawamoto, "Watakushi ga Chō Sakurin o koroshita," 196; Kikkawa, *Arashi to tatakau tesshō Araki,* 83.

59. The Guandong Army may well have known of the railway agreements in spite of doubts expressed by Machino ("Chō Sakurin bakushi no zengo," 79) and Shinmyō ("Shōwa seiji hishi," 196), for Yamamoto Jōtarō visited General Muraoka on 30 May, according to Major General Saitō's diary. Usui, "Chō Sakurin bakushi bakushi no shinsō," 32.

60. Confirmed in Arita, *Bakahachi to hito wa iu,* 45–46.

61. Kikkawa, *Arashi to tatakau tesshō Araki,* 87. Also see Tazaki, *Hyōden Tanaka Giichi* 2: 619.

62. In the army ministry and the general staff headquarters in May 1928, the Ugakibatsu held all five major posts: Shirakawa, army minister; Hata Eitarō, vice minister; Abe, chief of the military affairs bureau; Suzuki Sōroku, chief of staff; and Minami, vice chief of staff. Only Mutō, the inspector general of military training from Saga, did not represent the Ugaki mainstream. By inference all these "establishment" officers were linked to Tanaka and the Chōbatsu. Ugaki was himself a military affairs councillor.

63. When the army leaders transferred Araki, they replaced him in the operations division with Hata Shunroku, Eitarō's younger brother and fellow member of the Ugakibatsu. Hayashi Katsura, another Ugaki man, replaced Hata as chief of the 4th division of the general staff. Both of Araki's section chiefs were transferred at the same time. One of these was Obata Toshishirō of the Futabakai, now a vocal convert to Araki's cause.

64. Matsushita Yoshio reminds us that Tanaka himself cannot be absolved from blame in the assassination of Zhang Zuolin. "It goes without saying that in this incident Prime Minister Tanaka had no direct responsibility. However, if one considers the imperialist ideas Tanaka espoused from before and the Siberian Expedition, the Shandong Expeditions, and the Eastern Area Conference, which were all pursued on the basis [of those ideas], and the formation of a Tanaka clique by an amalgamation of Chōbatsu and Rikudaibatsu [elements], then one cannot say categorically that this incident, perpetrated in the name of plans for a military

administration over Manchuria, was completely unconnected with Tanaka. One might say that this incident was one for which Tanaka sowed the seed." Matsushita, *Nihon gunbatsu no kōbō* 3: 64.

65. Technically, the Issekikai was not formed until spring 1929, almost a year after Kōmoto murdered Zhang. Kōmoto was a charter member of the Issekikai, but at the time of the assassination he was a member of the Futabakai only.

66. Takamiya, *Gunkoku taiheiki*, 46–47.

67. The text of Zhang's announcement and a news report of the event appear in Takakura, *Tanaka Giichi denki* 2: 948–49.

68. Machino, "Chō Sakurin bakushi no zengo," 79.

69. Simplified composite of verified facts from the accounts in Usui, "Chō Sakurin bakushi no shinsō," 35–36; Takamiya, *Gunkoku taiheiki*, 46; Nihon Kokusai Seiji Gakkai, *Taiheiyō sensō e no michi* 1: 308–9; Mori, *Senpū nijūnen*, 11–17; Takakura, *Tanaka Giichi denki* 2: 950. There are several accounts in English. Dull, "Assassination of Chang Tso-lin," is generally excellent, but facts uncovered later make it out-of-date.

70. Takamiya, *Gunkoku taiheiki*, 46.

71. Mori, *Senpū nijūnen*, 15.

72. Usui, "Chō Sakurin bakushi no shinsō," 34. Nihon Kokusai Seiji Gakkai, *Taiheiyō sensō e no michi* 1: 308–9, gives credence to the story that the plot originated with Lieutenant General Muraoka himself.

It is said that Commanding General Muraoka, who had at last come up to Mukden, considered a plan to assassinate Zhang Zuolin using the North China Garrison Army, and he tried to communicate his feelings secretly to Tatekawa, the attaché, without the knowledge of either Saitō, his chief of staff, or Kōmoto. But Kōmoto persuaded Maj. Takeshita Yoshiharu, an officer attached to the army headquarters who had divulged Muraoka's plan to him, to pass off the bombing plan to Tatekawa not as Muraoka's but as one he [Kōmoto] had made himself since, in addition to wanting to create the opportunity for the Guandong Army to subjugate Manchuria by force of arms through the murder of Zhang, he regarded it as an utmost necessity to cloak its execution in secrecy.

(Actually, Takeshita was assigned to general staff headquarters and stationed in Manchuria to do [intelligence] research on China. Nihon Kindai Shiryō Kenkyūkai, *Nihon rikukaigun no seido*, 45.)

73. This cover story forms one of the more bizarre aspects of the case. Kōmoto, through his excellent contacts with the China *rōnin* (Japanese adventurers), provided the men at the murder site with three Chinese dressed appropriately for a secret mission. Two sacrificed their lives by being bayoneted to death in accord with the scenario, but the third managed to escape. Grenades and letters placed on the bodies linking them to anti-Zhang elements completed the clumsy fiction that others like them might have killed Zhang. According to the generally accepted version, the third intended victim later told his story to Zhang Xueliang, confirming what the young man already suspected to be the truth of his father's death. Morishima, *Inbō*, 21–22.

74. The man in charge at the murder site, who actually detonated the explosive charge, was Capt. Tōmiya Tetsuo, a company commander in the 2nd Indepen-

dent (Railway) Guard Battalion (Nihon Kindai Shiryō Kenkyūkai, *Nihon rikukai-gun no seido,* 50), whose men were supposed to be guarding the overpass. Kōmoto had recruited Tōmiya for the assassination plot, compromising the guard system.

75. At this time they knew neither that Zhang had died nor that Japanese army officers were responsible for the deed. Ugaki commented to his diary, "There should be none among my countrymen such fools as to plan and participate in the bomb attack on Zuolin." Ugaki, *Ugaki Kazunari nikki* 1: 664 (entry for 7 July 1928).

76. Takakura, *Tanaka Giichi denki* 2: 956–57; Usui, "Chō Sakurin bakushi no shinsō," 36.

77. Text of the release in Takamiya, *Gunkoku taiheiki,* 44–46.

78. Takakura, *Tanaka Giichi denki* 2: 1028.

79. Kikkawa, *Arashi to tatakau tesshō Araki,* 87.

80. Takakura, *Tanaka Giichi denki* 2: 1028.

81. Nihon Kokusai Seiji Gakkai, *Taiheiyō sensō e no michi* 1: 319.

82. Koiso, *Katsuzan kōsō,* 491. Koiso, who had been a friend of Kōmoto's for years, went to meet him at Tokyo Station when he arrived from Manchuria. There Koiso unexpectedly ran into Araki and Obata, who had also come to meet Kō-moto. After Kōmoto arrived, the four repaired to a restaurant in Kojimachi, where Kōmoto unburdened himself. (Araki had been Kōmoto's section chief [*kutaichō*] in the military academy.)

83. The most detailed account of the evidence presented to Tanaka appears in Takakura, *Tanaka Giichi denki* 2: 1029. The reports correctly singled out Kōmoto as the master planner.

84. Nihon Kokusai Seiji Gakkai, *Taiheiyō sensō e no michi* 1: 320. My narrative closely follows pages 318–27 of this volume. Suzuki Teiichi, then working for Araki in the operations division of the general staff headquarters, explains his part in the cover-up in Kido Nikki Kenkyūkai, "Suzuki Teiichi-shi danwa sok-kiroku" 1: 70–73. The decision to insist on an administrative disposition of the case was never meant to embarrass Tanaka or topple his government, according to Suzuki.

85. Takakura, *Tanaka Giichi denki* 2: 1030; Tazaki, *Hyōden Tanaka Giichi* 2: 695.

86. Harada, *Saionji-kō to seikyoku,* 10; Tazaki, *Hyōden Tanaka Giichi* 2: 696.

87. Okada, *Okada Keisuke kaikoroku,* 39; Nihon Kokusai Seiji Gakkai, *Taiheiyō sensō e no michi* 1: 321.

88. Nihon Kokusai Seiji Gakkai, *Taiheiyō sensō e no michi* 1: 322. To his diary military affairs councillor Ugaki admitted that he at first advocated stern measures against those who assassinated Zhang, but now he had changed his mind. Tanaka had known the truth about the incident since October but did nothing about it until December. (Ugaki had been with Tanaka on an army maneuver in Morioka when Tanaka received Mine's report. Ugaki, *Ugaki Kazunari nikki* 1: 698; Ugaki, *Shōrai seidan,* 317.) Ugaki saw Tanaka, whose positive policy he now violently opposed, attempting to shift the blame for the stalemate in Sino-

Japanese relations completely to the shoulders of the army in order to escape his own folly. Ugaki considered the cabinet dispute between Tanaka and Shirakawa "disgraceful in the extreme." Ugaki, *Ugaki Kazunari nikki* 1: 702 (entry for 25 Nov. 1928), 704 (entry for 24 Dec. 1928).

89. Takeuchi, *War and Diplomacy*, 276. This work carries an excellent account of the Diet debate, 275–81.

90. Yamaura, *Mori Kaku*, 641. Adachi and Egi were powerful figures in the Minseitō. Ugaki acknowledged meetings with the two men in his diary, but he did not specifically link the talks with an effort to unseat Tanaka. Ugaki, *Ugaki Kazunari nikki* 1: 709 (entry for 10 Feb. 1929). Adachi could well sympathize with Kōmoto's plight. He had plotted the brutal assassination of Queen Min of Korea in 1895. Like Kōmoto's, Adachi's "patriotic" murder escaped punishment.

91. Nihon Kokusai Seiji Gakkai, *Taiheiyō sensō e no michi* 1: 322.

92. Ugaki, *Ugaki Kazunari nikki* 1: 684–85 (entry for 25 Aug. 1928).

93. Lt. Gen. Abe Nobuyuki replaced Lt. Gen. Hata Eitarō in this position on 10 August 1928. Nihon Kindai Shiryō Kenkyūkai, *Nihon rikukaigun no seido*, 131.

94. Takakura, *Tanaka Giichi denki* 2: 1037.

95. Ibid.

96. Ibid., 1039; Okada, *Okada Keisuke kaikoroku*, 37, 40–41; and Harada, *Saionji-kō to seikyoku*, 11. Some versions had Tanaka in tears. See Takamiya, *Gunkoku taiheiki*, 56. Actually, no one knows exactly what was said between the emperor and the prime minister; not even Grand Chamberlain Suzuki was present when the two men spoke. All reports of their conversation are hearsay. In other words, it is not clear whether Tanaka lied to the emperor and told him that the army was uninvolved in Zhang's assassination or whether he merely told the emperor that the army would handle blame in the matter of Zhang's death internally. See Suzuki, *Suzuki Kantarō jiden*, 254–55; Tazaki, *Hyōden Tanaka Giichi* 2: 707–10; and Titus, *Palace and Politics in Prewar Japan*, 144–47. According to material made public in January 1989, in March 1946 the emperor told a group including the deputy grand chamberlain of that day that he had reprimanded Prime Minister Tanaka, saying, "That's different from what you told me before. It might be best for you to submit your resignation." "Kushita Michio Nikki," quoted in Ōe, *Chō Sakurin bakusatsu*, 119–20.

97. Nihon Kokusai Seiji Gakkai, *Taiheiyō sensō e no michi* 1: 327. All four men left the service.

8. Conclusion

1. There is a myth that persists in attributing the narrow-mindedness of the Japanese army officer at least in part to the fact that he saw so little of the outside world. (To what might we attribute the narrowness of the European and American army officer of the same period?) Actually, the imperial army has a far better record in constructive overseas service for its future leaders than one might imagine. My own random sampling of 50 officers bears this out. My first sample, 25 lieutenant generals and generals holding high military posts in the years 1918–29,

revealed that only one (Ōtani) had never been to Europe on assignment or for study. Four others, Honjō, Koiso, Minami, and Suzuki Sōroku, had not served in Europe, but they had all traveled extensively there. The remaining 20 had considerable-to-long periods of European experience. Ōi, for one example, spent nine years in Germany; Muraoka's service, for another, was confined to Turkey. My second sampling was among 25 representatives of the Futabakai-Issekikai group. Of these men only Kōmoto had no European experience. Seven others had only traveled in Europe. The remaining 17 had extensive European — or, in one case (Watari), American — experience. The older group had averaged a longer time in their overseas assignments, but many of the younger men had additional experience in China. This survey included no wartime combat service or service in troop units in China for either group.

As a second check among a wider body of officers, I looked at the records of staff college graduates from the 1st class (1885) to the 50th (1938). During the first phase of the college's operation, to 1898, when no graduating class exceeded 17 members, an average 33 percent of the graduates went to a European assignment immediately upon graduating. During the second phase, 1899–1908, when classes did not exceed 45 members, only about 17 percent went to Europe after graduation. In the long third, or modern, phase of college history a steady average of 20–25 percent of the graduates left for assignments in Europe or the United States until the year 1935. In 1936 only 1 officer went overseas — to Great Britain. In 1937 and subsequent years none served in overseas assignments after graduation because Japan was at war. This survey included only officers sent overseas to European and American assignments immediately upon graduation from the staff college. Others went in later years. One can say tentatively, then, that roughly 25 percent of the elite staff college group experienced service in advanced foreign nations from 1885 until the China Incident, and in general this 25 percent were the top graduates of the staff college, who later formed the top stratum of army leadership. It is true that few line officers served in such assignments, but the staff, not the line, became the decision makers or those whose work most influenced the decision makers. One can assume, then, that the officers' overseas experience confirmed rather than refuted the commonly held view of Japan's place in the world and of the violently competitive nature of nation-states.

2. Dore and Ōuchi, "Rural Origins of Japanese Fascism," 201–3.

3. Araki, *Uehara Yūsaku den* 2: 164.

4. Inaba, *Okamura Yasuji taishō shiryō*, 368–69. Okamura clearly shows that the demise of the Futabaki/Issekikai had at its root the bitter personal rivalry between Nagata and Obata, but he categorically denies that it had any factional overtones.

5. In this day of great horizontal mobility in our own society, we tend to forget the tremendous difficulty any person faced in changing employment or profession in the Japan of the 1920's. For most Japanese the course of their lives and their careers was pretty well set at an early age. Young people of high intelligence and low economic station who received enough education to enter a profession usually had but one choice. If this one choice was a bad one, they had to live with it. The

army's *yōnen gakkō* system locked bright youngsters into an army career at the age of twelve. As late as 1956 I met an officer in the Japan Self-Defense Force so discontent with his calling that it showed in everything he did. His colleagues told me sympathetically that he was a *machigai gunjin* — a soldier by mistake. Having unfortunately chosen the military service as his profession, and finding out later that he disliked the life, he could do nothing but live with his mistake.

For this reason few people voluntarily resigned their commissions even in extraordinarily bad times. Leaving the military service for another occupation was no safety valve for the system. As a result, pent-up discontent tended to mount within the confines of the army itself. There were exceptions, of course. Several dedicated radicals of the "young officers movement" did leave the service. "Young officers" Muranaka Kōji and Isobe Asaichi resigned in 1935. Nishida Mitsugi's retirement may have been in accord with his own desires. Shibukawa Zensuke, a brilliant cadet and scion of a well-to-do family, declined his commission.

6. Gordon, *Labor and Imperial Democracy in Japan*, characterizes this process as the collapse of imperial democracy. See especially chaps. 9 and 10.

Bibliography

Araki Sadao, ed. *Gensui Uehara Yūsaku den* (Biography of Marshal Uehara Yūsaku). 2 vols. Tokyo: Gensui Uehara Yūsaku Denki Kankōkai, 1937.

Arita Hachirō. *Bakahachi to hito wa iu* (People call me Hachi the Fool). Tokyo: Kōwadō, 1959.

Ayakawa Takeji. *Kindai shisō to guntai* (Modern ideas and the army). Tokyo: Heisho Shuppansha, 1929.

———. *Shōrai no sensō to kindai shisō* (Future war and modern ideas). Tokyo: Heisho Shuppansha, 1931.

Banba Nobuya. *Manshū jihen e no michi: Shidehara gaikō to Tanaka gaikō* (Road to the Manchurian Incident: Shidehara diplomacy and Tanaka diplomacy). Tokyo: Chūō Kōronsha, 1972.

Barnhart, Michael A. *Japan Prepares for Total War: The Search for Economic Security, 1919–1941.* Ithaca: Cornell University Press, 1987.

Bendix, Reinhard. "Preconditions of Development: A Comparison of Japan and Germany." In R. P. Dore, ed., *Aspects of Social Change in Modern Japan.* Princeton: Princeton University Press, 1967.

Bōeichō, Bōei Kenshūjo, Senshishitsu. *Senshi sōsho: Daihon'ei rikugunbu* (War history series: Imperial headquarters, army section). Vol. 1, *Shōwa jūgonen gogatsu made* (Up to May 1940). Tokyo: Asagumo Shinbunsha, 1967.

Bowen, Roger W. *Rebellion and Democracy in Meiji Japan: A Study of Commoners in the Popular Rights Movement.* Berkeley and Los Angeles: University of California Press, 1980.

Brown, Delmer M. *Nationalism in Japan.* Berkeley and Los Angeles: University of California Press, 1955.

Butow, Robert J. C. *Tojo and the Coming of the War.* Princeton: Princeton University Press, 1961.

Byas, Hugh. *Government by Assassination.* New York: Knopf, 1943.

Clyde, Paul H. *International Rivalries in Manchuria, 1689–1922.* 2d rev. ed. Columbus: Ohio State University Press, 1928.

Colgrove, Kenneth W. *Militarism in Japan.* Boston and New York: World Peace Foundation, 1936.

Cook, Theodore Failor, Jr. "The Japanese Officer Corps: The Making of a Military Elite, 1872–1945." Ph.D. diss., Princeton University, 1987.

Coox, Alvin D. *Nomonhan: Japan Against Russia, 1939.* 2 vols. Stanford: Stanford University Press, 1985.

———. *Tojo.* New York: Ballantine, 1975.

———. *Year of the Tiger.* Tokyo and Philadelphia: Orient/West, 1964.

Coox, Alvin D., and Hilary Conroy, eds. *China and Japan: A Search for Balance Since World War I.* Santa Barbara and Oxford: ABC-Clio, 1978.

Crowley, James B. "From Closed Doors to Empire." In Bernard S. Silberman and H. D. Harootunian, eds., *Modern Japanese Leadership: Transition and Change.* Tucson: University of Arizona Press, 1963.

———. "Japanese Army Factionalism in the Early 1930's." *Journal of Asian Studies* 21 (1962): 309–26.

———. *Japan's Quest for Autonomy: National Security and Foreign Policy, 1930–1938.* Princeton: Princeton University Press, 1966.

———, ed. *Modern East Asia: Essays in Interpretation.* New York: Harcourt, Brace and World, 1970.

Daitōa (taiheiyō) sensō senshi sōsho, vol. 8, appendix 8. Tokyo: Asagumo Shinbunsha, 1967.

Dore, Ronald P., ed. *Aspects of Social Change in Modern Japan.* Princeton: Princeton University Press, 1967.

Dore, Ronald P., and Tsutomu Ōuchi. "Rural Origins of Japanese Fascism." In James William Morley, ed., *Dilemmas of Growth in Prewar Japan.* Princeton: Princeton University Press, 1971.

Dull, Paul S. "The Assassination of Chang Tso-lin." *Far Eastern Quarterly* 11 (1952): 453–63.

Duus, Peter. "The Era of Party Rule, 1905–1932." In James B. Crowley, ed., *Modern East Asia: Essays in Interpretation.* New York: Harcourt, Brace and World, 1970.

———. *Party Rivalry and Political Change in Taisho Japan.* Cambridge: Harvard University Press, 1968.

Duus, Peter, Ramon H. Myers, and Mark Peattie, eds. *The Japanese Informal Empire in China, 1895–1937.* Princeton: Princeton University Press, 1989.

Duus, Peter, and Daniel I. Okimoto. "Fascism and the History of Pre-War Japan: The Failure of a Concept." *Journal of Asian Studies* 39 (1979): 65–76.

Earl, David M. *Emperor and Nation in Japan.* Seattle: University of Washington Press, 1964.

Fifield, Russell H. *Woodrow Wilson and the Far East: The Diplomacy of the Shantung Question.* 1952. Reprint. Hamden, Conn.: Anchor, 1965.

Fujiwara Akira. *Gunjishi* (History of military affairs). Tokyo: Tōyō Keizai Shinpōsha, 1961.

———. "Sōryokusen dankai ni okeru Nihon guntai no mujun" (Contradictions in the Japanese army in the era of total war). *Shisō,* no. 399 (Sept. 1957): 22–32.

Fukuchi Shigetaka. *Gunkoku Nihon no keisei: Shizoku ishoku no hatten to sono shūmatsu* (The formation of militarist Japan: The development of samurai consciousness and its result). Tokyo: Shunjūsha, 1959.

Fukushima, Shingo. "The Building of a National Army." In Tobata Seiichi, ed., *The Modernization of Japan*, vol. 1. Tokyo: Institute of Asian Economic Affairs, 1966.

Funaki Shigeru. *Shina hakengun sōshireikan: Okamura Yasuji Taishō* (China expeditionary army commanding general: General Okamura Yasuji). Tokyo: Kawade Shobō Shinsha, 1984.

Gaimushō. *Nihon gaikō nenpyō narabi shuyō monjo* (Chronology and principal documents in Japanese diplomacy). 2 vols. Meiji hyakunenshi sōsho, vols. 1–2. Tokyo: Hara Shobō, 1965–66.

Garon, Sheldon. *The State and Labor in Modern Japan*. Berkeley and Los Angeles: University of California Press, 1987.

General Headquarters, Supreme Commander for the Allied Powers, Civil Intelligence Section. "The Brocade Banner: The Story of Japanese Nationalism." Sept. 1946. Mimeo.

Gordon, Andrew. *Labor and Imperial Democracy in Prewar Japan*. Berkeley and Los Angeles: University of California Press, 1991.

Hackett, Roger F. *Yamagata Aritomo in the Rise of Modern Japan, 1838–1922*. Cambridge: Harvard University Press, 1971.

Hall, John W. "Changing Conceptions of the Modernization of Japan." In Marius Jansen, ed., *Changing Japanese Attitudes Toward Modernization*. Princeton: Princeton University Press, 1965.

Hara Kei. *Hara Kei nikki* (Diaries of Hara Kei), vols. 7–9. Hara Kei'ichirō, ed. Tokyo: Kengensha, 1950–52.

Harada, Kumao. *The Saionji-Harada Memoirs*. Tokyo, 1947.

———. *Saionji-kō to seikyoku* (Prince Saionji and the political situation), vol. 1. Tokyo: Iwanami Shoten, 1950.

Hata Ikuhiko. *Gun fuashizumu undōshi* (A history of the military fascism movement). Tokyo: Kawade Shobō, 1962.

———. "Nihon guntai no kensetsu to hatten" (The Japanese army's establishment and progress). *Chūō kōron*, Nov. 1962, pp. 211–21.

———. "Sanbō Ishiwara Kanji" (Staff Officer Ishiwara Kanji). *Jiyū*, Aug. 1963, pp. 140–49; Sept. 1963, pp. 140–49; Oct. 1963, pp. 123–31.

Hata Shinji. *Teikoku no kokubō* (Defense of the empire). Tokyo: Senshinsha, 1932.

Hayashi Gonsuke. *Waga shichijūnen o kataru* (Talking over my seventy years). Tokyo: Daiichi Shobō, 1936.

Hayashi Katsuya. *Nihon gunji gijitsushi* (A history of Japan's military technology). Tokyo: Aoki Shoten, 1957.

Hayashi Masaharu. *Rikugun taishō Honjō Shigeru* (Army General Honjō Shigeru). Tokyo: Seishōkai Rikugun Taishō Honjō Shigeru Denki Kankōkai, 1967.

Hayashi Saburō. *Taiheiyō sensō rikugun gaishi* (Outline history of the army in the Pacific War). Tokyo: Iwanami Shoten, 1951.

Hayashi, Saburo, in collaboration with Alvin D. Coox. *Kōgun: The Japanese Army in the Pacific War*. Quantico, Va.: Marine Corps Association, 1959.

Hayashi Shigeru, ed. *Dokyumento Shōwashi* (Documents on Shōwa-era history), vol. 1, *Shōwa Shonen* (Early Shōwa). Tokyo: Heibonsha, 1975.

"Himerareta Shōwashi" (Hidden Shōwa history). *Chisei*, supplementary issue, Dec. 1956.

Hirata Shinsaku. *Rikugun tokuhon* (An army reader). Tokyo: Nihon Hyōronsha, 1932.

Hiroe Genzaburō. *Guntai shakai no kenkyū* (A study of military society). Tokyo: Shūeikaku, 1925.

Holtom, Daniel C. *Modern Japan and Shinto Nationalism*. Rev. ed. Chicago: University of Chicago Press, 1947.

Honjō Shigeru. *Honjō nikki* (Honjō diary). Meiji hyakunenshi sōsho, vol. 13. Tokyo: Hara Shobō, 1967.

Humphreys, Leonard A. "The Imperial Japanese Army, 1918–1929: The Disintegration of the Meiji Military System." Ph.D. diss., Stanford University, 1974.

I Hyon Chiyoru (Lee Hyong Cheol). *Gunbu no Shōwashi* (History of the military in the Shōwa era). Vol. 1, *Gōhōteki kansetsu shihai e no michi* (The road to legal indirect leadership). Tokyo: Nihon Hōsō Shuppan Kyōkai, 1987.

Iizuka Hiroji. *Nihon no guntai* (Japan's army). Tokyo: Tōdai Kyōdō Kumiai Shuppanbu, 1950.

Ike, Nobutaka. "War and Modernization." In Robert E. Ward, ed., *Political Development in Modern Japan*. Princeton: Princeton University Press, 1968.

Ikei, Masaru. "Japan's Response to the Chinese Revolution of 1911." *Journal of Asian Studies* 25 (1966): 213–27.

———. "Kindai Nihon ni okeru gunbu no seijiteki chii" (The political position of the military in modern Japan). In Keiō Gijuku Daigaku Chiiki Kenkyū Gurupu, ed., *Hendōki ni okeru gunbu to guntai* (The army and militarists in a time of change). Tokyo: Keiō Tsūshinkan, 1968.

Imai Seiichi. "Taishōki ni okeru gunbu no seijiteki chii" (The political position of the military in the Taishō era). *Shisō*, no. 402 (Dec. 1957): 106–22.

Imai Seiichi and Takahashi Masae, eds. *Kokkashugi undō* (The nationalist movement), vol. 1. Gendaishi shiryō, vol. 4. Tokyo: Misuzu Shobō, 1963.

Imamura Hitoshi. *Imamura Hitoshi kaikoroku* (Imamura Hitoshi memoir). Vol. 1, *Ori no naka no baku* (The caged tapir). Tokyo: Jiyū Ajiasha, 1960.

———. *Imamura Hitoshi kaikoroku* (Imamura Hitoshi memoir). Vol. 2, *Kōzoku to kashikan* (The prince and the sergeant). Tokyo: Jiyū Ajiasha, 1960.

Imamura Takeo. *Takahashi Korekiyo*. Tokyo: Jiji Tsūshinsha, 1958.

Imanishi Eizō. *Shōwa rikugun habatsu kōsōshi* (Disputes among army factions in the Shōwa era). Tokyo: Dentō to Gendaisha, 1975.

Inaba Masao. "Manshū jihen" (The Manchurian Incident), part 1. *Kokubō*, June 1962.

———, ed. *Daihon'ei* (Imperial general headquarters). Gendaishi shiryō, vol. 37. Tokyo: Misuzu Shobō, 1967.

——, ed. *Okamura Yasuji taishō shiryō* (General Okamura Yasuji historical materials). Vol. 1, *Senba kaisōhen* (Battlefield reminiscence section). Meiji hyakunenshi sōsho, vol. 99. Tokyo: Hara Shobō, 1970.

Inaba Masao, Kobayashi Tatsuo, and Shimada Toshihiko, eds. *Zoku Manshū jihen* (More on the Manchurian Incident). Gendaishi shiryō, vol. 11. Tokyo: Misuzu Shobō, 1965.

Inoue Kiyoshi. *Nihon no gunkokushugi* (Japanese militarism). 9 vols. Tokyo: Tōkyō Daigaku Shuppankai, 1954.

Iriye, Akira. *Across the Pacific: An Inner History of American–East Asian Relations.* New York: Harcourt, Brace and World, 1967.

——. *After Imperialism: The Search for a New Order in the Far East, 1921–1931.* Cambridge: Harvard University Press, 1965.

——. "The Ideology of Japanese Imperialism: Imperial Japan and China." In Grant K. Goodman, comp., *Imperial Japan and Asia: A Reassessment.* New York: Columbia University, East Asian Institute, 1967.

——. "Japan's Foreign Policies Between World Wars—Sources and Interpretations." Review article on *Gendaishi shiryō,* vols. 7–13. *Journal of Asian Studies* 26 (1967): 677–82.

Ishida Morimasa. *Ōshū taisenshi no kenkyū* (A historical study of the Great War in Europe). 9 vols. Tokyo: Rikugun Daigakkō Shōkō Shūkaisha, 1925.

Ishiwara Kanji. *Sensōshi taikan* (An outline of the history of war). Tokyo: Chūō Kōronsha, 1941.

Itagaki Seishirō Kankōkai. *Hiroku Itagaki Seishirō* (Secret memoirs of Itagaki Seishirō). Tokyo: Fuyō Shobō, 1972.

Itō Keiichi. *Heitaitachi no rikugunshi: Heiei to senba seikatsu* (The soldier's military history: Life in barracks and battlefield). Tokyo: Banchō Shobō, 1969.

Itō Kobun. *Meiji kokka ni okeru seigun kankei—guntai to kokka no kankei no ichijirei kenkyū—* (The connection between the political and military worlds in the Meiji state—a study of one instance of the relationship of army and state). 2 parts. Bōeironshū, vol. 7, nos. 2–3. Tokyo: [Bōeichō], 1968–69.

Itō Masanori. *Gunbatsu kōbōshi* (The history of the fall of the military clique). 3 vols. Tokyo: Bungei Shunjū Shinsha, 1958.

——. *Kokubōshi* (National defense history). Kindai Nihon bunseishi, vol. 4. Tokyo: Tōyō Keizai Shinpōsha Shuppanbu, 1941.

——, ed. *Katō Takaaki* 2. Tokyo: Katō-haku Denki Hensan Iinkai, 1929.

Itō Miyoji. *Suiusō nikki* (The Suiusō diary). Tokyo: Yuhikaku, 1963.

Itō Takashi. *Shōwa shoki seijishi kenkyū* (A study of political history in the early Shōwa era). Tokyo: Tōkyō Daigaku Shuppankai, 1969.

Itoya Hisao and Inaoka Susumu. *Nihon no sōran hyakunen* (A hundred years of disturbances in Japan), vol. 2. Gendaishi shiryō, vol. 6. Tokyo: Gendai Hyōronsha, 1969.

Iwabuchi Tatsuo. *Gunbatsu no keifu* (Genealogy of the military clique). Tokyo: Chūō Kōronsha, 1948.

Izu Kimio [Akabane Hisashi] and Matsushita Yoshio. *Nihon gunji hattatsushi*

(The history of the development of the military in Japan). Tokyo: Mikasa Shobō, 1938.

Jansen, Marius B., ed. *Changing Japanese Attitudes Toward Modernization*. Princeton: Princeton University Press, 1965.

Johnson, Chalmers. *Peasant Nationalism and Communist Power: The Emergence of Revolutionary China, 1937–1945*. Stanford: Stanford University Press, 1962.

Jordan, Donald A. *The Northern Expedition: China's National Revolution of 1926–1928*. Honolulu: University Press of Hawaii, 1976.

Kantō Daishinsai 50 Shūnen Chōsenjin Giseisha Tsuitō Gyōji Jikkō Iinkai Chōsa Iinkai. *Rekishi nō shinjitsu: Kantō daishinsai to Chōsenjin* (Historical truth: The great Kantō earthquake disaster and the Koreans). Gendaishi shiryō, vol. 6. Tokyo: Misuzu Shobō, 1963.

Katogawa Kōtarō. *Sanjūhachi shiki hoheijū: Nihon rikugun no shichijūgonen* (The mark 38 rifle: The 75 years of the Japanese army). Tokyo: Hakkin Shobō, 1975.

Kawabe Torashirō. *Ichigayadai kara Ichigayadai e* (From Ichigaya Heights to Ichigaya Heights). Tokyo: Jiji Tsūshinsha Shuppankyoku, 1962.

Kawamoto [Kōmoto] Daisaku. "Watakushi ga Chō Sakurin o koroshita" (I killed Zhang Zuolin). *Bungei shunjū*, vol. 32, no. 18 (Dec. 1954): 194–201.

Keiō Gijuku Daigaku Chiiki Kenkyū Gurupu, ed. *Hendōki ni okeru gunbu to guntai* (The army and militarists in a time of change). Tokyo: Keiō Tsūshinkan, 1968.

Kennedy, Malcolm D. *The Changing Fabric of Japan*. London: Constable, 1930.

——. *The Estrangement of Great Britain and Japan, 1917–35*. Berkeley and Los Angeles: University of California Press, 1969.

——. *The Military Side of Japanese Life*. London: Constable, 1924.

——. *Some Aspects of Japan and Her Defense Forces*. London: K. Paul, Trench, Trubner, 1928.

Kido Nikki Kenkyūkai, Nihon Kindai Shiryō Kenkyūkai. "Inada Masazumi-shi danwa sokkiroku" (Oral record of Mr. Inada Masazumi). Nihon kindai shiryō sōsho, vol. B-2. Tokyo: Nihon Kindai Shiryō Kenkyūkai, 1969. Mimeo.

——. "Nishiura Susumu-shi danwa sokkiroku" (Oral record of Mr. Nishiura Susumu). 2 vols. Nihon kindai shiryō sōsho, vol. B-1. Tokyo: Nihon Kindai Shiryō Kenkyūkai, 1968. Mimeo.

——. "Suzuki Teiichi-shi danwa sokkiroku" (Oral record of Mr. Suzuki Teiichi). 2 vols. Nihon kindai shiryō sōsho, vol. B-4. Tokyo: Nihon Kindai Shiryō Kenkyūkai, 1971. Mimeo.

Kikkawa Manabu. *Arashi to tatakau tesshō Araki* (Philosopher General Araki who braved the tempests). *Shōgun Araki no shichijūnen* (General Araki's seventy years), vol. 2. Tokyo: Araki Sadao Shōgun Denki Hensan Kankōkai, 1955.

——. *Hiroku rikugun rimenshi* (A secret inside history of the army). *Shōgun Araki no shichijūnen* (General Araki's seventy years), vol. 1. Tokyo: Yamato Shobō, 1954.

Kinoshita Hanji. *Nihon fuashizumushi* (A history of Japanese fascism), vol. 1. Tokyo: Iwasaki Shoten, 1951.

Kitaoka Shin'ichi. "China Experts in the Army." In Peter Duus, Ramon H. Myers, and Mark Peattie, eds., *The Japanese Informal Empire in China, 1895–1937*. Princeton: Princeton University Press, 1989.

——. *Nihon rikugun to tairiku seisaku, 1906–1918* (The Japanese army's continental policy, 1906–1918). Tokyo: Tōkyō Daigaku Shuppankai, 1978.

Kobayashi Jun'ichirō. *Rikugun no konpon kaizō* (Basic reform of the army). Tokyo: Jiyūsha, 1924.

Kobayashi Tatsuo and Shimada Toshihiko, eds. *Manshū jihen* (The Manchurian Incident). Gendaishi shiryō, vol. 7. Tokyo: Misuzu Shobō, 1964.

Koiso Kuniaki. *Katsuzan kōsō*. Tokyo: Koiso Kuniaki Jijoden Kankōkai, 1963.

Kojima Noboru. *Shisetsu Yamashita Tomoyuki* (Yamashita Tomoyuki in historical perspective). Tokyo: Bungei Shunjū, 1969.

Kono, Tsunekichi. *The Japanese Army*. Tokyo: Institute of Pacific Relations, Japanese Council, 1929.

Kōno Tsunekichi. *Kokushi no saikokuten* (The blackest page in national history), vol. 1. Tokyo: Jiji Shinpōsha, 1963.

Kublin, Hyman. "The 'Modern' Army of Early Meiji Japan." *Far Eastern Quarterly* 9 (1949): 20–41.

Kurihara Ken, ed. *Tai-Manmō seisakushi no ichimen* (One aspect of the policy toward Manchuria and Mongolia). Meiji hyakunenshi sōsho, vol. 10. Tokyo: Hara Shobō, 1966.

Lehmann, Jean-Pierre. *The Roots of Modern Japan*. New York: St. Martin's Press, 1982.

Lockwood, William W. *The Economic Development of Japan*. Princeton: Princeton University Press, 1954.

——. *The State and Economic Enterprise in Japan*. Princeton: Princeton University Press, 1965.

Lory, Hillis. *Japan's Military Masters*. New York: Viking, 1943.

Ludendorff, Erich. *My War Memories, 1914–1918*. 2 vols. Original German ed. 1919. 3rd English ed. London: Hutchinson, n.d.

McCormack, Gavan. *Chang Tso-lin in Northeast China, 1911–1928: China, Japan, and the Manchurian Idea*. Stanford: Stanford University Press, 1977.

Machino Takema. "Chō Sakurin bakushi no zengo" (Before and after Zhang Zuolin's assassination). *Chūō kōron*, vol. 64, no. 9 (Sept. 1949): 72–80.

Maeda Haruyori. *Shōwa hanranshi* (A history of the rebellions of the Shōwa era). Tokyo: Nihon Shūhōsha, 1964.

Maejima Shōzō. *Shōwa gunbatsu no jidai* (The period of the Shōwa military cliques). Tokyo: Minerva Shobō, 1969.

Majima Ken. *Gunbatsu antō hishi: Rikugun hōkai no ichidanmen* (A secret history of the military cliques: One aspect of the army's collapse). Tokyo: Kyōdō Shuppansha, 1946.

Maki, John M. *Japanese Militarism: Its Cause and Cure*. New York: Knopf, 1945.

Maruyama Masao. *Gendai seiji no shisō to kōdō* (Thought and behavior in modern politics), vol 1. Tokyo: Miraisha, 1956.

——. *Thought and Behavior in Modern Japanese Politics*. Ivan I. Morris, ed. and trans. London: Oxford University Press, 1963.

Matsumoto Seichō. *Shōwashi hakkutsu* (Unearthing the history of the Shōwa era), vols. 1–3. Tokyo: Bungei Shunjū Shinsha, 1965–72.

Matsumura Shūitsu. *Miyakezaka—gunbatsu wa ikan ni shite umaretaka* (How was the military clique born?). Tokyo: Tōkō Shobō, 1952.

Matsushita Yoshio. *Chōheirei seitei no zengo* (Before and after the enactment of the conscription law). Tokyo: Kaikosha, 1932.

——. *Chōheirei seiteishi* (The enactment of the conscription law). Tokyo: Naigai Shobō, 1943.

——. *Gunjishi monogatari* (The Story of military affairs). Tokyo: Kokumin Tosho Kyōkai, 1939.

——. *Gunsei kaikakuron* (The debate on the reform of military administration). Tokyo: Seiunkaku, 1928.

——. *Hansen undōshi* (A history of the antiwar movement). Tokyo: Gengensha, 1954.

——. *Kindai Nihon gunjishi* (A history of military affairs in present-day Japan). Tokyo: Kigensha, 1941.

——. *Meiji gunsei shiron* (A historical essay on Meiji military politics), vol. 2. Tokyo: Yuhikaku, 1956.

——. *Meiji gunsei shironshū* (A collection of essays on Meiji military politics). Tokyo: Ikuseisha, 1938.

——. *Meiji no guntai* (The Meiji army). Tokyo: Nihon Rekishi Shinsho, 1963.

——. *Nihon gunbatsu no kōbō* (The fall of the Japanese military clique). 3 vols. Tokyo: Jinbutsu Ōraisha, 1967.

——. *Nihon gunjishi sōwa* (A collection of stories on Japanese military affairs). Tokyo: Tsuchiya Shoten, 1963.

——. *Nihon gunjishi zatsuwa* (Random stories on the history of Japanese military affairs). Tokyo: Tsuchiya Shoten, 1966.

——. *Nihon gunsei to seiji* (The military and politics in Japan). Tokyo: Kuroshio Shuppan, 1960.

——. *Nihon no gunbatsuzō* (Portraits of Japan's military leaders). Tokyo: Hara Shobō, 1969.

——. *Nihon rikukaigun sōdōshi* (A history of the strife between the Japanese army and navy). Tokyo: Tsuchiya Shoten, 1966.

——. *Rikukai gunji shiwa* (Historical talks on army and navy military affairs). Tokyo: Shikai Shobō, 1938.

——. *Rikukaigun sōdōshi* (A history of strife between the army and navy). Tokyo: Kuroshio Shuppan, 1959.

Maxon, Yale C. *Control of Japanese Foreign Policy*. Berkeley and Los Angeles: University of California Press, 1957.

Mitarai Tatsuo, ed. *Minami Jirō*. Tokyo: Minami Jirō Denki Kankōkai, 1957.

Mori Shōzō. *Senpū nijūnen* (Twenty years of the whirlwind), vol. 1. Tokyo: Masu Shobō, 1945.

Morishima Morito. *Inbō, ansatsu, guntō* (Intrigue, assassination, military swords). Tokyo: Iwanami Shoten, 1950.

Morley, James W., ed. *Dilemmas of Growth in Prewar Japan*. Princeton: Princeton University Press, 1971.

———. *The Japanese Thrust into Siberia, 1918*. New York: Columbia University Press, 1957.

Morris, Ivan I. *Nationalism and the Right Wing in Japan*. London: Oxford University Press, 1957.

Morton, William F. *Tanaka Giichi and Japan's Foreign Policy*. New York: St. Martin's Press, 1980.

Murakami Hyōe. *Japan: The Years of Trial, 1919–52*. Tokyo: Japan Culture Institute, 1982.

———. *Konoe rentaiki* (The flag of the guards regiment). Tokyo: Akita Shoten, 1967.

Nagata Tetsuzan. *Kokka sōdōin* (State general mobilization). Osaka: Ōsaka Mainichi Shinbunsha, 1928.

Nagata Tetsuzan Kankōkai, ed. *Hiroku Nagata Tetsuzan* (Nagata Tetsuzan's secret memoirs). Tokyo: Fuyō Shobō, 1972.

Naimushō. *Nihon kakushinron taikō* (Fundamentals of the reform controversy in Japan). Tokyo: [Naimushō], ca. 1933.

Naimushō, Keihokyoku. *Fuashizumu no riron* (The theory of fascism). Tokyo: [Naimushō], 1932.

———. *Shakai undō no jōkyō* (The situation of the social movement). Annual publication. Tokyo, 1927/1928 and 1929.

———. *Shuppanbutsu o tsujite mitaru Nihon kakushinron genkyō* (Present conditions in the Japan reform controversy as seen through published materials). Tokyo: [Naimushō], 1933.

Najita, Tetsuo. *Hara Kei in the Politics of Compromise, 1905–1915*. Cambridge: Harvard University Press, 1967.

Nakamura Kikuo. *Manshū jihen* (The Manchurian Incident). Tokyo: Nihon Kyōbunsha, 1965.

———. *Shōwa rikugun hishi* (A secret history of the army in the Shōwa era). Tokyo: Banchō Shobō, 1968.

———. *Tennōsei fuashizumu ron* (A theory of emperor-centered fascism). Tokyo: Hara Shobō, 1967.

Nakane, Chie. *Japanese Society*. Berkeley and Los Angeles: University of California Press, 1970.

Nakano Masao. *Hashimoto Taisa no shuki* (The handwritten notes of Colonel Hashimoto). Tokyo: Misuzu Shobō, 1963.

Nakano Tomio. *Tōsuiken no dokuritsu* (The independence of the Supreme Command). Tokyo: Yuhikaku, 1934.

Nara Takeji. "Nara Takeji Taishō kaikoroku sōan" (General Nara Takeji's memoirs, draft). 1928.

Narita Atsushi. *Rikukaigun udekurabe* (Comparing the muscles of the army and navy). Tokyo: Dai-Nihon Yūbenkai, 1928.

National Archives of the United States, Modern Military Records Division, Records of the War Department General Staff, Record Group 165.

Nihon gunkoku shugi (Japanese militarism). *Shisō*, nos. 399, 400, and 402 (Sept., Oct., and Dec. 1957).

Nihon Kindai Shiryō Kenkyūkai, comp. *Nihon rikukaigun no seido, soshiki, jinji* (The system, organization, and personnel of the Japanese army and navy). Tokyo: Tōkyō Daigaku Shuppankai, 1971.

Nihon Kokusai Seiji Gakkai, Taiheiyō Sensō Gen'in Kenkyūbu, ed. *Taiheiyō sensō e no michi: Kaisen gaikōshi* (The road to the Pacific War: Diplomatic history to the outbreak of war). Vol. 1, *Manshū jihen zenya* (The eve of the Manchurian Incident). Tokyo: Asahi Shinbunsha, 1962.

———. *Taiheiyō sensō e no michi: Kaisen gaikōshi* (The road to the Pacific War: Diplomatic history to the outbreak of war). Vol. 2, *Manshū jihen* (The Manchurian Incident). Tokyo: Asahi Shinbunsha, 1962.

Nishida Mitsugu. "Sen'un o sashimaneku" (Beckoning the war clouds). In Tanikawa Ken'ichi, Tsurumi Shunpo, and Murakami Ichirō, eds., *Hangyakusha* (The dissidents). Vol. 3 of *Dokyumento Nihonjin* (Documents of the Japanese people). Tokyo: Gakugei Shorin, 1968.

Nitobe, Inazo. *Bushido, the Soul of Japan: An Exposition of Japanese Thought.* New York: Putnam's, 1905.

Nitobe Inazo et al. *Western Influences in Modern Japan: A Series of Papers on Cultural Relations.* Chicago: University of Chicago Press, ca. 1931.

Nukada Hiroshi. *Rikugunshō jinjikyokuchō no kaisō* (Recollections of a war ministry personnel bureau chief). Tokyo: Fuyō Shobō, 1977.

Ōe Shinobu. *Chō Sakurin no bakusatsu: Shōwa Tennō no tōsui* (The bombing death of Zhang Zuolin: The Shōwa emperor's command). Tokyo: Chūō Kōronsha, 1989.

Ogata Sadako. *Manshū jihen to seisaku no keisei katei* (The Manchurian Incident and the process of policy formation). Meiji hyakunenshi sōsho, vol. 12. Tokyo: Hara Shobō, 1966.

Ogata, Sadako N. *Defiance in Manchuria: The Making of Japanese Foreign Policy, 1931–1932.* Berkeley and Los Angeles: University of California Press, 1964.

Okada Keisuke. *Okada Keisuke kaikoroku* (Okada Keisuke's memoirs). Tokyo: Mainichi Shinbunsha, 1950.

Oki Shūji. *Yamashita Tomoyuki.* Tokyo: Akita Shoten, 1968.

Ōtani Keijirō. *Shōwa kenpeishi* (A history of the military police in the Shōwa era). Tokyo: Misuzu Shobō, 1966.

Otsu Jun'ichirō. *Dai-Nihon kenseishi* (Constitutional history of Greater Japan). 10 vols. Tokyo: Hōbunkan, 1927–28.

Ozaki Yoshiharu. *Rikugun o ugokashita hitobito* (The men who moved the army). Odawara: Hasshōdō Shoten, 1960.

Ozaki Yukio. *Nihon kenseishi o kataru* (Talking about Japan's constitutional history). 2 vols. Tokyo: Monasu, 1938.

Patrick, Hugh T. "The Economic Muddle of the 1920's." In James William Morley, ed., *Dilemmas of Growth in Prewar Japan*. Princeton: Princeton University Press, 1971.

Peattie, Mark. *Ishiwara Kanji and Japan's Confrontation with the West*. Princeton: Princeton University Press, 1975.

Presseisen, Ernst L. *Before Aggression: Europeans Prepare the Japanese Army*. Tucson: University of Arizona Press, 1965.

Pyle, Kenneth B. "Some Recent Approaches to Japanese Nationalism." In Irwin Scheiner, ed., *Modern Japan: An Interpretive Anthology*. New York: Macmillan, 1974.

————. "The Technology of Japanese Nationalism: The Local Improvement Movement, 1900–1918." *Journal of Asian Studies* 33 (1973): 51–65.

"Rikugun (Gen'eki shōkō dōsōtokan) jitsueki teinen meibō" (Army [active duty officers and civil officials] retirement lists). Materials in Bōeichō, Bōei Kenshūjo, Senshishitsu. Annual publication. 1927.

Rikugun shikan gakkō (The military academy). Tokyo: Akimoto Shobō, 1969.

Rikugun Shikan Gakkō. *Rikugun shikan gakkō no shinsō* (The truth about the military academy). Tokyo, ca. 1926.

Rikugunshō. *Gunrei, riku, daijūshichigō, guntai naimusho* (Military order, army, no. 17, army interior regulations). Tokyo, 1908.

————. *Guntai naimusho kaisei riyūsho* (Paper on the reasons for changing the army interior regulations). Tokyo, 1908.

————. "Guntai naimusho, Meiji yonjūichinen junigatsu tsuitachi, Taishō shichinen nigatsu nijūhachinichi kaitei" (Army interior regulations, 1 Dec. 1908, changes to 28 Feb. 1918). Unpublished material in Bōeichō, Bōei Kenshūjo, Senshishitsu.

————. *Meiji sanjūshichinenshi Taishō jūgonen rikugunshō enkakushi* (A history of the army ministry from 1904 to 1926). 3 vols. Tokyo, 1929.

————. *Naimusho kaisei riyūsho* (Paper on the reasons for changing the interior regulations). Tokyo, 1921.

————. "Seido chōsa ni kansuru shorui" (Documents relative to the examination of systems). Jan. 1924. Materials in Bōeichō, Bōei Kenshūjo, Senshishitsu.

————. *Teikoku rikugun gaiyō* (An outline of the imperial army). Tokyo, 1917.

Sakamoto Kizan [Tatsunosuke]. *Nihon gaisenshi* (A history of Japan's foreign wars). Tokyo: Banchōshōsha, 1935.

Sakurai Tadayoshi. *Human Bullets: A Soldier's Story of Port Arthur*. Tokyo: Teibi, 1907.

————. *Nikudan* (Human bullets). Gendai Nihon bungaku zenshū, vol. 49. 1906; Tokyo: Kaizōsha, 1929.

Sanbōhonbu. *Taishō shichinen naishi jūichinen Shiberia shuppeishi* (A history of the Siberian Expedition from 1918 to 1922). 6 vols.; 1924. Facsimile reprint in 3 vols. Tokyo: Shinjidaisha, 1972.

Sasaki Tōichi. *Aru gunjin no jiden* (Autobiography of a soldier). Tokyo: Keisō Shobō, 1963.

Satō Kiyokatsu. *Manmō mondai to waga tairiku seisaku* (The Manchuria-Mongolia problem and our continental policy). Tokyo: Shunjūsha, 1931.

——. *Teikoku kokubō no kiki* (The crisis in the defense of the empire). Tokyo: Nihon Senshi Kenkyūkai, 1931.

Satō Kōjirō. *Guntai to shakai mondai* (The military and the social problem). Tokyo: Seibundō, 1922.

——. *If Japan and America Fight*. Tokyo: Meguro Bunten, ca. 1921.

——. *Kokubōjō no shakai mondai* (The social problem from the standpoint of national defense). Tokyo: Seibundō, 1920.

Satō Rokuhei. *Kokubō genron* (The principles of national defense). Tokyo: Heiyō Tosho, 1930.

Scalapino, Robert. *Democracy and the Party Movement in Prewar Japan*. Berkeley and Los Angeles: University of California Press, 1962.

Scheiner, Irwin, ed. *Modern Japan: An Interpretive Anthology*. New York: Macmillan, 1974.

Shidehara Heiwa Zaidan. *Shidehara Kijūrō*. Tokyo: Shidehara Heiwa Zaidan, 1955.

Shigemitsu, Mamoru. *Japan and Her Destiny: My Struggle for Peace*. New York: Dutton, 1958.

——. *Shōwa no dōran* (Upheavals of the Shōwa era). 2 vols. Tokyo: Chūō Kōronsha, 1952.

Shillony, Ben-Ami. *Revolt in Japan: The Young Officers and the February 26, 1936, Incident*. Princeton: Princeton University Press, 1973.

Shimada Toshihiko. *Kantō gun: Zaiman rikugun no dokusō* (The Guandong army: The creation of the army in Manchuria). Tokyo: Chūō Kōronsha, 1965.

Shinmyō Takeo. "Shōwa seiji hishi — Chō Sakurin bakusatsu" (Secret political history of the Shōwa era — Zhang Zuolin's assassination). *Chūō kōron*, vol. 69, no. 4 (Apr. 1954): 190–201.

Shinobu Seizaburō. *Taishō demokurashiishi* (A history of democracy in the Taishō era). 3 vols. Tokyo: Nihon Hyōron Shinsha, 1954–59.

——. *Taishō seijishi* (A political history of the Taishō era), vol. 3. Tokyo: Kawade Shobō, 1952.

Silberman, Bernard S. "Bureaucratic Development and the Structure of Decision-Making in the Meiji Period." *Journal of Asian Studies* 27 (1967): 81–94.

Silberman, Bernard S., and H. D. Harootunian, eds. *Modern Japanese Leadership: Transition and Change*. Tucson: University of Arizona Press, 1963.

Singer, Kurt. *Mirror, Sword, and Jewel: A Study of Japanese Characteristics*. New York: George Braziller, 1973.

Smethurst, Richard J. *A Social Basis for Prewar Japanese Militarism: The Army and the Rural Community*. Berkeley and Los Angeles: University of California Press, 1974.

Smith, Thomas C. "Japan's Aristocratic Revolution." *Yale Review* 50 (1961): 370–83.

Smith, Warren W., Jr. *Confucianism in Modern Japan: A Study of Conservatism in Japanese Intellectual History*. Tokyo: Hokuseidō, 1973.

Stanley, Thomas A. *Ōsugi Sakae, Anarchist in Japan: The Creativity of the Ego*.

Harvard East Asian Monographs, vol. 102. Cambridge, Mass.: Harvard University, Council on East Asian Studies, 1982.

Stimson, Henry L. *The Far Eastern Crisis: Recollections and Observations*. New York: Harper, 1936.

Storry, Richard. *The Double Patriots: A Study of Japanese Nationalism*. Boston: Houghton Mifflin, 1957.

Suematsu Tahei. "Aomori hohei daigo rentai no kiroku" (A record of the 5th Infantry Regiment in Aomori). In Tanikawa Ken'ichi, Tsurumi Shunpo, and Murakami Ichirō, eds., *Hangyakusha* (The dissidents). Vol. 3 of *Dokyumento Nihonjin* (Documents of the Japanese people). Tokyo: Gakugei Shorin, 1968.

———. *Watakushi no Shōwashi* (My history of the Shōwa era). Tokyo: Misuzu Shobō, 1963.

Suzuki Hajime, ed. *Suzuki Kantarō jiden*. Tokyo: Jiji Tsūshinsha, 1968.

Suzuki Teiichi. "Hokubatsu to Shō-Tanaka mitsuyaku" (The northern clique and the Chiang [Kai-shek]–Tanaka [Giichi] secret agreement). *Chisei*, supplementary issue, Dec. 1956.

Takahashi Masae, ed. *Kokkashugi undō* (The nationalist movement), vol. 2. Gendaishi shiryō, vol. 5. Tokyo: Misuzu Shobō, 1964.

———. *Niniroku jiken* (The February 26th [1936] Incident). Tokyo: Chūō Kōronsha, 1965.

———. *Shōwa no gunbatsu* (The military cliques of the Shōwa era). Tokyo: Chūō Kōronsha, 1969.

Takakura Tetsuichi, ed. *Tanaka Giichi denki* (The biography of Tanaka Giichi). 2 vols. Tokyo: Tanaka Giichi Denki Kankōkai, 1958–60.

Takamiya Tahei. *Gunkoku taiheiki* (The record of a military paradise). Tokyo: Kantōsha, 1951.

———. *Jungyaku no shōwashi*. Reprint of *Gunkoku taiheiki*. Tokyo: Hara Shobō, 1971.

———. "Rikugun o nibun shita kōdōha-tōseiha" (The Kōdōha and Tōseiha, which split the army). *Chisei*, supplementary issue, Dec. 1956, pp. 114–27.

Takeuchi, Tatsuji. *War and Diplomacy in the Japanese Empire*. Chicago: University of Chicago Press, 1935.

Tanaka Giichi. "Rokoku kakumei shokan" (Impressions of the Russian revolution). *Kaikōsha kiji* 515 (June 1917): 1–3.

Tanaka Ryūkichi. *Nihon gunbatsu antōshi* (A history of secret strife in the Japanese military cliques). Tokyo: Seiwadō Shoten, 1947.

Tanaka Sōgorō. *Nihon fuashizumu no genryū* (Japanese fascism wastes away). Tokyo: Hakuyōsha, 1949.

———. *Nihon no gunbatsu* (Japan's military cliques). Tokyo: Shinkō Shuppansha, 1945.

Tanikawa Ken'ichi, Tsurumi Shunpo, and Murakami Ichirō, eds. *Hangyakusha* (The dissidents). Vol. 3 in *Dokyumento Nihonjin* (Documents of the Japanese people). Tokyo: Gakugei Shorin, 1968.

Tanin, O., and E. Yohan. *Militarism and Fascism in Japan*. New York: International Publishers, 1934.

Tateno Nobuyuki. *Shōwa gunbatsu* (The military cliques of the Shōwa era). Vol. 1, *Bōkōhen* (Violence). Tokyo: Kōdansha, 1963.

Tazaki Suematsu. *Hyōden Mazaki Jinzaburō* (A critical biography of Mazaki Jinzaburō). Tokyo: Fuyō Shobō, 1977.

———. *Hyōden Tanaka Giichi* (A critical biography of Tanaka Giichi). 2 vols. Tokyo: Heiwa Senryaku Sōgō Kenkyūjo, 1981.

Teikoku Zaigō Gunjinkai Honbu. *Teikoku zaigō gunjinkai sanjūnenshi* (The thirty-year history of the Imperial Reservists Association). Tokyo, 1944.

Teidemann, Arthur E. "Big Business and Politics in Prewar Japan." In James William Morley, ed., *Dilemmas of Growth in Prewar Japan*. Princeton: Princeton University Press, 1971.

Titus, David Anson. *Palace and Politics in Prewar Japan*. New York: Columbia University Press, 1974.

Tokutomi Iichirō. *Kōshaku Yamagata Aritomo den* (The biography of Prince Yamagata Aritomo). 3 vols. Tokyo: Yamagata Aritomo-kō Kinen Jigyōkai, 1933.

Tōyama Shigeki, Imai Seiichi, and Fujiwara Akira. *Shōwashi* (Shōwa-era history). Tokyo: Iwanami Shoten, 1959.

Tsuchikata Kazuo. " 'Gunjin seishin' no ronri — toku ni Shōwaki ni okeru sono henkō" (The logic of the military's [emphasis on] spirit — especially the changes [in it] in the Shōwa period). *Shisō*, no. 400 (Oct. 1957): 22–36.

Tsukushi Kumashichi. *Kokumin hidoku: Gunshuku no daiippo e* (The people bitter: The first step toward arms reduction). Tokyo: Tōa Insatsu K.K. Shuppansha, 1923.

Tsunoda Jun, ed. *Ishiwara Kanji shiryō* (Historical materials of Ishiwara Kanji). 2 vols. Meiji hyakunenshi sōsho, vols. 17–18. Tokyo: Hara Shobō, 1967.

Uehara Yūsaku Kankei Monjo Kenkyūkai. *Uehara Yūsaku kankei monjo* (Letters to Uehara Yūsaku). Tokyo: Tōkyō Daigaku Shuppankai, 1976.

Ugaki Kazunari. *Shōrai seidan* (Stories told among the pines). Tokyo: Bungei Shunjū Shinsha, 1951.

———. *Ugaki Kazunari nikki* (Ugaki Kazunari [Kazushige]'s diary). 2 vols. Tokyo: Misuzu Shobō, 1968.

———. *Ugaki nikki* (Ugaki's diary). Tokyo: Asahi Shinbunsha, 1954.

U.S. Department of State. *Papers Relating to the Foreign Relations of the United States, 1928*. 2 vols. Washington: U.S. Government Printing Office, 1943.

Unterberger, Betty M. *America's Siberian Expedition, 1918–1920: A Study of National Policy*. Durham, N.C.: Duke University Press, 1956.

Usui Katsumi. "Chō Sakurin bakushi no shinsō" (The truth about the assassination of Zhang Zuolin). *Chisei*, supplementary issue, Dec. 1956.

Uzaki Rojō. *Satsu no kaigun Chō no rikugun* (Satsuma's navy, Chōshū's army). Tokyo: Seikyōsha, 1913.

———. *Rikugun no go-daibatsu* (The army's five great cliques). Tokyo: Tōkyōdō Shoten, 1915.

Wakatsuki Reijirō. *Wakatsuki Reijirō jiden: Kofūan kaikoroku* (The autobiography of Wakatsuki Reijirō: Kofūan memoirs). Tokyo: Yomiuri Shinbunsha, 1950.

Wald, Royal Jules. "The Young Officers Movement in Japan, ca. 1925–1937: Ideology and Action." Ph.D. diss., University of California at Berkeley, 1944.

Ward, Robert E. *Japan's Political System*. Englewood Cliffs, N.J.: Prentice-Hall, 1967.

——. "Political Modernization and Political Culture in Japan." *World Politics* 15 (Oct. 1962–July 1963): 569–96.

——, ed. *Political Development in Modern Japan*. Princeton: Princeton University Press, 1968.

Watanabe Hisashi and Akamatsu Kanbi. *Gendai oyobi shōrai no sensō* (Wars, present and future). Tokyo: Kaikōsha, 1925.

Wilson, George M. "Kita Ikki's Theory of Revolution." *Journal of Asian Studies* 26 (1966): 89–99.

——. *Radical Nationalist in Japan: Kita Ikki, 1883–1937*. Cambridge, Mass.: Harvard University Press, 1969.

Yamagata Aritomo. *Rikugunshō enkakushi* (A history of the army ministry). Tokyo: Nihon Hyōronsha, 1942.

——. *Yamagata Aritomo ikensho* (Yamagata Aritomo's opinion papers). Meiji hyakunenshi sōsho, vol. 16. Tokyo: Hara Shobō, 1966.

Yamamoto Yoshinosuke. *Nihon o horoboshita mono* (The fellows who ruined Japan). Tokyo: Shōkō Shoin, 1949.

Yamaura Kan'ichi. "Bōshō Mori Kaku" (Mori Kaku, the mastermind). *Bungei Shunjū*, vol. 33, no. 6 (June 1955): 60–65.

——. *Mori Kaku*. Tokyo: Mori Kaku Denki Hensankai, 1941.

Yokoyama Shinpei. *Hiroku Ishiwara Kanji* (Ishiwara Kanji's secret memoirs). Tokyo: Fuyō Shobō, 1971.

Yoshihashi, Takehiko. *Conspiracy at Mukden: The Rise of the Japanese Military*. New Haven: Yale University Press, 1963.

Yoshino Sakuzō. *Gendai kensei no un'yō* (The working of present-day constitutional government). Tokyo: Ichigensha, 1930.

Young, A. Morgan. *Imperial Japan, 1926–1938*. London: G. Allen and Unwin, 1938.

——. *Japan in Recent Times*. New York: W. Morrow, 1940.

——. *Japan Under Taisho Tenno, 1912–1926*. London: G. Allen and Unwin, 1928.

Young, C. Walter. *The International Relations of Manchuria*. Prepared for the 1929 Conference of the Institute of Pacific Relations in Kyoto, Japan. Reprint. New York: Greenwood Press, 1969.

——. *Japan's Special Position in Manchuria*. Baltimore: Johns Hopkins University Press, 1931.

Young, John W. "The Hara Cabinet and Chang Tso-lin, 1920–1." *Monumenta Nipponica* 27 (1972): 125–42.

Index

In this index an "f" after a number indicates a separate reference on the next page, and an "ff" indicates separate references on the next two pages. A continuous discussion over two or more pages is indicated by a span of page numbers, e.g., "pp. 57–58." *Passim* is used for a cluster of references in close but not continuous sequence.

Library of Congress Cataloging-in-Publication Data

Humphreys, Leonard A.
   The way of the heavenly sword : the Japanese Army in the 1920's /
Leonard A. Humphreys.
      p.   cm.
   Includes bibliographical references and index.
   ISBN 0-8047-2375-3 (acid-free paper)
   1. Japan. Rikugun — History — 20th century.   2. Japan —
History — 20th century.   1. Title.
UA847.H86   1995
355'.00952'09042 — dc20   94-15612
                                                              CIP

⊗ This book is printed on acid-free, recycled paper.